--- Praise for *Finding Sara* ---

"What a jewel of a book Margaret Edds has written—
a loving and honest memoir about a mother she never knew.
In order to bring this book to us, Margaret had the good
fortune to be born into a literate family. Then she was gifted
with an Aunt Eleanor who possessed the good sense to know
what to toss and what to keep. Finally, Margaret was blessed
with the sensibilities to come to know her mother, Sara,
from the inside out and the talent to bring her to us complete.
Thank you for taking us across Big Black Mountain and back
to a time and place nearly lost to memory. I loved every
line of this book and reading it really took me home."

—Linda Scott DeRosier, author of *Songs of Life and Grace*,
Appalachian Writers Association Book of the Year

"*Finding Sara* reminds you to never underestimate the
significance of a handwritten letter, and that in
finding someone we sometimes find ourselves."

—Lynne Hughes, Founder and CEO,
Comfort Zone Camp

Finding Sara

A Daughter's Journey

Margaret Edds

Butler Books
Louisville, Kentucky

ISBN 978-1-935497-06-6
Library of Congress Control Number: 2009937792
Printed in Canada

Designed by Eric Butler

Library of Congress Cataloging-in-Publication Data
  Edds, Margaret, 1947-
    Finding Sara : a daughter's journey / Margaret Edds.
      p.   cm.
    Includes bibliographical references.
    ISBN 978-1-935497-06-6 (alk. paper)
  1. Edds, Sara, 1915-1950. 2. Edds, Sara, 1915-1950—Correspondence.
3. Mothers and daughters—Tennessee—Biography. 4. Edds, Margaret, 1947-
5. Tennessee—Biography. I. Title.

  CT275 . E276E33 2009
  976.8'053092—dc22
  [B]
                          2009040935

Published by:

Butler Books
P.O. Box 7311
Louisville, KY 40207
(502) 897-9393
fax (502) 897-9797
www.butlerbooks.com

For Rachel

Contents

Acknowledgments ix

Prologue xi

One   Delina, Tennessee, 1915–1932 1

Two   Petersburg, Tennessee, and Bowling Green,
Kentucky, 1939–February 1942 17

Three   Lynch, Kentucky,
March 1942–May 1943 35

Four   Oak Ridge, Tennessee,
June 1943–December 1943 71

Five   Oak Ridge, Tennessee,
January 1944–September 1944. . . . 103

Six   Greenville, Texas,
October 1944–October 1945 149

Seven   Lynch, Kentucky,
January 1946–June 1948. 165

Eight Lynch, Kentucky,
Summer 1948–March 1950 199

Nine Lynch, Kentucky, and Delina, Tennessee,
April 1950–November 7, 1950 231

Ten 1950–2009 249

Ideas for (Re)Discovering Your Mother . . . 275

Bibliography 277

Acknowledgments

When you live for several years with a book project as intimate as this, almost everyone you know impacts the result in some way—a word of encouragement, a spark of inspiration, an insight, a criticism, a shared laugh or tear. It would be nearly impossible to list all those who deserve and receive my gratitude. The fear of inadvertently leaving someone out discourages me from trying. Dear friends, I thank you all.

For those who played a direct role in the publication of the book, I add a note of additional acknowledgment. Friends Barbara and Stephen Fleming first encouraged me to consider the letters as not only a personal resource, but a historical one, worthy of sharing with a larger audience. The initial readers of the manuscript—Laura LaFay, Glenn Frankel and Stephen Fleming—raised probing questions and made thoughtful suggestions, as did many other later readers. Mary Fran Hughes-McIntyre and Charlotte Davenport talked with me at length about the enduring consequences of losing their own mothers at an early age, and therapist Anne Lane provided a check on my understanding of human psychology. Historian Betsy Brinson opened the door to valuable resources in Kentucky, as did Theresa Osborne, folklorist and facilitator in the Appalachian Program at the Southeast Kentucky Community & Technical College. Cardiologist Dave Propert provided crucial medical expertise. Former Lynch neighbors Barbara Tiabian and Pauline Nunn provided essential links to an earlier era, as did my father's dear friend and Benham resident Paul Graham, whose death before the publication of *Finding Sara* saddens me. Cousins Jane Barnes Tilford, Bill Barnes, Sandra Garrison Cooper and Elizabeth Edds Rock shared helpful memories and insights, as well as enthusiasm. Kathy Benham and brother-in-law Elliot Lieberman lent their talent and expertise in selecting images. Editor Viqi Wagner's clear, elegant style and voice proved an enormous gift. Bob Hiett, Nancy Wright Beasley, Connie Lapallo, Jason Smith and Carol Butler all contributed in essential ways to the production of the book.

In this writing and all else, my family remains my anchor. Heartfelt thanks to Kate and Mark Garabedian; Sharon, Brett, Taylor and Lauren Halsey; Adam Lipper; Elliot Lieberman, and Margaret and Jerwaine Simpson. My husband, Bob Lipper, buoyed me with unwavering belief in the project, a sharp editing pencil, humor and good sense. I could never have undertaken this journey without the complete support and encouragement of my sister, Rachel Edds, who lived it with me. First and last, the spirit of Eleanor Barnes Murray permeates every page. Who else not only would have kept every letter and clipping, but sorted them into files? This book is a tribute to her extraordinary devotion.

Prologue

The summer after our father died, my sister and I crossed Big Black Mountain, driving west from the Virginia side toward Lynch.

We loaded husbands and children into a van and navigated the steep ascent over Kentucky's highest peak, past hairpin turns, perilous drops and dazzling overlooks, until the road leveled into the narrow seam where I was born and experienced my first, deepest loss.

My father and I had traveled this highway of memories together a few times in the twenty-odd years after he retired from a furniture sales job in Nashville and moved back to his paternal grandfather's farm in Lee County, Virginia, near Cumberland Gap. But those quick, sporadic visits focused on his memories, not mine.

Now, Rachel and I planned to find the house where we lived together, the four of us, for three years, two months and twenty days. That was my age on November 7, 1950, the date my beautiful young mother died. Rachel was exactly two years older, minus nine days, which turns out to be a significant span of time. She remembers things I do not, a look, a touch, a moment, a laugh.

Mother has, for her, a physical shape, a form. For me, mother is a black-and-white photograph, a concept, an eternal longing, a swirl of energy just past the edge of consciousness that can never be grasped or contained, try as I might.

We found the house. No one answered. We posed for photographs, forced the children to take note, embraced our husbands in a circle of nostalgia and drove on. "Wait," one of us corrected the others moments later. "That was the wrong house." We had just reached the Lynch schoolhouse, boarded against vandals, where we used to play and where Rachel dreamed of entering first grade. In this company-built coal town in which every home followed one of a dozen models, ours was still to come. Now we saw it, the familiar rectangular box containing four rooms, a living room to the right where you entered, the kitchen behind, two bedrooms on the left, how plain a repository for so much vitality and life.

This time, an owner answered our knock, inviting us in. The room was cozy, nice, unfamiliar. In the bedroom that my sister and I once shared, we paused.

"My crib was against that wall, I think," I said. "Your bed was there."

"That's right," she answered.

In the front bedroom, my heart raced. Here my mother lay confined to bed rest on doctor's orders many of the months after I was born. "I have the vaguest memory of climbing into bed with them one night," I said. I was between them, safe, secure.

Was that real? Imagined? A dream?

Impossible to know.

"You're toddling along when you're three, and suddenly, wham. Your whole world is turned upside down. You don't know why," a therapist once told me.

I had come to her because of a paralyzing anxiety that sometimes gripped me when I envisioned the catastrophes that could befall my children. In most ways, I have a certain bravery, or at least confidence, toward life. I have knocked on strange doors in low-income housing projects in the middle of the night because I needed to find someone. I have explained calmly to a robber why it would be helpful if he took the cash and left the photos and credit cards behind. After my father's stroke, I learned to administer crushed pills through a feeding tube, to dress and undress a man unable to stand, to handle blood and vomit and human waste, all because I loved him and it had to be done. But when my children failed or suffered heartache or strayed, I saw less the promise of growth than the potential for an unraveling, a collapse from which no one—neither they nor I—would rebound.

The therapist smiled, amused no doubt that a woman of reasonable intelligence could be so dense. "Have you ever mourned your mother?" she asked. Well, sort of, sometimes, not really.

At my next visit, we arranged photographs and lit candles. She read from Kahlil Gibran and talked about the pictures, how my mother's arm encircled me in one, how my parents stood glowing during their courtship days, filled with the promise of life. She talked; I sobbed. Improbable as it might sound, that was one of the best hours of my life.

I was fifty years old at the time.

Once earlier, I had felt the full emotional weight of my mother's death. I was much younger then, about twenty-five, and in the throes of a disintegrating first marriage. On the night of my deepest sorrow, it came to me in a jolt, a moment of unexpected clarity, that my grief was not just for my departing husband, but for her. It was no surprise that her passing had left a void. As a child, I defined myself in part by her absence. "My mother died when I was three" was a birthmark, both magnetic and repellent, not unlike the mole on my right leg. Who could forget the flimsy school projects cobbled together without an adult's touch, the homemade costume that nearly fell apart during a school dress-up day, the gaps in routine knowledge? I learned far later than most girls of my generation how to scramble an egg, how to use a tampon, that doing laundry meant separating colors and whites, not just piling every dirty item into a single load. But I experienced my mother as a blank space, not as an authentic person once present and now gone. That night, I saw otherwise. The primal force of her loss erupted from some unknown cavern in my soul, as when in a dream your subconscious hits on a truth your conscious mind would never have revealed. Buried deep inside me, there she was.

My childhood lacked neither stability nor affection—far from it. My father provided constancy and devotion. With Tom, "I could add 2 and 2 together and know that the answer will come out four," my mother wrote in a 1943 letter to her closest sister, Eleanor, explaining why he was rising to the top of her pack of suitors. She chose well.

Tom was not perfect; no one is. Many days, he worked too many hours. His lifetime commitment to my deceased mother deprived him—and by extension, my sister and me—of joys and insights a second marriage might have allowed. But as a parent, he was a quiet, unwavering presence. On the morning of my second marriage, he was up at daybreak to mow the meadow where we planned to wed. That is how he was, guiding me more by his actions than by any spoken words. When I needed him, Tom was there. In the interim, he never seemed to doubt my competence to stand alone.

Aiding him were the aunts, eight counting the in-laws, each

with a distinct femininity, each modeling some unique blend of opportunity and limitation to a child. None lived around the corner, or even in the next town, but my sister and I saw them on holidays and for month-long summer visits. It was not the same as daily interaction. In youth, I rarely observed the ongoing, familiar intimacy of friendship in a group of women or the communication skills that develop between a man and a woman who live together, day in, day out. Later, I had to sort out those patterns on my own, sometimes to ill effect. But if I know what it means to suffer tremendous loss at an early age, I know equally well what it is to be adored. None of my mother's sisters, Virginia, Eleanor, Katherine, had children of their own. If I was in want of a mother, they had space in their lives for a child.

Inevitably, perhaps, the image I gleaned of my mother in that setting was of a perfect creature, forever youthful, spirited, unencumbered by human frailty, bad temper, selfishness or age. No compliment loomed larger than "that reminds me of your mother" or "that would make your mother proud." I strove mightily, usually with good result, never to displease or disappoint.

Into that cocoon, unexpectedly, the letters appeared.

I discovered the first stash on a summer day, sometime during my teens. They lay in a box atop my father's bureau, two neat stacks, each envelope addressed in Sara's small, square handwriting to S/Sgt. Tom Edds, Greenville, Texas. Her return address, across from the three-cent stamp, read Oak Ridge, Tennessee. For a time during World War II, she worked as a secretary in that so-called secret city outside Knoxville, created almost overnight in a mad rush to develop a method of enriching uranium for production of the atomic bomb. Like most Oak Ridge residents, she knew nothing of that fateful mission, only that the town's charge was of the utmost urgency and secrecy. Some 120 letters to my father span the months from January to September 1944. The first was written two months after their marriage, the last just days before she joined him at Majors Field, an Army Air Forces base northeast of Dallas where he was assigned to a personnel unit. I immersed myself in the treasure, stealing the box into my room during long hours when my father was at work.

Would he have minded that his daughter had found a window into the first year of his long-distance, wartime marriage? Perhaps not. Asking was not a risk I chose to take, for I had discovered something too precious to relinquish—my mother's unfiltered voice, revealed to me by no one but herself. Reading the letters as a teenager, I loved her saucy, strong-willed independence ("It really does me good to go to church, for I can always look at the preacher and be glad he didn't marry us!"), the romantic teasing ("My dentist said I had one of the nicest figures in Oak Ridge and that I carried myself beautifully. Shall I get a new dentist?"), the promise that my own dull social life was not a lifetime sentence ("Better be glad you didn't know me at 18. You'd not have noticed me, much less liked me. But I'd have loved you at any age").

I relished the glimpses of her minor rebellions from a strait-laced, Bible belt youth, not so far removed from my own. Even if she seldom missed a Sunday morning slipping into a church pew, she loved late-night bridge parties and dances and even a cocktail now and again. "I'm afraid I don't share your total antipathy toward alcoholic beverages," she wrote. "Maybe I'm wrong in thinking that a discriminating taste along those lines isn't unpleasant." I devoured the hints of sexual intimacy. "Today, nine days late I menstruated," she wrote after his furlough in the summer of 1944. "I'd about decided I wasn't going to and to tell the truth was almost disappointed when I did." And later, "Didn't we have a good time? I loved hiding in the tree when the rain came . . . and our washing dishes together and playing croquet . . . the nice, clean smell of you when we'd go to bed, and people saying Sara and Tom as though the two names had always gone together."

I found in the letters a certain release, an approval to be myself.

Four decades passed before I delved into those letters again. By then, my father had been dead a half dozen years; Eleanor was gone too, and I had long since become an adult. This time, I saw layers of complexity beneath Sara's cheerful surface—loneliness at times, altruism limited by parochialism in her worldview, uncertainty as she forged a marriage with fountain pen and ink. "Your letter yesterday scared me a little in that you seemed disappointed in my 'vim, vigor, and vitality,'" she wrote six months into their marriage. "It made me feel again though that because you had known me on only 'high occasions' that you might not like the everyday me as well as you thought."

Some years earlier, Eleanor had sent me another stash of Sara's letters, written mostly to Eleanor or their mother. Busy with my own family and work, I had dashed through the pack. But one night after my children left home, the youngest to college, time and interest finally collided in full. Unable to sleep that evening, I extracted Eleanor's letters from an old trunk and, for hours, found myself transfixed. I had never realized how complete a record existed, in Sara's own hand, of the decade preceding her death at age thirty-four. Here, on paper, was a young woman evolving from heady independence to the chosen responsibilities of a marriage and children to a sober and brave defiance of her own mortality.

A few weeks later, during a Thanksgiving visit to my sister's home in Baltimore, Rachel and I plowed through a roomful of boxes carried from my father's farm. We recovered the 1944 wartime letters, plus additional ones from before their marriage, as well as a box of previously unknown gems: her high school and college diplomas, a hand-written autobiography of her first sixteen years and a collection of treasured letters, one from her dearest childhood friend, several from my father and assorted cards and notes from intimate friends and former beaus. I knew vaguely from my aunts that my mother once had a significant, failed romance. Now, here were a half dozen of Bud's letters, illuminating her heartbroken account to Eleanor of their last meeting. "Maybe he could hold anybody like that and kiss them like that but I don't see how it would be possible without loving them. . . . I guess you'd better not leave this letter around. Just burn it up."

I began to piece together the dates, the events that propelled her unlikely journey from her family farm and a teaching job in southern Tennessee near the Alabama border to the Appalachian coal-mining town where I was born. In the 1930s Harlan County, Kentucky, spawned bloody battles between John L. Lewis's United Mine Workers and distant coal operators as they fought for shares of the mineral wealth buried deep beneath mountain rock. But when Sara arrived in March 1942 in Lynch, a planned town created by a subsidiary of the U.S. Steel Corporation for an unlikely blend of European immigrants, relocated Deep South blacks and native mountain men, it was as if she had discovered a personal Camelot. "Now you stop thinking about me being pinned in by mountains, as I always did love mountains," she reassured my worried grandmother in a postcard home. And to Eleanor: "I am so 'blooming' happy. . . . It just seems everything is lovely." For the first time, I realized how narrowly she and my father overlapped in Lynch—by mere weeks—before he left for the army and how much of their nineteen-month courtship was conducted by mail.

As I read, a vanished world unfolded, a time and place when women in the rural South, prodded in part by the disruptions and demands of a world at war, were venturing beyond their mothers' horizons to cities and communities bustling with purpose and adventure. Still, even a woman who kept the writings of Greek philosophers on her secretarial desk and reported "today I amused myself by rereading the old classic myths" yielded to professional constraints. The options, although expanding, were limited primarily to teacher, secretary or nurse. Wife-and-mother was the ultimate ambition. With society in flux, marriages formed on a wing and a prayer. Airplanes joined the automobile, trains and buses in transporting masses of people thither and yon. "Which is the most powerful, the urge of patriotism or the craving for adventure?" quipped my father in referring to some members of the Women's Army Auxiliary Corps (WAAC) who'd just arrived at his base "to help fight the battle of Greenville." Big-band radio sounds drifted out of Oak Ridge dormitory windows late into hot summer nights and a week rarely passed without a movie or two or three. "Monday night Virginia, Emily, Mary and I tore home from work, rushed through supper without even going back for a second helping of anything, and raced up to the Theater— all so that we might sit rather than stand and see Bette Davis and Miriam Hopkins in 'Old Acquaintance,'" Sara reported to Eleanor in March 1944. "It was very good, Bette being her usual slick self—only I believe I mean sleek in this instance."

Her vivacity stood in bold relief against the backdrop of war. "In a newsbroadcast the announcer is saying that Paris, the world's third largest city, is free again tonight, free after four years," Sara wrote Tom in August 1944:

It seems a long, long time since June of 1940. Johnny and I were just home from U.T. [the University of Tennessee in Knoxville], our last quarter there, and it was the first summer since 1934 and probably the last forever that we'd all been home for the whole summer. In the laughter and gaiety there, Paris seemed very far away, and even in the stunned realization of its fall, war still seemed far from America.

By the next autumn, Sara and Tom were returning with postwar optimism to Lynch, a world where even simmering labor strife could not squelch the excitement of a new Frigidaire, a Bendix washing machine and a pressure cooker that could can fourteen quarts at once or the security of a community where a four-year-old and a two-year-old could walk to the store alone. Penicillin had surfaced as well. "That penicillin is kindly wonderful stuff," she wrote nine months into her illness. No magic elixir could stem the heartbreak ahead.

Eventually, my stack of letters to, from and about Sara grew to more than three hundred, a paper window on the life's journey of a person I had thought impossible to know. The briefest were one-cent postcards, crammed with writing so meticulous and condensed that the word count rivals a brief college essay; Sara's longest epistle was thirteen pages, recording every detail of Christmas Day 1949. Fountain pens produced a rich, full script in many of the letters. The font in others hammered out on manual typewriters has a squiggly, uneven quality, primitive by modern standards. Most of the paper is commercial grade, but for special occasions—a birthday, a holiday or a vow of love—Sara switched to a heavy, buff-colored stock that signaled the consequence of the moment as surely as a dab of perfume or a bright new lipstick.

Over the next months, I supplemented the letters' narrative with the remembrances of Sara's friends and acquaintances.

Most were now in their eighties and nineties, and the list was dwindling fast. Why did I wait so long to ask? I combed streets she would have walked in Lynch and Oak Ridge, studied her pictures, read books she loved. I tried to imagine myself in her company. I wanted to glimpse her mind. I dreamed of feeling her beside me, a physical presence. The story I unearthed contains little of the dysfunction that peppers many modern family narratives. There is no divorce, no alcoholism, no incest, no abuse. Birth and death frame lives defined by good intention. The anguish is in the brevity of existence, the redemption, if it can be found, in the churning that propels bits and pieces of one generation on to the next. The envelopes, I realized as weeks passed, opened a window not only to Sara but to some part of me as well. What does it mean to lose your mother before memories become fixed? What of her do I carry in my genes, my nature, my outlook? What did I lose—or gain—through her death? A living mother, I know, can be an obstacle as well as a channel to a healthy life. How different would I be had mine lived?

As I write, I am nearly three decades older than Sara when she died. In multiple ways, my life has been happy and fulfilled. I feel cherished by a husband, children, relatives and friends. How is it then that I carry a sore spot deep in my soul for something lost so long ago? I cannot say why, only that this is true. On rare moments, I am again three, wishing for my mother more than anything in the world.

In the cheery rambling of Sara's earliest known letter, opportunity beckons.

I.

Delina, Tennessee

1915–1932

Dear Virginia,

What are you doing tonight?

I haven't studied any, tonight.

We got a letter from Eleanor and you both today.

Daddy is playing "Mumble Peg."

Katherine is studing.*

John O's in bed and asleep, and Mamma is writeing to you.

When you go out and hunt bugs you should faint gracefully when you find one.

I finished "Jo's Boys" Sunday afternoon. I read a little on "The Bishop of Cottentown." I've been reading "David Copperfield" but haven't read any in it for three or four days. And then I've been reading "Little Women" too but I don't think I've read any on it for two or three days either.

---

* While the collected letters are intelligent and articulate, I elected to preserve rare misspelling or misplaced punctuation (particularly in Sara's earliest writing) to preserve the flavor of the correspondence.

We didn't go to church Sunday it was so rainy.
I will be perty glad when school is out. Won't you? Guess I'll stop.
Love, Respectily, Yours truly, lovingly, Your sister,
    Sara
    Bruce
    Barnes

Nighttime at Hilltop View farm, Delina, Tennessee, 1927.

Eleven-year-old Sara Barnes describes the evening's activities to Virginia, the oldest of her four siblings, who is attending high school in Lewisburg, the nearest sizable town.

I envision the family in the two-story, white frame farmhouse, some seventy-five miles southeast of Nashville. They gather in the sitting room where an assortment of rockers and ladder-backed chairs cluster near the fireplace. A double bed occupies a spot in a back corner of the room, available for visiting relatives. Books, papers and games crowd various chests and tables. In daylight, floorboard-to-ceiling windows reveal a row of maple trees and a rock-wall fence separating the front yard from a steep hillside that leads down to an unpaved county road.

Rural electrification did not come to that corner of south-central Tennessee until the mid-1930s, so as Sara writes, kerosene lamps and a coal fire light the room. Her father, John O. Barnes Sr., a farmer and fruit-tree salesman whose territory ran as far west as Texas, occupies his usual spot in a cane-bottomed rocker to the left of the fireplace, long legs crossed, feet steadied against the mantle, a pipe close at hand.

My grandmother, Jennie May Downing Barnes, a teacher and gentle soul who gave birth to five children after marrying at twenty-eight, has finished the dinner chores and prepared the next day's school lessons. This year she is Sara's sixth-grade teacher at the

Delina school, a mile-or-so walk to the south. A tall, plain woman with steady blue eyes, a narrow nose and thin mouth, Jennie May combined strong faith and a kind heart. Her children spoke of her reverently. She died the spring after I was born.

I know this setting because each summer in the 1950s and early 1960s, Rachel and I spent several weeks in the farming community of Delina, playing Rook and Flinch for hours, soaring as high as the squeaky porch swing would carry us, concocting dress-up versions of fancy balls and pretend college, wading the creek, devouring novels, exploring the barn's intricate web of stalls and feeding chutes.

My stern grandfather bought us orange Dreamsicles at the crossroads store and, elevating us far above our ordinary status back home, introduced us importantly as "Sara's girls." Our aunts put bobby-pin curls in our hair, mended our clothes and— depending on the aunt—read us long passages of Laura Ingalls Wilder or allowed us to paint our mouths with tiny red and pink lipstick samples.

At thirteen, during one magical summer visit, I experienced my first, backseat kiss from a local boy while driven home from a Delina Methodist Church youth cookout. At the end of another visit, I lay awake far into the night, praying for the headlights of our father's car to crest the hill, stricken at the thought of an accident. If one parent can die, why not two?

"Living on a farm has its advantages and disadvantages," Sara wrote. "There are not many boys and girls at home to run around with and at times my life seems very lonely. But at other times it is unspeakably lovely."

I retain only one memory of my mother at Delina. Even that recollection contains no clear image of her, only a fit of activity with her at its core. So the discovery more than a half century

after her death of an account of her first sixteen years was to me
as miraculous as the unearthing of a personal Rosetta Stone. The
thirty-six yellowed, handwritten pages, composed for a college
class probably in about 1933, illuminate our differences. She
came of age in a lamp-lit, 1920s farmhouse, I in a post-Sputnik
Nashville suburb. She was surrounded by a large and active
family. Aunts, uncles and cousins lived a short Model T ride away.
Days seldom passed without a visitor for dinner or the night. My
father, sister and I lived in a setting at once more populated and
more isolated. School, work and church provided social outlets.
Neighborhood playmates came and went. But overnight visitors,
parties and dinner guests were rare events. Minus a mother, our
household was quieter, more shuttered by far.

Even so, I see glimmers of myself in the pages. For both of us,
reading was an early and deep love. "I have never loved another
character in the same way that I loved Dora, David's child wife [in
David Copperfield]," Sara wrote. "My favorite author is Victor Hugo
and my favorite book is 'Les Miserables' which I read when I was
thirteen years old. I have read 'Jane Eyre' twice and each time
I was scared for days afterwards." I read *Jane Eyre* twice also and
loved Edward Rochester each time. For Sara, as for me, books
were a ballast, imagination a transport, writing a release. She,
too, saw herself as a shy young girl, and though I believe her later
vivacity far exceeded mine, we each grew more extroverted with
time. We both loved school and liked to excel, both vowed to see
distant horizons, both knew solitude and, at times, loneliness. I
recognize in myself the fierceness of her attachments to those she
loved; I see in my sister Sara's strong, independent will.

*I was a late Christmas gift. Or so I always call myself for I was born
on the day after Christmas in 1915. . . . My first recollection is the*

time I locked Eleanor and Katherine in the spring house. I only did
it for fun and I meant to let them out in a few minutes but I had no
sooner turned the lock than I saw one of our cows that was a well
known butter coming toward me. I ran to the fence, leaving my sisters
in the spring house. I do not know what I would have done if Virginia
had not come along and let them out.

Sara's older sisters, Virginia, Eleanor and Katherine, were the
mainstays of her early social life. Virginia came first.

In August, 1909, a tiny little baby girl was laid in Mother's arms. She
was called Virginia. Not only was she adored and petted by Mother
and Daddy but she was also petted by all the relatives. Virginia, as the
eldest, has always been the leader of the other children. She finished
High School at Lewisburg at the age of sixteen years. The next two
years she attended Martin College [in Pulaski, Tennessee]. *Then,*
after teaching two years at Ebenezer, she finished college at Vanderbilt.

In later life, Virginia melded certitude with self-doubt.
Strikingly handsome in a severe, frowning sort of way, she
rejected two offers of marriage from local farmers, preferring
to pursue her dream—an English degree from Vanderbilt
University. A celebrated student, she found herself devastated
by inability to manage unruly students in her first post-degree
teaching job. A switch to library science, a natural choice given
her appreciation of literature, provided safe haven. Virginia
agonized over decisions, an outgrowth perhaps of her station as
the eldest child of a domineering father, but she never wavered
in her politics (Adlai Stevenson Democrat), her philosophy
(antiwar, antisegregation), her matinee idol (Clark Gable) and
her insistence on truth ("I believe you look the worse for wear,"

she announced with typical frankness after the birth of my second child).

In 1910, fourteen months after Virginia's birth, Eleanor arrived. "Eleanor seems to have more initiative and leadership than any of the rest of us. She has that happy gift of making friends with everyone." Valedictorian of her senior class, winner of top honors at a local junior college, Eleanor later excelled as a teacher and guidance counselor. Saddened by her inability to have children after marrying in her late thirties, she showered energy on other people's offspring, semi-adopting several young people in difficult straits, mentoring scores of others. Gracious and poised in public settings, she often had her hand in so many pies that we privately accused her of being "in a dither." I retain an early memory of guests arriving for a party while Eleanor, in a housedress, was in the backyard snipping zinnias for bouquets. She grieved suffering in any form, whether next door or on a distant continent, which made it all the more surprising when a competitive streak transformed her into a shark at cards or Scrabble. Eleanor scripted and produced scores of class plays, could quote long stanzas of Wordsworth and Yeats and seldom let a visitor leave without a glass of homemade grape juice or a cup of spice tea. Mutual admiration and devotion made Eleanor and Sara the closest of siblings and Eleanor the nearest mother substitute for Rachel and me after our mother's death.

"Katherine is my third sister and my playmate. She does not care especially for books and school but she has her own talents. Katherine is the only member of our family that has ever been ill a great deal. This sickness has made her nervous." Less accomplished academically and professionally than her more ambitious siblings, Katherine did elaborate needlework, showed a facility for making friends and, when not saddled with a "sick headache," engaged in appealing playfulness. She slipped Rachel and me chewing gum and Coca-Colas, and on summer nights as we splashed in the bathtub at Delina, Katherine impersonated an Evil Troll hiding outside the window: "Trip-trap. Trip-trap. Who's that walking over my bridge?" We screeched in fright.

Next came Sara, followed by the baby and only boy, John O. Jr. (Johnny). "As he is the baby, he has been spoiled and petted a great deal, especially by Virginia and Eleanor. He is a regular boy who loves football and thinks he dislikes school." In later years, John O. would become an accomplished local orator and educator, facing perhaps his greatest challenge as superintendent of schools in Marshall County, Tennessee, during their racial integration. He told stories of deflecting white parents trying to escape court orders and moral dictates. John O.'s position as the only boy and youngest child in a world of sisters instilled a lifelong confidence. It also left him headstrong at times and hard to challenge. A childhood accident nearly crippled him for life. "He and I were playing with long jumping poles. While he was jumping his pole broke and he fell heavily." An increasingly pronounced limp resulted in a trip to a noted Nashville orthopedic specialist. "The thought that my little brother might be a cripple for life almost killed me." After six months in a plaster cast, Johnny was able to walk, although with a lifetime limp.

However settled life appeared at Hilltop View, America in the 1920s was a nation in tumult. Modernism clashed with tradition in music, literature and the arts. Sigmund Freud redefined the nature of human relationships. Jazz roared. Economic prosperity and optimism collided with the lawlessness of Prohibition and the rise of radical political movements. Women gained the right to vote; the Ku Klux Klan attracted numbers unprecedented since its 1865 founding in Pulaski, Tennessee, one county removed from

Delina. And a few hours' drive to the east in Dayton, a county seat town not unlike Lewisburg, William Jennings Bryan and Clarence Darrow in July 1925 faced off in the trial of the decade, an epic battle between the forces of science and religion. Two years before Sara's letter advising Virginia to "faint gracefully" when encountering a bug, the Tennessee legislature made it unlawful "to teach any theory that denies the story of divine creation as taught by the Bible and to teach instead that man was descended from the lower order of animals." The decision of John Scopes, a twenty-four-year-old biology teacher, to teach evolution in defiance of that law led to his famous trial. Eventually, the Tennessee Supreme Court absolved Scopes by throwing out the statute on a technicality.

Sara's writings say nothing of politics. They describe a southern, rural girlhood light-years removed from anarchists and psychoanalysis, flappers and bathtub gin.

One of my chief joys lay in visiting my grandmothers, who lived only a short distance from one another. First I would visit Grandma Downing and Aunt Lillie. There was always plenty to do there. The attic was filled with interesting pictures and books and trunks. But most wonderful of all was the staircase, which I never tired of sliding down. . . . I could run down the hill to my uncle's and play with my cousins, A.M. and Edwin Downing. After spending a day (or two) with Grandma Downing I would visit Grandma Barnes. Another cousin, Doyle Harris Curry, and myself had wonderful times together. In the springtime we would gather strawberries and eat them. Later we would go to the orchid and climb the trees to the very tops until we had picked the choicest apples. One day we made little apple pies and had a store. Another day we took three or four apples apiece and a bottle of water and went on a long expedition. When we were tired of playing Auntie would take me on her lap and Doyle at her side and read stories. At night we played with blocks and dolls or curled up on the divan and listened to the victrola. However happy these visits might be, I could never stay away from home long.

One of my favorite games was swimming dandelions. In the springtime when on every side dandelions were seen peeping out, was the time for this sport. We would find us a long pole and select the biggest dandelion we could and go down behind the large barn to the creek that danced merrily along. After due consideration we would throw our dandelions in the water and, with the use of our sticks, guide them down the stream. . . . How gay, how happy, how blessed we were.

In the orchid below our house was a large June apple tree. Its branches were so low that I could climb it quite easily. Every summer delicious red striped apples were abundant on the tree. This tree was a haven to me. Each day I would lie among its branches and muse, munching apples all the while. When I was tired, the tree seemed to rest me. When I was sad the tree could comfort me. Even yet in the summer time I go to this June apple tree when I want to be alone.

I know that I read too much when I was a child. I did not play enough with other children; consequently I am too reserved and shy with boys and girls. Reading has also made me very imaginative. When I was a child I was always trying to picture myself with blue, blue eyes and long, golden curls and a fascinating smile and dimples. But reality is not to be done away with so easily and before long I would realize that I was only a plain little girl with straight brown hair.

My first teacher was Mrs. Lizzie Smith. Mrs. Lizzie was not only my teacher but also my neighbor. I usually walked to school with Virginia, Katherine, Eleanor and all the neighboring girls. However at times Mr. and Mrs. Smith would stop on their way to school and let us ride. One morning I, with several others, was late to school. Mrs. Lizzie lined us all up before her, and beginning with the first one, asked us all why we were late. When she asked me, I replied "Because you didn't let me ride." . . . When I entered Delina school the fourth year Miss Mary Dee Ellis was my teacher. The first day of school she wore a black taffta dress trimmed in gold. Each day she wore a new dress. I privately told mother that she had more pretty clothes than anyone I had ever seen.

When I was in the fifth grade I went to Goshen school with mother as my teacher. One day at school we were all discussing what we would do if the school building should get on fire. About this time one boy shouted that the school house was really on fire. The ceiling was so high we couldn't get water to it. We all worked with twice our usual strength and when the building fell in every desk and book was out. Mother finished the school in a vacant house.

Another memorable event was the burning of my birthplace [from which the family moved when Sara was three]. *One clear morning before I had arisen I heard excited voices downstairs. I dressed quickly and ran down. Someone told me that my old home was burning. I ran almost half a mile until I came in sight of the house. The fire had already gained too much headway to be stopped. So I saw my beloved home falling to ashes, leaving only a chimney standing as a symbol of all this home had meant to me. The great old oak trees that had probably stood there for centuries were badly burned and when the next spring came there were no green buds on their branches. The yard quickly grew up in weeds; the fence soon began to sag and all that was left of my childhood home was a beautiful rose bush that did its best each summer to make the spot less desolate.*

Soon, a larger sadness would intrude on Sara's sheltered world.

During this time Elizabeth Sullivan was my best girlfriend. . . . Elizabeth was the best girlfriend I ever had. She is the only one to whom I have been able to tell all my secrets. Elizabeth knew how well I love hickory nuts and many are the mornings that she has come to school with her pockets full of hickory nuts for me. She also brought me apples when she had them. She and I were in the same school most of the time and we finished Delina High School [which ended at the tenth grade] *together. The next year we started to Morgan together. After two weeks Elizabeth became ill and had to stay at home a few days. The next Sunday someone told me she had had a hemorrage. It was all too true. Elizabeth never went to school another day during her life. The doctor told her to stay out of school one year so that she might be well and strong the next term. That Christmas she sent me handkerchiefs for a Christmas present. At the end of that school term when I received twenty-five dollars for the highest scholarship Elizabeth called me as soon as she heard of it to tell me how glad she was. The next year I was a senior in High School. Elizabeth did not start to school as she had planned. In fact, she was no better. I wrote her frequently and at times I sent magazines, fruit, cake and anything she might like to her. Mildred Sullivan, her sister, was going to Morgan school at this time so I always knew how she was getting along. Several weeks before the next Christmas Elizabeth wrote me a letter. It was not long but I will always cherish it.*

• • •

Petersburg, Tennessee
November 18, 1931

Dearest Sara,

I'm starting this to-day but will be probably a week before I finish but anyway here goes! I have to stay in bed most of the time. I sit up some times but not every day during the afternoon. When are you coming to see me. I do wish you all would come sometime when you are coming to Petersburg.

Do you have much time for reading now? Did you ever read "Moby Dick." If you haven't read it and want it I'll send by Mildred. I can't read very much it makes my fever come up.

You were speaking of clothes they are a thing of the past with me. I haven't a dress this year but I don't go anywhere. But I'd like something new occasionly but this depression.

Thurs morn: I intended to finish this yesterday afternoon but I had the headache.

Tell Mrs. Jennie Mai to write me again and tell me about her pupils if nothing else. I enjoyed the pears very much. I still have some I kept them till they got mellow.

Well I know you "mostest" bored to the utmost with this so I'll say answer when you can.

Love,

Elizabeth

. . .

The tuberculosis was now working fast. Each time I received word from her she was worse. One morning I asked Mildred how she was and Mildred began to cry. That morning when I went to chemistry class I could not speak for the sobs that choked me. At twelve o'clock they came for Mildred, saying Elizabeth was worse. I went out to the front of the schoolbuilding with Mildred. She turned to me with the most pitiful look in her eyes that I have ever seen and said "Oh, Sara, can't you come to see her—soon?" At that moment I made up my mind to go with her. The ride out to her home is memorable. It was a cold day and I was bareheaded and without a coat. I had not even told my teachers I was going. But I did not think of these things until we were already started. Mildred cried on my shoulder most of the way while I tried to comfort her. The short drive was over and I was going in the room where Elizabeth lay. Not the old Elizabeth, but one who was deathly pale and oh! so thin. Her mother leaned over her bed. Her brothers and sisters were gathered in the room. I crossed the room to where she lay and the next moment I had her in my arms. Her mother asked her if she knew me and she shook her head. Then she told her it was Sara. Never, never shall I forget what followed. Elizabeth did not know her own brother but she knew me. Weakly, oh, so weakly, she put her arms around me and said in a broken whisper, "I love you, I love you." Just those six words and then she sank back on the bed. A little later I took one last look at my friend and then left never to see her again in this world. That night as I was studing chemistry mother came in and told me that Elizabeth had gone—quietly. I put away my book and went to bed, but not to sleep. I lay awake and remembered the things we had done together. No, for her sake, I would not call her back but at times I cannot help but long "for the touch of a vanished hand and the sound of a voice that is still."

· · ·

December 19, 1931
Petersburg, Tennessee

Your sympathy and
the beautiful flowers in
this time of bereavement
are greatly appreciated.
    Mr. and Mrs. Jones Sullivan
    and family

Educationally, Delina residents enjoyed a rare bonanza. Because the local school ended at the tenth grade, the county picked up the tab for both boys and girls to attend the Morgan

School for Boys, an elite private school located in the nearby
village of Petersburg. The younger Barnes children, Katherine,
Sara, and Johnny, joined their neighbors for the eight-mile school
bus ride. By the end of her senior year, Sara was blossoming into
the attractive woman she would become.

*During fourth year High Katherine George was a good friend of mine.
We studied Vergil together and got more humor out of it than Vergil
had intended for us to. The summer I was fifteen Katherine and I had
a lawn party. There were thirty boys and girls present and we had a
jolly time. I was really very much excited though I wouldn't admit
it to anyone. We served punch and little pink cakes. I do not care
particularly for parties yet I have been to some that I have enjoyed
extremely. One was a party at home, given by Eleanor and Virginia.
There were eight boys and eight girls. We played bug, a game that will
bring a smile to any face. There was one boy whom I had never met
before but had heard quite a bit of him. Ray P. was tall and good-
looking and the life of any party. We played dates and I had two with
Ray. All in all, I had a wonderful times that night.*

*No one ever had a better school to attend than I. This prep school
is known as one of the best prep schools for boys in the South. My
classmates this [senior] year were from all parts of the union. There
were eight girls and about twenty-five boys in the senior class. My
class work was very hard. I had signed up for fourth year English,
second Spanish, fourth History, Chemistry and Vergil. I worked hard
on all my subjects and made good grades.*

*Commencement week was something that was looked forward to
for a long time before it actually came. Weeks before, all the fourth
year students had met and chosen our speakers for senior night. We
chose A.M. Downing for valedictorian, and Raymond Phillips for*

salutatorian. I was elected class prophet [which required writing a fanciful prophecy for all the students]. *The night came, beautiful and serene. I wore a light pink satin evening dress and white slippers. When the music began to play the entire class marched slowly out on the stage and sang our alma mater. I was not at all frightened when it was time for my prophesy:*

"The sun was just below the western horizon, while night had already begun her march in the East. There was no sound of busy feet or call of the wild life of the woodland; 'and all the air a solemn stillness held.'

"The Time: A summer twilight

"The Place: A garden of magic wonders

"All the world was shrouded in that mystic drapery which only twilight can reveal. I was wrapped in the wonder and the mystery of it all, when Lo! From out of the shadows—I knew not from whence— came slowly—yes sadly too—the figure of an unknown being—A Man.

"The man of weird mien approached and spoke. Said he with a voice as deep as the roar upon the ocean surf: 'I am Future. Here my daughter is a scroll. Take it and read what is written thereon to thee, 1932 member of the Morgan H.S.' . . ."

An annual occurrence at Morgan was a school picnic just a few days before the close of school. On the morning of the picnic day the whole school gathered in the chapel and elected the Maid of Beauty and Bachelor of Ugliness. Each pupil had one vote which they might cast for anyone in the whole school. On this morning Katherine George and myself led the other girls and Raymond Phillips and J.W. Loyd led the boys for the first vote. When the second votes were counted Raymond Phillips was elected Bachelor of Ugliness and I was elected Maid of Beauty, beating Katherine by only two points. Although I was very happy, I was never "puffed up" over it.

Every year the Jeffersonian and Crescent Societies have a debate at the close of school. Heretofore, I had always been for the Jeffersonian society, but this year I was for the Crescents. The reason for my changing might have been because my brother was a Crescent but more likely it was because Raymond was a Crescent. It is a custom at Morgan that the Bachelor of Ugliness must hold the Maid of Beauty's hand on the night of the debate, so for a few brief seconds Raymond held my hand. All this seems silly and childish to anyone else, but it does not seem so to me. For me it was the happiest night I had ever known and always, no matter what happens in the future, I shall remember that night as one of poignant sweetness and beauty.

And now the last day of school was come. Soon we would receive our diplomas and then—goodbye. The girls wore white dresses with a little touch of color. Gravely we walked in and took our seats. I was sitting between Woodrow Pilot and Raymond. I received both a Morgan diploma and a state diploma. I received five dollars for having the highest scholarship of any girl.

School was over. Commencement week had been happy but it was now gone. Now my plan is to become a teacher of foreign languages but plans can be uprooted in a second and my course in life may be far different from this. I want to travel and see with my own eyes those places so richly described in books.

If in the course of time I shall marry and God sees fit to send me little ones then I pray that I may be such a mother to them as my mother has been to me. The past is gone; the future is uncertain; the present is all I have. May I so live today that my tomorrows may be happy ones.

Sara was either sixteen or seventeen years old, in her first year at Martin College, when she wrote those words. She would have just that many years again to fulfill her dreams. Her life was half over.

2.

Petersburg, Tennessee, and Bowling Green, Kentucky

1939–February 1942

Sunday Night

January 21, 1941

Petersburg, Tennessee

Dear Eleanor,

It's 9:30, my morning coal and kindling are laid, the grapefruit is cut and sugared, pants are washed, bath is taken, clothes are hung up, and so I'm like a contented Cheshire cat.

Your fire yesterday made me wish that I would or could have one too, and sure enough when we got here Miss Dixie had me one. Not having been hungry either for breakfast or dinner I had developed a ravenous appetite and notwithstanding the lunch you had packed nothing would do Bud but that we drive to Fayetteville and eat, which we did, eating a huge steak, french fried potatoes, coffee, hot biscuits, and ice cream, it being very good. Well, after we got back from Fayetteville and got in my morning coal it was already dark. Our light in the room had gone kaflooey and wouldn't burn so we tinkered with that awhile with no results. To make a long story short Margaret and Charles arrived after 8 o'clock and Bud was still here, but he left soon after they came. I'm really sorry it was so late, because it was a long way to go.

My hack's about gone. The "runny" stage came today but I think it's better too and now Margaret and I are wanting to go to Nashville tomorrow night and see Katharine Hepburn in "A Philadelphia Story." We probably won't manage it, but there's always a possibility.

I talked to Katherine tonight and she thinks mother is much better. It was lucky for me you were there this weekend as I don't see how I could have managed. Thank you for being the most sweet and helpful sister. Bud is coming back in four weeks. I have to jot him a line or so tonight and do a school letter so will close. Hope everything's in good shape.

> *Love,*
>
> *Sara*

Bud. Who is this man? And what is he doing in my mother's life?

Worse, why is he on the verge of breaking her heart—although in hindsight I can see the benefit? "Sara and Tom" would never have combined, most likely, had Bud been a less mercurial sort. I could have warned Sara off before she traveled too far down this road. Here's the clue. Bud's first letter, dated August 26, 1939, was postmarked October 10, 1939. A man who crams four pages full of words and then neglects to mail them is more enchanted with himself than the recipient. I once knew a man similarly nonchalant about staying in touch. Unfortunately for me, he became my first husband. Consider yourself lucky, Sara. Eventually, she did.

Not, however, before enduring the worst stretch of her young life. "Not for anything in the world would I have you go through a year equivalent to my 1941," she wrote Eleanor after the misery began to fade.

They met at the University of Tennessee in Knoxville. After graduating in 1932 from Morgan School at age sixteen, Sara followed the footsteps of her older sisters. She spent two years at Martin College, a Methodist junior college an hour-or-so drive from Delina; received an elementary-school teaching certificate, and headed for a seventh-grade Petersburg classroom with forty students. By the summer of 1937, she was taking classes in Knoxville toward a baccalaureate degree, paying her own way with her teaching checks. Unlike her sisters, who selected the more sedate campuses of Vanderbilt University and George Peabody College in Nashville, Sara joined her brother, Johnny, in Knoxville, where academics and good times entwined. Bud was waiting.

I think I know how he looked—flirty, confident, a touch of a Casanova, a bit of a rogue. I'm not making this up. That's the face staring back at me from the picture frame unearthed from an old suitcase of Sara's. Most of the contents are innocuous: powder; some children's clothing; a long, hand-stitched, flowered-blue dress that must once have been lovely and probably took a twirl on a dance floor or two. Tucked among the items is this photograph of no one I know. He is wearing a letter sweater and a polka-dot tie, both tinted apple green, and the dark, wavy hair and broad, ain't-I-swell grin all scream BUD. My father, I am happy to say, would never have stooped to wearing green polka dots. Score one for Tom.

Nor would he have written the letters that followed, either the self-centered portions (score two for my dad) or, as Tom's more formal love letters later attest, the ardent, romantic parts (score one, I fear, for Bud).

Saturday morn, August 26, 1939
[Postmarked: October 10, 1939]
Knoxville, Tennessee

Dear Sara,

Thought I'd write you the news before it gets cold and I might remember some of it incorrectly at a later date. I had a nice long visit with the fat boys at city jail but finally got out about 6:30 that morning.

[What in the world is he talking about? Apparently, a speeding ticket while traveling through North Carolina.]

I called my preacher brother to come get me out of jail. Isn't that a fine mess for a fellow like myself to get into. No they really never put me in jail, but they allowed me the exquisite pleasure of conferring with them until my brother got down. By borrowing a little money from my brother I paid them $15 and kissed them good-bye. I can go back Sept. 6th and stand a trial if I wish too. I don't think it worth fooling with cause I was guilty, therefore I'll just forget it. That will serve as a reminder in future years to respect the law and never go so far into the country again.

As I remember I didn't make myself any too gentleman like when I left you at bus. Think I left you and baggage parked outside the bus. Lack of sleep, the preceding night, and boys waiting on me all tended to unstablize my coordination of mind and muscle. I trust that you will think nothing of my uncouth or unthoughtful behavior at bus as I have so perfectly excused myself.

[Blah, blah, blah.]

Now may I say a word or two about you. The first impression I had of you was that you were a neatly dressed, graceful girl, rather good looking and having an extraordinary face. The unusual part of the face is not its beauty because of a correctly curved nose, thin lips and pretty teeth but primarily because of the unusual expressions.

That open countenance, facial expressions apparently stimulated by heart-felt realities within ones very soul, and the "sweet" manner in which you conduct yourself, all together make up a being that I am very glad to have known.

I think you caught the idea that I liked you because you were something different to the average girl. That happens to be the real truth of the matter. You were my girl in Knoxville during the summer of '39. The only girl that I am really glad to have known. Unless something happens you will be my girl in Knoxville in Spring.

Be a sweet girl always. Be nice to the little kids and write old Bud a nice letter.

Love,

Bud

Sara, Sara, run while you still can. Too late.

The next spring, she returned to the University of Tennessee. Their relationship thrived. In June 1940 she graduated with a bachelor's degree and a certificate to teach high school English, Latin and math. Her sister Katherine's diary records several visits by Bud to Delina that fall, and his letters to Sara are increasingly passionate, although marred by odd notes of discord here and there.

August 31, 1940
Bells, Tennessee

Dear Sara,

The sun is sinking low, it's cool and pleasant, everything is quiet and beautiful, but I have a feeling of lonesomeness down deep inside of me that I've never quite had before. What would I give to just talk to you now? I'd like to tell you I love you so much it hurts. I'd like to tell you that the love I have for you has never been quite as strong as it is at this time. I'd like to say that I'm truly sorry for those crabbed or rather sarcastic hours we spent together. I cannot describe the nature of those hours but you know what I mean.

When I have said to you "if I ever marry, it will be you" I have been quite sincere and I now believe it more than ever before. I do love you because you are more than a girl. Ah! The inadequacy of words to express feelings. When I should have told you in unmistakable language that no man ever before loved a girl any more than I do you, I didn't.

I'd like to be at the rocks or the elm tree at your house that are near and dear to your memories of your childhood and girlhood. I'd like to tell you for hours that every bit of it has a touch of sacredness about it because you loved it and love it. I'd like to lay out front on the quilt and look at the stars, possibly say nothing, look at you, and feel that sweet deep emotional feeling that we've allowed ourselves to enjoy a few times.

You are the sun, moon, stars, trees and everything that I contact. I wouldn't feel lonesome tonight if I knew you were happy, smiling and in love with me. I can't wait till I see you again. I'll write you a sensible letter later. Until then, at that time, and in the future, you are my wife that I have not married,

I love you,

Bud

. . .

September 13, 1940
Gadsden, Tennessee
SPECIAL DELIVERY

Dear Sara,

I'll see you this Fri. at your school. The moon changed my mind.

Bud

. . .

November 4, 1940

Knoxville, Tennessee

Dear Sara,

Got into Knoxville about 1:00 and finished a fairly good nights sleep in the bed. Feel fairly good today but not exactly too full of vitality.

Sara I enjoyed the weekend very much but I'm not sure but what I enjoy the after effects better. Somehow you look forward to some things with much anticipation and pre-arrangement of conversations etc. and they never quite materialize. A few weeks ago I'd think of lots of things I wanted to say to you if everything came out O.K. I didn't say lots of things I thought of but in short I do appreciate you, feel deeply thankful for a girl like you, realize that you are so far above the average person that there's no comparison, and I hope you will never regret having done what you have to keep us from breaking apart.

We didn't get around to a nice heart to heart talk like I wanted to. Somehow we didn't or couldn't make a change in so short a while from the ridiculous to the sublime. At the same time a more or less perfect understanding of each others innermost feelings and desires is the only thing that will satisfy me in that capacity. I want our love to be the strongest in the world, our home the best, anything we do as a unit must be tops.

I hated to leave you Sun. night in that room without a roommate. It looked a bit lonesome and I thought of times you've spent like that when your thoughts were far from pleasant. For every night we're apart from now on we'll be together about sixty. For every night we're apart from now to Christmas we'll live together a year. For every minute of unhappiness and misery you've had I want you to have months of happiness and pleasures. As long as you live, *beginning now, I hope that you'll never close your eyes at night or open them in the morning without feeling that you are the most precious thing in the world to someone.*

I love you,

Bud

. . .

November 14, 1940
Knoxville, Tennessee

Dear Sara,

There is a very pretty moon tonight and the cool weather makes it all the prettier. That fall atmosphere makes me think of home and feel a kind of longing. . . . My lady I promise you the wide open spacious free country, the stars and moon above, the soil, grass and trees below. Do you remember my promising you all these things over at the library one night last spring?

Rainy days, moonlight nights, the freshness of spring and the beauty of fall. It is a great life Sara and I'm not sure but that I love it more every day. We're young, full of life, emotional, passionate and hopeful. Lets enjoy life at its best and in its fullest.

Was happy to hear from you to-day. I'm proud of you, I'm looking forward to seeing you in the near future and, I think Christmas this year will be about the best one I've ever spent. Good-night and I love you.

Bud

So when did Sara stop being the "sun, moon, stars, trees and everything that I contact," not to mention the "wife that I have not married"? And why? Sara herself does not appear to have known. Katherine's diary for December 23, 1940, includes the notation,

"Sara told us that she and Bud had quit." But three weeks later, he was visiting and there is no hint of strain in Sara's January 21, 1941, letter to Eleanor. Bud's letter immediately after that visit—the last Sara saved from him for many months—also makes no mention of a breakup, although it could be read as dwelling more on the past than the future:

> To go into the usual procedure of saying how much I enjoyed seeing you etc. seems futile. . . . I love you, and I miss you when not with you. I will add that the happiest and richest days of my life have been spent with you. I refer here most especially to those days in Knoxville during the [1940] spring quarter. That feeling of companionship, understanding, love, mutual interests, the sharing of ideals peculiar to the best that is within us and that feeling (though not consistent) that you were mine and entirely mine cannot be satisfactorily displaced by anything less real, worthwhile and beautiful.

Somehow that spring of 1941, passion turned to distance. Two souls—or at least one soul, Bud's—disengaged. Family and friends believed the separation was linked to Sara's discovery (I do not know when) that Bud had been married previously. To whom, for how long, and whether a child was involved remain mysteries. But reading between the lines of later letters, it seems clear that Bud, not Sara, changed the relationship and that the knowledge of an earlier marriage did not drive her away. The intensity of his language ("A more or less perfect understanding of each others innermost feelings and desires is the only thing that will satisfy me"), coupled with his vacillating commitment makes me question his emotional grounding. The strongest support lies in a letter to Sara from a man she dated briefly a year later. He alludes to either jealousy or distrust on Bud's part, neither of which appears warranted in any way. "I can't see why he would misunderstand you if he's really in love with you," her friend wrote. "Listen, if I were engaged to you and as little as I've been with you, I could trust you without the least of fear." He advises her "to forget everything before it worries you too much" if Bud can't demonstrate his confidence in her.

No paper trail documents how the deteriorating relationship affected Sara in the spring of 1941, but her actions affirm the impact. She announced to her stunned family that she planned to quit teaching and take a nine-month business secretarial course at Bowling Green College of Commerce in Kentucky. At Hilltop View, the ominous news from Europe of Adolf Hitler's April sweep through Yugoslavia and Greece, and the downward spiral of the British economy after months of bombings and blockades, paled beside the small drama in which a daughter defied counsel and expectations. The career change mystified a family of teachers and the distance distressed them. Dissatisfied with teaching ("My dear, in our life together, I shall do most anything that is needed, with the exception of teaching, or keeping boarders," she once wrote my father), and determined to dispel her melancholy, she threw aside caution and risked change. I admire her spirit and see as a defining trait the spunk that carried her farther from the family circle than any of her siblings. Years later, her brother, Johnny, recalled driving her to Bowling Green. He was supposed to be helping their father thresh wheat, and the senior Barnes— used to having his own way—was livid about Sara's strong-headed independence, despite an apparent soft spot for his youngest daughter. Parental objections aside, she set off on a course that would redirect her life.

A county school official, as well as her family, rued the choice.

                                        June 16, 1941
                                        Petersburg, Tennessee

Dear Miss Barnes:

    Glad to hear from you but sorry of the action
you have taken. I'm not going to believe yet tho'
you won't be back for at least one more year. Why
don't you take three months this summer, come back
another year and then finish your business course
next summer? You know what I think of your teaching
and if you don't come back I want you to know I
certainly appreciate your work here and at any time
I can help you will be only too glad to do so.

    I don't know what this war is going to do to
everything. You know what you want to do tho' but
I would like very much to see you back with us.

        Sincerely,

        Ralph W. Askins

        President, Petersburg Commercial Club

Throughout the summer of 1941, diplomats and congressmen
quarreled over the merits of isolationism versus European
intervention as German troops pressed toward Moscow. But for
Sara Barnes, like millions of her fellow Americans, the clatter of
daily life quieted the rumbles of distant war. Soon, she was writing
home from her new address with a determined cheerfulness. Only
in later letters ("I thought when I left Petersburg I never wanted
to go back") did she openly address the despair of that period.
Instead, she encouraged Eleanor in her almost humorously long-
suffering relationship with a local boy, even as Sara privately sifted
through the rubble of her own romance.

August 31, 1941

402 12th St.

Bowling Green, Kentucky

Dear "Miss Eleanor,"

My day has consisted in rising at nine—Naturally I had company overnight (I've got so I'm right sociable). We dressed leisurely at first and then frantically the last five or ten minutes, but managed to get to church on time—a feat accomplished only 2 or 3 times since I've been here—being on time I mean. We went to the Baptist Church, the main feature consisting of a little 13-year-old boy who sang "I come to the Garden Alone" beautifully—next dinner—a good chicken, corn, pea, potato, tomato, cucumber pickle, macaroni, lettuce, asparagus, ice cream and cake affair. Then home, chatting a few minutes, practicing "The Soldiers Song," "The Wayside Rose" and "America" for about an hour (I've started learning a really pretty version of "Silent Night" so I can have it memorized by Christmas), next an hour's typing and now letters. I owe nine or ten but I'll probably settle for two or three this afternoon. I really do like the whole course here. Naturally I haven't set any worlds on fire but I think (though it may be a one man's opinion) that I'm doing as well as anyone else who started June 9. I have every intention of finishing in February.

Today's hot—hotter than it's been lately. My tongue's dry with thirst, but I think I've motivated Georgia to go down to the midget kitchen (a Toddle House affair) and get us a couple of coca-colas, the friend of the common people.

Have you heard from Herman? I hope he found work that he likes. Yes, of course, I think you're too good for him but as far as that goes I think you're too good for anybody I know, so if you ever decide to be Mrs. H.—you can do so with my blessing. I think the fact that he has judgment enough to have loved you all his life is a great deal in his favor.

I do hope that you'll like your grade, your room, all the faculty, and Petersburg, and that this will be a happy year. I'll come see your room Christmas.

Love,

Sara

In October, Sara came home to Delina for her first visit since the move. Upon her return to Bowling Green, she wrote to Eleanor. Bud, she confided, still burdened her thoughts.

October 17, 1941

Bowling Green, Kentucky

Dear Eleanor,

Come Tuesday night 7 o'clock I was back in Bowling Green (having stopped in Nashville and seen two hours worth of "Honky-Tonk" with Clark Gable and Lana Turner and buying myself a "uplifting" brassiere for more allureness). As I wrote mother I found the holiday which was the basis for my visit home had been annulled, but I still was glad I left. Everybody here tells me I look better after being home and everybody there told me I look better after being here so I can't draw any conclusions. Either I looked liked Ned to begin with or else I'd better start going back and forth more often.

I wanted to sit down and write you when I got back, the first night. Even if I am your sister, I guess I can tell you what I think. You have so much more than most people—a spark of difference which practically everybody feels. I'm not like you but I've always wanted to be and everybody that I've ever loved has some time or other told me that you were the person I tried most to be like. . . . I've thought a lot of you and Herman in the last few days. And I do not know definitely and conclusively just what I want. But I am glad he is there. And I think I want you to marry him next summer. You're fitted to be a wife and a mother, you were made for that, and I want that for you. Anything short of that just wouldn't be enough for you.

Don't worry about my going to Knoxville and again I'd rather you wouldn't say anything about it. It's not that I care for mother knowing or anyone as far as that goes, but I don't want her to worry about me. I may not see him at all, and if so it will be for only a few minutes, but I want to see him so badly that I have to make some effort. I wish I could stop loving him but I don't believe I can. At least I haven't.

I really feel better about mother. She didn't seem nearly so frail as in June or July. I will write her a letter the first of the week. As you see this is hardly a family letter.

I'm trying to get to bed earlier, so must stop, wash a little and get to bed.

Love,

Sara

By her next letter, she had indeed gone to Knoxville, meeting Bud on the way.

Once again, she elevated her heart's desire above societal convention—though to no happy end.

November 19, 1941

Bowling Green, Kentucky

Dear Eleanor,

It's rather late so I'll write hurriedly—and mostly about myself I guess. First, though this isn't a real answer to it, I was very happy to get your letter because you were so happy. I am glad you've made your mind up really and truly and I believe you'll be very happy.

I went to Knoxville last week-end, and I wouldn't be much surprised if the Murrays don't write something about it to Mrs. Lucille as I went by to see them a few minutes Sun. morning. If they do, you will just have to tell mother that I went up to see Estie, but if they don't mention it I'd still rather you wouldn't.

The Sunday before I went I wrote Bud and told him I was coming through Crossville, would get there at 11:25 Friday night and would like to see him if he wasn't busy, asleep, or out of town. He wrote right back that he would meet the bus and would "suggest" that I spend the night in Crossville. So that I won't build you up for a let-down, I'll say now that my going didn't make any difference, as of course, I knew deep down that it wouldn't. I just had to take the chance though.

Well he met me and took me over to his office and explained all about his work. He has a nice office, really likes his work and is making $3000 a year. $2300 of that is straight salary and $800 or thereabouts mileage on his car, etc. Then we went over to where he boards (where I spent the night—in his room). We took off our coats and he took me in his arms and kissed me as though he'd never stop, but he didn't say anything but "Sara" and "Sweetheart," just over and over. I didn't say anything at all. The next morning I went down to his office with him. He really is good for the place and all the people coming in seemed to think so very much of "Mr. C." We ate dinner in Crossville, then he took me to Knoxville—I saw Estie a few minutes, then went to supper with Bud and we went back to Norris to see his brother. We got back about 12. You can't imagine the different expressions on some of the people's faces who saw us. His cousin who goes to school up there saw us in the cafeteria. We told her we were married and she believed it. Sun. morning about 9 we went to Norris again, had dinner with his brother's family and he brought me back to Crossville where I got on the bus and came back to B.G. Got here at 11:30.

What did we talk about all that time? Well, most of the time we just laughed at us. There seemed no point in not. He never said "I love you" as of course, he doesn't. Except for the first night, he

*didn't kiss me much. Just before we got back to Crossville Sun. aft.,
he stopped at some falls and did again. I just can't quite understand
it. Maybe he could hold anybody like that and kiss them like that but
I don't see how it would be possible without loving them.*

*He gave me a nice box of candy just before I left. Again, as before
he told me he really believed I was the best person in the world and
the most broad-minded. He also said that he had almost written me
many times and meant to come up and see me if I had answered his
letter of this summer in a favorable mood.*

*Concerning his family's opinion of our quitting, I thought they
would all be glad. He said that on the contrary they were shocked
and couldn't believe it and finally decided that I must have found out
about his having been married and quit him. He told them that wasn't
the reason but wouldn't tell them anything else. I guess he just likes
me but doesn't love me.*

*I guess you'd better not leave this letter around. Just burn it up.
I suppose I was a nut to go up there when I had no money.*

I must go to bed.

Love,

Sara

What is *this*? Sara spent the *night* in his room? Am I to take that
literally or as a euphemism for sex? And what of Bud's obscure
reference a year earlier: "I hope you will never regret having done
what you have done to keep us from breaking apart." What can
he mean? Knowing something of Sara's ideals and the times,
I suspect that, more likely than not, she remained chaste. But
passion has ever clashed with convention and often won. All I can
say for sure is that she willingly gambled on love. Good for her.
She lost, but her willingness to follow her heart shines through.

When she wrote again, six days before the Japanese bombed

Pearl Harbor, Sara did not mention inner turmoil, though later letters confirm that her heart had not yet healed. Her spirits had revived sufficiently to relate a joke about a traveling preacher and urge Eleanor to pick out a simple piano duet that they could learn together at Christmas. She thanked her sister for a small loan: "I think I had 13 cents when it arrived, so you can have an idea of the welcome it received." And she was beginning to plan for life after Bowling Green. "One of my friends here has just got a TVA [Tennessee Valley Authority] job in Knoxville—Oh, boy—Gosh! Wish it was me. No, I don't know whether I want there or not, but believe I do."

Just before 8 o'clock on the morning of December 7, as American sailors savored the Sunday morning reverie, a wave of Japanese fighter planes appeared in the skies over Pearl Harbor, Hawaii. Barely two hours later, eight U.S. battleships and more than a dozen other vessels had been sunk or badly damaged, 188 aircraft destroyed and more than 2,400 American lives lost. All pretense of American neutrality in the spreading global conflict was silenced; the nation was at war. No letter preserves Sara's reaction to the carnage, but when she wrote again on January 27, 1942, the world had turned. With sisterly concern, she shifted her focus to Eleanor and the possibility that Herman might be drafted:

Lincoln County's quota may already be reached for awhile and if so he won't likely be called before next fall or winter and maybe not then. So I imagine I'd do (in your shoes) what you're probably intending to—wait now till school is out and then marry right away. If he should be drafted before then I don't think I'd let him leave without marrying no matter how short the notice. As you've always wanted everything about marrying to be so perfect, I wish you could have June weather and roses and a long dress and a full moon and a

*world at peace, but they're not the important things after all, so if you
just get married quickly and without preparation, I don't think any of
the beauty or sweetness or memories of it would be lacking. . . . P.S.
Did I ever tell you I always have a glad feeling when I come in and see
a letter addressed to me in your handwriting?*

The warmth of such letters illuminates for me what I missed
years later when my first marriage collapsed for reasons as elusive
and inexplicable as Bud's retreat. Sara would have understood,
I think, better than most the helplessness in facing seemingly
irrational behavior and the imperative not to be overwhelmed.
Because it was in her nature, I believe she would have come
running to my side, on a "cold day . . . bareheaded and without
a coat." I hope I would have welcomed her hard-won insights.
That is part of what mothers can offer daughters: wisdom and a
model against which to measure themselves. Instead, it was Rachel
who made the journey. As Sara and Eleanor knew, sisters offer
consolation powers of their own.

Unraveling the chronology of Sara's failed romance resolves
one small mystery. Some years back, a Bible given to Sara by
her mother came into my possession. To my disappointment,
it contained nothing revealing—no personal comments or
underlined passages—anywhere in the text. The only writing was
a seemingly innocuous inscription: "Sara Barnes. May 14, 1941.
Mother." Now, I realize the consequence of the date. The gift
coincided with Sara's decision to abandon everything familiar and
set off on an unknown course in Bowling Green. Jennie May must
have been deeply worried. She herself was not in good health. As
a mother, she could not shelter her child from pain. Instead, she
offered her strongest solace, the wisdom of her lifetime—faith
that, even in adversity, life can be moving to a better place.

3.

Lynch, Kentucky

March 1942–May 1943

March 19, 1942
Lynch, Kentucky
Lynch Hotel

Dear Mother,

How I did enjoy your letter which I've just finished reading. Now you stop thinking about me being pinned in by mountains, as I always did like mountains, and besides I could leave here after work any day and be home by 11 the next day. Last night I went to St. Patrick's tea at the Methodist Church, then to a show and tonight to a show at Cumberland. It's nice not to have work at night and though I miss you all, I don't have time to get lonesome. My job is grand and I had my first paycheck today for five days' work. I'm always glad to get mail, but specially from you.

Love to all,

Sara

Sixty-four years and one month after Sara arrived in Lynch, I telephoned Bob Lunsford long-distance to ask if he'd give me a tour of the southeastern Kentucky town. A local historian and raconteur, Bob readily agreed. Though we'd never met and I'd just learned his name through a random call to the town hall, this veteran mine welder and native son could not have been more welcoming. Yes, he remembered Lynch in the 1940s, and he'd be glad to describe the buildings that were gone and show me what remained. But first, Bob needed to write down my name and telephone number, and for that he put his wife, Wanda, on the phone. His hearing aids distort telephone conversations these days. After Wanda took my information and returned the phone to Bob, I could hear her speaking in the background with growing recognition about my father. "Tom Edds . . . Tom Edds . . . Tom and Sara. Why, that's Tom and Sara's girl!" She took the phone back. "Honey," she said, "Your mother was a beautiful woman, and it just about killed us all when we lost her."

For a moment, I couldn't speak. The depth of sentiment from a stranger left me stunned. I'd heard glowing remembrances of my mother from her family and friends over the years. But for someone totally unknown to me to remember her so warmly more than a half century after her death seemed an especially poignant affirmation. She lived. She died. Someone remembers. I carried the afterglow with me a few weeks later when my husband, Bob, and I met Bob Lunsford in the parking lot outside the converted train station across from Portal 31, the entrance to the original Lynch mine, and began our trek back through time. I wanted to know the place where my mother spent six of the happiest years of her adult life, wanted to sense what drew her there and to imagine her in all the stages and settings of that time.

Hulks of Goliath-sized, soot-blackened stone buildings, windows boarded against the elements, stood out like ruins in a Tuscan village as we drove down the main street. On a hillside behind the old post office and bank, Bob pointed out the site of the grand hotel where Sara boarded, its graceful portico, spacious lobby and long corridors demolished some years back to the consternation of local residents. Faint indentations in the hillsides traced the paths of streets long since reclaimed by ironweed and pines. A thousand or so Lynch residents bravely persevere in the fight against further decay. Late that afternoon, in a community gathering at the train station, over cornbread and soup beans and with fiddles tuning up in the background, I glimpsed the spirit and pride that still live in Lynch, carried forward on the echoes of an earlier time.

Sara captured a segment of that long-ago world in back-to-back letters to her mother and Eleanor during her first days in Lynch. She described a coal town that, from a corporate vantage point, was lively and even vaguely cosmopolitan, a "dressy little place" that could scarcely be imaged driving through eastern Kentucky today.

March 18, 1942
Lynch, Kentucky
Lynch Hotel

Dear Mother,

A week ago I arrived, but as Aunt Harriett would say, it seems longer than that. However, we wouldn't have the same meaning, because it's been a very pleasant time for me. I got your letter mailed Friday on Sunday morning, and gathered that when I mailed one here Wed. morning you got it on Thursday. That isn't bad mail connections.

Mr. McCorpin continues to be such a nice person to work for. Everyone who works at the store (and there's myriads) has been so considerate of "the new secretary." By now I about know all of them and quite a few people in town besides.

There's a theater facing the hotel. It gets the best shows and even earlier than Knoxville, changes five times a week. So, Katherine, that's five things for you to do the week you spend with me.

There's a lovely country club here about a mile above the town, all fitted for games and everything. It's so beautiful inside I was amazed to find they had such a one here. Mr. McCorpin is this year's president of it. I've been up three times and have been asked to join, but won't for awhile anyway. Believe it or not, debts are going to come first with me for quite a while. Last night was "ladies' night" at the club and Mr. Mac's sister-in-law asked me as her guest. They had a beautiful looking (as well as tasting) dinner in St. Patrick's colors. Bridge afterwards. This is a dressy little place. I wore the new suit, and how I love it. It's positively the prettiest thing I've ever had.

Katherine, you should really have been here Fri. night, because you'd have had as much fun out of this as I did. Jimmie Lunceford's (colored) orchestra played at the Negro schoolhouse. They're an orchestra from New York who are touring the country. March 18 they played in Knoxville, so the Negro school here put up $300 and got them to come up here and play for a Negro dance. They sold tickets also to white people who wanted to spectate and one of the boys at the store took me. I've never seen such dancing in all my life. The Negroes were dressed up fit to kill and of all the jitterbugging, congo-ing, and such! They all looked like professionals. In the orchestra there was a grand soloist, who sang "This Love of Mine," "South of the Border," "Blues in the Night," and more.

Sunday morning I went to church (Meth.). It's a pretty good looking church with a flowery preacher, excellent choir, and large membership. Sunday afternoon a crowd took me up to the state line in Virginia to see the Blue Ridge Mts. It's a beautiful view, and of course, there's still snow on the top. The weather here has been very warm since I came. The electrical storm and heavy rain of last night *has cooled the air a good deal. It's been being so hot that with all my windows up, I still don't need cover for awhile at night.*

Well, it's nice being new as I have something to do every night. I imagine that'll wear off.

Love,

Sara

One of the most popular swing bands of the 1930s, Jimmie Lunceford and his showy troupe rated alongside Duke Ellington and Count Basie with contemporary audiences. That he found his way to an eastern Kentucky coal camp telegraphs the unique status of that town.

In a separate letter to her sister, Sara added more personal details about her arrival in Lynch. She offered advice about Eleanor's ongoing, emotional seesaw with Herman and—my personal treasure—recorded her first, fateful encounter with her future husband, my father.

Easter, 1942

Lynch, Kentucky

Lynch Hotel

Dear Eleanor,

Happy Easter and I hope it's been as beautiful a Sunday at home as it has been here.

I was "that" proud to get your letter and would have written sooner, but wanted to wait 'til I wouldn't have to just "dash" a letter off. I've thought a lot of what you said in your letter. Naturally I feel that your feelings about Herman and yourself are just the natural slump which comes in the lives of everybody every now and then and doesn't mean a thing. I'm sure he wouldn't wait for you 15 years for nothing. But also I realize that you couldn't help feeling bad. Not for anything in this wide, wide world, and I say it with all sincerity, would I have you go through a year equivalent to my "1941." You are the balance wheel around which pivots all which is stable and good and normal. I couldn't feel right about anything if I didn't feel that you are there, always loving and wise, and mine.

Now as to how much you've heard and read about this new job, I don't know. But here's the facts, briefly stated. It's the most wonderful job in the world. I like it from the minute I slit open the letters in the morning to the moment I put the cover on the typewriter at night. I like Mr. McCorpin—in fact, I think he's wonderful. He is so kind, and thoughtful, and he is such a comfortable sort of person if you know what I mean. Next, I like the town. The people I've met here are equal if not superior as a whole in education, culture, or what have you to the people as a whole anywhere else I've lived. Because money is made and paid here, there is the cream of the crop in the line of officials, and teachers, etc.

Thirdly, I wouldn't be human if I didn't feel like this, I like the attention I've received. Now since Feb. 27, when I sorta woke from the daze, I would have been happy anywhere. In fact, I think it's the fact that I am so "blooming" happy that has caused so many nice things to happen. But it just seems that everything is lovely. Even my Negro waiter sometimes brings me ham and eggs for breakfast instead of the bacon and eggs the others get!

Here's the nicest thing of all, but it can't last on account of the war. When I first came I sort of looked the town over, masculinely speaking, and decided that if I had my pickings I'd take the manager of the service station. He's, I'd say, about 28 and has the kind of intelligent face of Mr. Ross. The whole town and especially Mr. McCorpin "sings his praises." But here was the rub and after I heard it, I stopped thinking. Everybody said he cared nothing about going with girls and in fact didn't. So I think the town got as big a surprise

*as me (these little things do spread you know) when he called me up
for a date. He has a lovely Buick with soft-colored red leather seats,
and he took me riding to Virginia—over Black Mt. to Appalachia and
Big Stone and Norton, Va., and I enjoyed it thoroughly. But, sad to
say, he's drafted and leaves tomorrow for the Army. And he went to
his home in Virginia the day after we had the date. But, I sorta feel
like he likes me, because he's coming back over here tonight to see me
and is going to leave from here in the morning. He won't be here till
about 8:30. He said he'd have a hard time getting away from his
home and I remembered how Mother would feel about Johnny and
should have told him not to come (But you bet I didn't).*

*The United Supply Co. gave a banquet for him last week (and
another department manager who is leaving) and gave them pay for
a two-week vacation and yesterday, Mr. Mac brought over two lovely
military wristwatches, waterproof and shock-proof, for me to wrap
for them and he told me I could give Tom (name—Tom Edds) his. So
again, I present a watch.*

*Well, having one woman-proof man ask for dates would have
been enough, but lo and behold the band leader in the High School
here, who finished at Western College, Bowling Green, and who,
again according to report, has not had any dates this year on account
of the girl back home, or somewhere, comes across Friday night and
takes me riding and then back to play bridge with the dentist here
and his wife. And last night he took me to the Easter Dance up at the
Club here. Eleanor, I had a wonderful time and I think I danced with
a million different people. During intermission Mr. Mac and wife,
her sister and the man she was with, took us over to his house—Mr.
Mac's—and they have a lovely home. To make a long story short I
danced from 11 till 5 and crawled in bed at 6 this morning. But it was
a grand time had by all.*

I got up at 10 this morning and went to Easter services. There were two pink hydrangeas (large), two other potted plants and two large green ferns. The altar looked beautiful and the whole service was good.

Well, 'scuse me for writing mostly about myself again. But I wanted you to know that I "like."

Is mother getting along all right? I feel uneasy about her since her last card. I wish I were nearer home for her sake. I hope you'll write again soon and tell me mostly that everything is all right, if it is, which I believe.

Now you be good, and don't you feel bad.

Lots of love, from Sara

Sara's winter of heartache was spent, and—war or no war, forbidding terrain or not—she was ready to bloom. Once again, her choice perplexed her family. Offered a job two hours from home in the familiar, manageable city of Nashville and another a sixteen-hour bus trip away in a Kentucky county known nationally for labor strife, its divisions chronicled by the literary likes of Theodore Dreiser and John Dos Passos, Sara did the unthinkable. She chose Lynch. "Several times she made choices that seemed very foolish to us—when she started off for U. T. when Eleanor and I were going to nearby Peabody—and particularly when she gave up her teaching job and took the business course, and then when she chose, of all places, to go to Harlan County," Virginia wrote to my father a few days after Sara's death. "We then wanted her to take the church job in Nashville. It seems to me now something of a miracle that you found each other."

Indeed. From a distance, now as then, it is hard to imagine a less likely decision. What in the stereotype of Appalachia—remote villages, undernourished children, greedy mine owners—would lure an attractive, young outsider with marketable skills?

Somehow, she saw in Lynch—or at least the *idea* of Lynch, as she arrived sight unseen—possibilities far beyond stereotype. Perhaps she was lured by articles such as a 1941 piece in a University of Louisville publication headlined "Lynch: Mining Metropolis of the Blue Grass." Perhaps a recruiter spun an appealing portrait of a vibrant, planned community featuring baseball leagues, ethnic dances, a resort-quality hotel and Fourth of July and May Day parades. That was an accurate, if incomplete, profile. Along with remarkably cohesive, family-oriented camaraderie, the town had a rawer, class- and race-conscious underside as well. Perhaps the salary offer outstripped other prospects. Perhaps Sara simply wanted the adventure and mystery of an unknown place.

Unquestionably, Lynch was an anomaly within "Bloody Harlan" County, best known as the site of one of the nation's most bitter Depression-era labor conflicts. With lyrics scribbled on the back of a calendar, coal miner's wife Florence Reese embedded the county in the national psyche after a 1931 coal strike: "They say in Harlan County, There are no neutrals there. You'll either be a union man, Or a thug for J.H. Blair . . . Which side are you on? Which side are you on?" First elected with miner support, Harlan County sheriff John Henry Blair switched to management, employing scores of company guards as deputies. Between spring 1931, when those company-paid deputies and union organizers fatally clashed near the small town of Evarts, and 1939, when abolition of the private-deputy system and federal pressures finally brought most of the county's miners under union contracts, six miners and five deputy sheriffs died in labor-related violence. Thirteen additional miners, two newsmen, three deputies and two national guardsmen were wounded in various fights, according to historian John Hevener. None of those killings or woundings occurred in Lynch, although tensions existed as U.S. Steel fought to stave off the United Mine Workers by forming a company union. My father himself would be injured in a deadly, labor-related episode in Lynch in 1949, eighteen months after I was born.

Lynch was not immune to the friction at its doorstep, but its regional status as a model town created by a major corporation determined to boost profits through a stable, content workforce cast it in a far different mold. Built from scratch in 1917 by U.S. Coal & Coke Company, a subsidiary of U.S. Steel, the Lynch that Sara encountered was a bustling, company-run community approaching ten thousand people living in relative harmony and comparative comfort. Of the more than twenty thousand coal camps and company towns established in the United States in the first six decades of the twentieth century, few surpassed Lynch in amenities. Urban studies professor Thomas Wagner, a Lynch scholar, distinguishes model coal towns from other coal camps and company towns. Lynch and next-door Benham, built by the International Harvester Company, were "an extraordinary form of company town," he writes. "They involved a great deal of intentional physical and social planning." The towns exemplified a turn-of-the-century progressive movement, known as "welfare capitalism," in which companies hoped to maximize profits by providing worker amenities. For U.S. Coal & Coke, better-than-average housing, superior education and health care and an array of churches and recreational opportunities were investments as critical to success as tipples and coal cars. In return for such rare accommodations, the company demanded steady labor and rigid adherence to its code of behavior. Those who strayed could expect to be fired, evicted from company housing and ushered out of town with little ceremony or notice.

August brings a mown-grass sweetness to the air of the Cumberland Plateau of the Appalachian Mountains, along with a penetrating heat. Deep fogs can chill the early mornings, and nights wrapped in inky blackness or a spectacular canopy of stars often call out for a quilt or blanket before dawn, even after the hottest days. But by mid-morning until the sun drops behind some ridge, an intense heat permeates man and beast. Into such a setting in August 1917, U.S. Coal & Coke deposited engineers, surveyors, carpenters and laborers, their mission to erect a mining community that would service U.S. Steel's Gary, Indiana, mills.

At its conception, "the plant location was in a wooded wilderness, with absolutely nothing at the site," records a U.S. Steel Corporation history. An early photograph shows a wide meadow with forested ridges rising steeply to each side. Planners named the new town for Thomas Lynch, U.S. Coal & Coke's first president. Driven by the government's wartime appetite for steel, the crew hauled equipment and supplies two to three miles upstream from Benham along Looney Creek and began blasting zig-zagging rows of streets into the mountainside. Using steam shovels, dump carts and mules, the men drilled wells, straightened and walled the creek channel, built four temporary tipples and set three sawmills buzzing. Along a narrow, two-and-a-half-mile-long valley floor and up both sides of the mountain, workers constructed some two hundred single homes, four hundred double homes and five boardinghouses with twenty-two bedrooms each. Except for a few concrete-block-and-stucco dwellings reserved for top officials, the houses were wooden, painted and trimmed in a variety of colors, distinguishing them from the monotony of most coal camps. Plastered interior walls, running water and an electric light—typically a single, drop cord—in each room set the early Lynch houses apart as well. Coal grates provided heat, except in some thirty "silk-stocking row" dwellings serviced by cleaner, hot-water central heat. Those fashionable houses, overlooking the town center, enjoyed indoor toilet and bathing facilities. Outdoor privies serviced typical laborer homes until sometime in the 1930s.

Soon, the company completed a 108-bedroom hotel to accommodate not only visiting officials but also many of the town's younger, professional staff; a fifty-four-bed hospital; a power plant; churches and recreational facilities. Between four hundred and five hundred Italian stonemasons chiseled native sandstone into a nearly indestructible fortress of core public buildings: a post office and bank, a four-level "Big Store" known as eastern Kentucky's finest, a schoolhouse for white students and the hospital, mine offices and churches. African American children attended school in a two-story brick building that today is one of the town's best-preserved major structures.

Hampered in the 1920s by post-World War I labor shortages, the company hired agents to meet immigrants at Ellis Island and direct them toward Lynch. A smorgasbord of humanity—Hungarian, Austrian, Serb, Greek, Scottish, Irish, Russian, Swedish, Spanish, Croatian—filled the boardinghouses and family homes. "Lynch is the melting pot of the Cumberlands," wrote freelance writer Rose Feld in the March 1926 issue of *Success Magazine*. "Thirty-two nationalities help season the pot that boils in the vastness of these American mountains." Other recruiters turned south, luring black field hands and industrial workers with promises of better wages and living conditions. "This was the promised land for people from the South," said Ronnie Hampton, a state mining inspector and former miner, whose grandmother traveled from Mississippi in about 1939 to do domestic work in a Lynch boardinghouse. His mother, then five years old, came too.

Within five months of the day in August 1917 that construction began in Lynch, nearly 1,500 men were on the payroll and twelve thousand tons of Black Mountain coal, desired for its low sulfur and ash content, had been shipped to Indiana. Three years later, the payroll had swelled to 2,300 and the population of Lynch to 5,350. By 1924 the Bank of Lynch had assets of over $1 million, as well as a foreign exchange department to serve foreign nationals. According to the *Harlan American* newspaper, the post office processed some thirteen hundred letters and two hundred parcels per day between 1921 and 1930, an annual flow of some half-million pieces of mail.

In oral histories stored at the University of Kentucky, Lynch residents of the 1920s and 1930s recall an almost idyllic atmosphere of neighborliness and self-sufficiency—dances at fraternal lodges and the hotel, Italian weddings with young couples trailing cornet players through town, traveling vaudeville shows and nickel movies at the Lynch Amusement Building, which doubled as a bowling alley, pool hall and restaurant. Blacks and whites sat in separate eating areas but were served the same food prepared in the same kitchen. In a 1985 interview, Verona Smith, a miner's daughter, described the Hungarian grape dances she attended as a young adult. Bunches of grapes tied with ropes dangled from the ceiling of a dance hall. "The girl would entice the man to get her some grapes. He got fined, $5, $10, $15, as much as $50" for the pilfered grapes, she said. A live orchestra played and couples swirled.

In another taped interview, Kathryn Overbeck, a former teacher, recalled the excitement of daily train arrivals from Louisville and points west. Young professionals clustered on the hotel verandah or relaxed in the lobby's leather and wicker chairs. "There was a big parlor upstairs [at the hotel] and a great big circle in the floor that you could look down and see everybody who came in off the train to register for the night. We could always get up a crowd and dance. There were a lot of young people in town."

Echoing Sara's delight upon arriving in Lynch, Overbeck added: "I just loved it. Everything about it appealed to me."

For many, the amenities overshadowed weekend fights and occasional shootings, particularly in Lynch's early days, at boisterous boarding houses where bootleg whiskey and gambling mixed. "Just before I came here [in 1922], they had a shooting in these apartments down here by the bathhouse and about four people were killed," Overbeck recalled. "I was a little afraid to come." Some of the early black Lynch miners were former convicts who brought with them an edge of lawlessness. The fact that African Americans were treated more evenhandedly by U.S. Coal & Coke than by many employers of the era did not erase the stigma and burden of segregation. Black miners for many years could not expect to become foremen; clear lines of separation existed in eating and recreational facilities.

Above ground comforts did not erase the danger that accompanied the Lynch miners in their daily toil beneath the earth's surface. A stone marker outside Portal 31 lists the names of the dead, an ageless tribute to the sacrifice of the fallen. Two hundred and thirty-eight men form a fraternity that makes no distinction for race or national origin. Their ghosts bear silent witness to the perils of their craft and the diversity of their origins. Among the roll call: William Brown, John Vasaki, Alex Kestukevich, Joe Tutak, Fred Washington, John Smith, Steve Salazi, Frank Supucke, Camillo Favaro, Albert Bordeau, Jose Penande, Manuel Marques, Pes Serafino, Howard Flanary, Emigdio Sandoval, James Barnes, Joe Govendish and John McGuire. The roster includes seven deaths from 1918, twenty from 1920, twenty-three in 1921, eight in 1924 and three—Pete Linsey, Will Culpepper, and Willie James Crawford—in 1942, the year Sara arrived in Lynch.

By then, eastern Kentucky had rebounded from the coal-mining slump of the 1930s. Three years earlier, after a long campaign, the United Mine Workers had gained recognition as the sole bargaining agent for Lynch miners. For a time, labor-management tensions escalated as the union sought to cement its clout by forcing higher wages and better working conditions. In 1941 that climate bred five work stoppages totaling sixty-four days. By March 1942, however, labor strife had taken a backseat to a more pressing demand, America's entry into a global war. According to U.S. Steel's history of Lynch, "The year 1942 started off with 4,091 employees on the payrolls, but due to the disturbed labor conditions and the war effort a great many men left Lynch for employment in defense plants and for military service. By the end of the year, the number stood at 2,923—a net loss of 1,168 men," including one Pvt. (soon to become Sgt.) Tom Edds.

Here's the story Tom told about Sara's arrival in Lynch. Rachel and I could never hear it enough. She was hired as secretary to the general manager of the United Supply Company, a U.S. Steel subsidiary that managed Lynch retail operations. My father, at work as manager of the service station next to the Big Store, noticed an unfamiliar woman, tall, dark haired, pretty, climbing the steps from the main street to the hotel one evening in early spring. As he watched, she ducked under the railing and picked a flower, probably a daffodil given the time of year. He smiled; his heart skipped a beat. The next day, someone joked: "Guess you'll be needing to go up and talk to Mr. Mac today." It took him a moment to get the drift. It wasn't the boss who needed checking out, but the new secretary. Later in the day, Tom found an excuse to do just that.

What caught his eye? Photographs are a limited substitute for the real person. No matter how many I scrutinize, I can't see the flow of her limbs, hear her voice, know the subtle shifts in carriage or inflection that spelled her moods. What I see on paper is a fresh, open face, wholesomely appealing, framed by thick, shoulder-length, curling hair. She is taller than many of her friends, only a couple of inches shorter than my six-foot father when they stand side by side. Nineteen-forties fashion favored a healthy roundness. Not until the end of her life did Sara look thin. Nothing in her face seems angular or shadowed or mysterious. Her smile radiates, and whether by coincidence or because she genuinely grew more lighthearted, it is after she arrived in Lynch that laughter most often leaps from the prints.

I had no idea how nearly Tom and Sara missed meeting. Katherine's diary and my father's army discharge papers preserved that morsel. Curious how much I failed to ask while those who knew the answers were alive. Is there an inverse correlation? One generation takes interest in the last, it seems, precisely when the elders die out. Katherine's diary records that Sara, her Bowling Green course complete, arrived home in Delina on Friday, March 6, 1942. On Saturday, she "sorted out her clothes and washed them," and on Monday "Daddy carried her to bus. Her first job at Lynch, Ky." According to a later letter, my parents' first date was on March 31. On April 7, Tom was inducted into the U.S. Army in Cincinnati, Ohio. A couple of weeks' shift in her arrival or his departure and, most likely, they never would have met.

If it was a miracle that Sara wound her way to Kentucky, it is no surprise that my father preceded her there. With his home place just across the mountain in Virginia and his father's profession, farming, a precarious source of income in the 1930s, coal camps offered tangible opportunity for a paycheck.

Thomas Harrison Edds was born on February 23, 1910, the third child and first boy in a family that would eventually grow to five children. My grandmother Lela, a Baptist minister's daughter, was barely sixteen when she married James Thomas "Tom" Edds and moved to a plot of land at the foot of a ridge, well back from the highway, deeded them by my great-grandfather. As a child, I found her age at the time of their marriage romantic. Long after she died I learned that isolation and childbearing took a toll. She briefly spent time in a sanatorium—the cure in that era for what appears to have been postpartum depression. Tom's oldest sister, Jewell, was a plain, retiring soul who never moved away from home. She devoted her life to the garden and the kitchen, turning out melt-in-your-mouth cornmeal hoecakes and blackberry jam on a wood-burning stove, though sometimes telegraphing resentment of her homebody role with a look or a snort. Next came Ruby, an elementary school teacher and wisp of a girl who never married. She was a playmate to her nieces and nephews, delighting us with trinkets from the Pennington Gap five-and-dime, dubbing us each with a fanciful nickname ("Texas Bluebonnet" for Rachel, "Kentucky Belle" for me) and mesmerizing us with stories about Daniel Boone as we drifted to sleep on a feather mattress. Lynette, whose gentle nature and frail heart lent her a gauzy sainthood, followed Tom. Whenever I hear of trapped miners, I relive the childhood shock of the day Lynette's husband, Coy, died in a mining accident. James brought up the rear. Mischievous and rambunctious as a boy, he was in many ways the polar opposite of my more serious, disciplined father. While they sometimes clashed (James could find my father bossy and self-righteous; Tom could find James exasperating), the bond never broke. Tom helped James through hard times; James—a classic mountain storyteller and musician—made my father laugh as few others could.

I carry an enduring image of the brothers on the night before

James died of a sudden heart attack in his late seventies. They are seated at Tom's kitchen table. James has just told a favorite story about a visiting preacher when they were boys, and his head is thrown back in laughter. Tom's grin, more subdued, conveys no less delight. I cannot say whether he was more tickled by the story or by James.

As a boy, I imagine Tom was like his adult self—a tireless worker, careful and patient about his tasks, enjoying games like checkers and baseball, but not before his work was done. His first job after high school was at a small mining camp on the Virginia side. Later, he completed a nine-month typing and bookkeeping course at Knoxville Business College and then earned a junior-college associate degree from Tennessee Wesleyan College. In later years, his old college friends teased him about being much sought after by girls during this period, but when Rachel and I pressed him for details, he demurred. He was interested in a couple of girls in high school and college, he said, but none who measured up to our mother.

By 1935, Tom was in Lynch, doing clerical work for the United Supply Company. His college plans had included dental school, but when the moment came to apply, he balked. Conscientious to a fault, conflicted about borrowing money from his aunts in the midst of the Depression, Tom nonetheless filled out the application. But when he got to the post office, the line was so long that it would have made him late for work. He turned and never went back.

World War II shook him loose from his Lynch moorings. Within weeks of his induction, he was at work in the personnel office at an Army Air Forces base in Sherman, Texas. Sara saved the first letter from a man who already appeared smitten.

April 26, 1942
Sherman, Texas

Dear Sarah,

By this time, you no doubt have the situation in Lynch under complete control. Starting out by dictating your own salary to the manager and demanding special privileges at the hotel is something very few people have gotten away with in that town. No, I don't blame you one bit. Ordinary people may be treated as such, . . . but in the case of special extraordinary people, they deserve special attention. My regret is that I cannot see that this special person is properly taken care of.

No kidding, Sarah, how are you liking the place by now? There are a fine lot of people in Lynch to work with. A few, I guess, are like a few you find everywhere. You must know them before you can really appreciate them. Does Charlie Russell smoke his cigars as short as he always did? Mr. Carter, Fred Kirby and Coy Brannon, of course, will never stop chewing, or Medley stop repeating jokes. Yes, and there is Scrip. You can never tell whether he gets more satisfaction from chewing his cigarette or from smoking it. Has Miss Rose persuaded him to wear suspenders? She used to worry for fear he might lose his pants.

I am wondering if the draft board has made another raid. There were Jimmie Medley, Earl Brannon, Ted Tremarathon, and Harley Mays who were expecting calls at any time. Tell them, if they want a real vacation, to get in the air corps. And there is Vinson Horne. Tell him that I have spoken to the commanding officer, and reservations are being made for him in the parachute troop.

I can't tell you a lot about this place since I don't know much myself. Perrin Field is a new air training school, and there are a lot of fine men here. It was a pleasure to learn that the officers here have a broader vocabulary than those at Fort Thomas. There, a command *was a barrage of curse words. That must be real Army life. Everyone, officers and enlisted men as well, tell us we are fortunate to be in the air corps. As to the food, I wouldn't want more nor better. At every meal we have just one kind of meat but always a large variety of vegetables and fruits and preserves. For breakfast we have a choice of from two to four cereals. Two and sometime three times during the week we have ice cream with cake for dessert. I still believe vanilla is better than chocolate unless maybe I had a certain pair of sparkling, should I say gray or pale blue, eyes to look at while eating it.*

Although we are not deep in the heart of Texas, our captain told us we could sing the song anyway. That reminds me, I can't get out to find those pear blossoms, and I refuse to search for the moon alone. I believe it would be much more beautiful rising over some mountain top than just coming up out of the ground.

By the way, I haven't asked about the claims department. If it isn't too overworked, sometime I have a great big one to make. Three weeks ago, about this time, I was making excuses for being late. Now I must say goodnight.

Sincerely,

Tom

Tom Edds, it turns out, wasn't the only Lynch man noticing those bright eyes, and some of the competition had easier access to the object of their desire. Meanwhile, Bud still held claim to Sara's heart. A brief flirtation with Lynch's high school band director ended when the man moved away in June. A farewell letter affirmed that each found the friendship enticing but felt a commitment to someone else. He urged her to clarify her relationship with Bud and expressed dismay at an apparent lack of trust on Bud's part. "Your honesty and frankness not only toward me your new acquaintance, but to all your friends, cannot be overlooked or overemphasized," he wrote. "I shall always remember you as that person with a friendly smile and a wonderful personality, those talking eyes and southern expressions accented by a dynamical resonating voice. I shall never forget how pretty you were on the dance floor in your evening gown and was very disappointed when I didn't get to stay over and have one more dance." A few weeks later Sara mentioned yet another beau in a letter home: "The pictures are the ones taken last Sunday week. They're not yours for keeps but I'll send them. The boy is [a local man whose father was a mine supervisor]. We went up to his home this Sunday aft. And it started raining as it has been doing off and on ever since Saturday, so we had Sunday night supper there—just one of the family!"

Meanwhile, sometimes for better, sometimes worse, Sara's awareness of the town and its novelties grew. With coal dust spread by home fires and daily train runs, "my clothes get dirty so fast I almost run out sometimes," she told her mother. "I got myself two white cotton blouses—kinda cute ones—and that will help as I've several jumpers and skirts." Navigating communications proved a challenge, as well. "I almost called you up yesterday, but didn't," she wrote after Easter. "One thing, there is not a very convenient place to call on Sunday. The telephone here is just a local one, though if necessary it can be plugged in with the long-distance phone at the police station."

In a community with strong eastern European roots, one where patriotism had been preached for years in lavish Independence Day celebrations, the war commitment flourished. If Sara paid attention to mining dangers and union strife during her early months in Lynch, her letters make no mention of it. But she was an enthusiastic enlistee in the war effort. "From Wednesday on last week I didn't do much of my regular work as all my time was taken in seeing and signing up people and typing cards for the

Defense Bonds," Sara wrote on June 10, 1942. "Everybody was very nice and we have gone almost 100 per cent in taking at least a little each month. The biggest amount signed for by any person was a $100 Bond a month. All in all, we're signed up for $930 a month for 'the duration' and I have still quite a few to see who were on vacation last week. The majority took $3.75 a month and even that is a good bit."

Sara also began a lengthy Red Cross training course, another wartime commitment.

> *Our first night they brought in an emergency case—a little Negro girl who had cut her foot terribly and several stitches had to be taken. I helped hold her on the table while the doctor sewed it up, and of all the yelling, screaming, twisting I've ever heard. . . . I know it was hurting her terribly. Tonight I took temperatures, respiration, and pulse counts, and filled ice collars and administered them (I never knew before that you put ice bags on the head of a pneumonia patient). You know how little I know about waiting on or taking care of sick people. I think by the time I've finished 44 hours in the hospital I'll at least know more than now.*

A few months later, a familiar scrawl appeared on an envelope. The writer's brief letter was as politely distant as his earlier ones were passionate.

> *September 20, 1942*
> *Crossville, Tennessee*
>
> *Dear Sara, .*
>
> *I am wondering if you are still at your same job and place. A Mr. Carroll Howard recently coming on my program informs me that he was acquainted with you.*

Surely Johnny won't have to go to the Army. You seemed to think so in your last letter but I'm hoping this isn't true. As far as I know now I'm just as far from the Army as I was when I last wrote you. Knowing you as I do I will not say anything regarding your nursing except this, Should you ever go into such a service you will be the best. I say that with all sincerity and appreciation for your integrity, ability and true worth.

I would like to come to see you but tires are such an item that I'd prefer to meet you in Knoxville some weekend in the near future. Please write your suggestions.

Love,

Bud

Thankfully, Sara was not living in an age of e-mail and text messaging. Otherwise, here, her life's story might have taken a far different twist. In a November 13, 1942, letter to Eleanor, she described a critical miscommunication with Bud, provided an update on the rest of her romantic interests (including Tom), and once again, sought to rally her sister's spirits regarding the ever-difficult romance with Herman.

November 13, 1942

Lynch, Kentucky

Dear Eleanor:

I seat myself upon the bed with pillow to back, radiator within touching distance, and typing paper at my side, and the night before me, to relate, rehash, (and forsooth to sympathize with) the happenings of the last two months and ½.

It doesn't take a smart person at all to know that right now you're more interested in talking about recent draftees than anything else. So—not to cheer you up falsely, but because it's the truth, I'll say I believe this is the best thing that could have happened for you all.

I don't think for one moment that Herman will ever have to go across. They just aren't sending the ones over 27 across. They want the boys around 21 and 22 because in the long run they will take more chances and are hardier than those a little older. And there's thousands of jobs they have to keep them over here for. Herman will do good on the intelligence test they give them and I believe they'll put him in personnel or office work. But he will get the basic training, and will probably be healthier than he's ever been by spending a few months in the Army. Few months? No, I'm not an authority, nor is Mr. McCorpin, in spite of his keeping mighty close tab on current events. However, he isn't especially an optimistic person, so I know he really means it when he says "I believe the boys will all be back home by this time next year." It certainly can't be denied that we've come further in the last two or three weeks than we ever have before, and it's just as true that we're just started in what we can do. And I too believe that it can't last much over a year if that long. And at the end of that time with how much more happiness and assurance you all can begin a married life.

The "slump" of the past summer was almost inevitable and probably forgotten by both of you by now. But a few months in the Army will make him appreciate, long for, and love you as he never has before. So with all my heart I believe that soon you'll have all the happiness that you deserve and plenty of time for rearing Jr. and Little Eleanor to boot!!

Now I'll begin on me and bring me up-to-date. To begin with, the letter that I got from Bud the last of Sept. was a short one but it was a kind, sweet one. He evidently thought my going into Red Cross work more important to me than it was. He said that he would say nothing concerning my nursing except that if I ever decided to go into such a service that I would be the best because of my integrity, ability, and true worth. He closed by saying that he would like to come to see me but that tires were such an item that he'd prefer to meet me in Knoxville some weekend in the near future if I could—Signed Love, Bud.

Now enters the villain in the form of the Methodist preacher here (albeit it, unknowingly). A day or two later he and his wife ask me to sit down in the Drug Store and have a coca-cola, which I do. They mention casually about going to Knoxville to see a Dr. the 2nd week in Oct. and tell me they'd be glad for me to go along anytime they were going that I could get off. Well, I tell them I might want to go the 2nd wk. in Oct. Then I wrote Bud and told him that weekend would suit me better than any other if it suited him and that I had a ride down Sat. In the meantime the preacher and wife change their minds about going. But I didn't get a letter from Bud so decided that it probably didn't suit him. So the Friday of the 2nd weekend arrives and when I get back to work I have a call from Crossville. Connection is bad, so Bud calls three times before I finally get to talk to him and by that time it's late afternoon. He, of course, was planning on coming and just taking it for granted that I still was. But my ride was off, Mr. McCorpin had already gone home, and there just wasn't anything to do but tell him I couldn't come. So that's finis! I think Bud thought I was just trying to be hard-to-get. I've been pretty disappointed about it all, especially since last month was such a pretty one and I had a pretty new suit!

Since I've started, I'll just talk about all the "fellows." Texas Tom is getting along fine, and is a Sgt. now. Yesterday he sent me a pair of silver wings which I'm wearing at this moment. They are as large almost as the whole necklace and very pretty. Sometimes I feel good because of him and sometimes I feel mean. For instance I felt a combination of good and mean when he wrote the following after

I had repeated to him some nice things that various people in Lynch had said about him, "It doesn't matter to me what the whole town may think so long as I know what a single person with whom none is comparable thinks. Remember a King once gave up a Kingdom for "The Woman I love."

And now to the 3rd member of my little trio—and that is [the local Lynch man]. *Sometimes I think that I couldn't be happy with Bud or Tom either because of him. Do you remember crying when I told you about him last summer. Well, sometimes I could do the same. I know beyond a shadow of a doubt that I never have been and never will be loved by anyone as I am by him and he is so unselfish about it is why it hurts me. He isn't going to be called, I don't think, until after Xmas. But when he volunteered for the Air Corps he told me just before he left that he had signed the $10,000 insurance that they have all to me. Of course, I told him he couldn't do that, but he just said that if anything happened to him he meant for me to have it and that it was the only way he could show his appreciation for what I'd done for him. (He is so handsome in his new suit that I almost love him when I see him.)*

Well, excuse this long monologue; it seems I got started and just couldn't stop.

I want to come Xmas, but am trying to "toughen up" so I won't be disappointed if I don't get to. At the most I couldn't stay but a day or so, and it's very likely not that. But if not then, I'll come in the spring.

I'll send this little line to Petersburg [where Eleanor was teaching]. *You can do as you like about taking it home. Sounds like the prattling of an egotistical brat, but a certain D.A.C.* [Bud] *took away any egotism I might have had.*

I do hope all of you are getting along all right. I do love you every one so much more than I can ever say or show.

Your sister,

Sara

*Oh Boy! Am I stream-lined!! I haven't missed a day for over 2
months taking exercise. And my hips are down to a paltry 36½ (by
stretching the tape) and I haven't lost a pound either!*

Once again, Bud shows his nature—or at least his casual
commitment to my mother. A man determined to keep a relationship alive would not have waited until the day before an arranged
meeting to confirm his plans to show up. The September 20 letter
from Bud is his last, at least the last Sara elected to save. I'm sorry,
dear. I know his loss hurt, but truly, good riddance. Now, as to the
remainder of Sara's "little trio." Clearly, my father needs to pick
up his pace. The local competition is edging him out. A couple
of dates and six months of letters don't substitute for an adoring
presence, close at hand.

Thomas's first furlough came later that month, just in the nick
of time. After it, he reported "the happiest moment of my life"—
their first kiss. Excellent. The letter also reveals qualities that she
probably had begun to recognize and appreciate, particularly his
devotion and sense of duty to his family.

November 29, 1942
Greenville, Texas

Dear Sara,

*Before, you said it was a month before you got a letter. Just now
I have been back in camp seven hours, have just gotten my things
from the supply room, hung my clothes, made my bed, read three
letters—two from home, one from you. Have you ever waited less
than thirty minutes to answer any of my letters? I'll be fairer than
that. I am not writing to answer that letter but to tell you again that
you gave me the happiest moment of my life.*

The trip back was not so tiresome as the one home even though there was nothing closer than four months away to look forward to. . . . Sara, it is hard to go back to the things you love, everything that has any bearing upon your life and then have to leave it again in such a short time. When I go home there are so many things I want to do to help them, it takes time to get over not being able to do so. I did feel pretty good over the fact Dad had only three or four more days of tobacco grading to do when I left. That was worth a whole week hunting, and I got one squirrel anyway.

Sara, I am proud of the picture you gave me, but I am prouder of the real you. One thing I can't agree with you is that you said you were no different from other girls. It is the difference that makes me like you so well. The best of everything is not good enough for you and there is so little I can offer anyone is what I meant by not feeling worthy. I can't forget the pressure of your head on my shoulder and the touch of your lips on mine.

I hope that I haven't lost by taking the furlough. Maybe my chances are less than they were before. Please don't change as rapidly as you said a person could change. The first time I left Lynch and asked that you not let Lynch change you, I meant just that. Anyone or anything you had known before coming to Lynch had priority upon you. Now I don't want anything to change the way you felt the last night we were together.

Always,

Tom

My father was a quieter, shyer sort than my mother, but they shared many values and core experiences. Each grew up in a farming family with four siblings. Life pivoted around crops, education and church, although my father reveled in hard labor and my mother joked about her talent for avoiding it. (Remarking during a visit to Delina on Katherine's skill at keeping their parents' house and yard in order, Sara added, "I'd rather sit around and giggle and exclaim and enjoy somebody else's good cooking.") Both cherished their home places and their extended families. I imagine they found familiar ground in each other's company as their relationship deepened. As Christmas 1942 approached, Sara lamented her first such holiday away from home.

December 20, 1942
Lynch, Kentucky

Dear Mother and all,

It's pretty late as I've been up to church to see the Christmas pageant and several people came in after I got back. The program was good and the church looked beautiful, with 6 lighted candles in each window, banked in a scene of snow (cotton) and real holly. A little girl not over 3 sang "May all your Christmases be White." It was precious.

Mother, I have the loveliest Christmas tree I almost ever saw. It's on a table covered with fluffy white cotton and it's just decorated with the icicles and lights. It's near the window and shows through when the shades are up. I also bought myself a Christmas present of a new bedspread—a rose one—as I did hate to have these hospitally-looking white ones for Christmas.

Buses and trains are coming in 4 hours late and more. With everything so crowded, it's by far best that I'm not trying to come home, as I might not get there and back even in 3 days.

Guess what I've been doing at the store for the last two days— wrapping presents the live long day for Dept. managers, telephone operators (about 20) who work at Harlan, and ever so many more that the Supply Company sends to. They wanted to send something to all the boys who did work for them and are in the Army, but we don't have all the addresses. I've enjoyed the wrapping, as there has been an abundance of paper, seals, stickers, ribbon etc. at my disposal.

I hope all the sickness is over now and that you all will have a good Christmas. It's irony that I couldn't work last Christmas when I really wanted and needed to and have to this Christmas when I want to come home so bad.

You know that I will be thinking of you all day long and hoping that you are happy and well.

I love you all,

Sara

Her family responded with a post-Christmas barrage, letters from her mother, two sisters and two aunts, crammed onto the fronts, backs and margins of five pages and stuffed into a single, three-cent envelope. They described every detail of the day, from the tabletop "Victory Tree" trimmed with red and blue icicles and Lux soap flakes to a list of presents: $1 books of stamps, a leather folder for protecting gas-ration books, coveted silk hose and a host of lotions, china and fruit. Johnny's new wife, Frances, made her debut and was pronounced satisfactory, "quick about her work, doesn't mind helping, and very nice without much ado." The letters elaborate, as well, on a unique present for Sara—a pair of antique bloomers from an elderly aunt, Jennie May's sister, Lillie. Perhaps only someone who grew up trying to think of gracious ways to reject hand-me-downs from aunts, as Rachel and I did, can appreciate the hilarity.

December 27, 1942

Delina, Tennessee

Dear Sara,

When Katherine met the mail the day your package arrived, Mr. W. told her she would have to bring the push cart, wheelbarrow or

something as she had so much mail. I've never seen such a deluge
of cards as has been this year. I didn't send any but received 2
doz. individually. You certainly were generous and thoughtful of
everybody. I had written a letter to Santa Claus and pinned on the
wall in Johnny's room and he nearly filled my bill. I asked for a knife.
He sent me two. I didn't have the heart to ask for stockings, in fact I
didn't expect to have another pair of silk ones as long as the war lasts.
I bought a pair of rayon hose in the fall, but I was mighty saving of
them. When they gave me a box with those nice honest-to-goodness
real silk hose, from Sara, I was so happy I didn't know what to do.

I resurrected some heirlooms and relics and gave to the family.
I gave Eleanor a pin tray dating back to 1903. Virginia, high top,
old-fashioned (imitation) tortoise shell. For Catherine I had a relic
of 1889, a jewelry case none very pretty. Now, I sent you a pair of
silk (supposed to be) bloomers of 20 years or more standing. Now if
you can't wear them if too long, send them on to Virginia. She said
she would use them. And they need to be used.

Thank you again and I love you,
Aunt Lillie

. . .

Dear Sara,

We were astonished as well as delighted to get your Christmas
letter yesterday in addition to your last two cards. The mails must
have "made a sudden sally" after the rush.

I feel like I'd better do a little interpreting on your latest
presents. . . . Then there are the undies!! Auntie Lillie was doubtful
about sending them. While I was packing the box, they were held up
for inspection and were greeted with a good bit of merriment. Maybe

it will be just as well if you don't have an audience when you open that package. We tried to get Aunt Lillie to keep them but she said she didn't wear them. We then voted with Mother and Frances being pro sending them, Johnny's vote controlled by Frances, and the rest of us con. I thought Aunt L. might feel a little bad if she didn't have something for you so we decided to send them on. You can return to Mother or me if you wish. . . .

    Lots of love,

      Virginia

. . .

Dear Sara:

    . . . We have all had a very happy Christmas. But we missed one familiar face with that million dollar smile. However when your letter came telling of so many nice things you had received, which I know you deserve, we were glad for you. . . .

    Thanks again and love,

      Auntie (Ozella)

. . .

Dear Sara:

    . . . Christmas has come and shall I say gone? . . . We all love you so dearly. It's no wonder they do there for you are dutiful and sweet. . . .

    Love,

      Mother

. . .

Dearest Bruce [Sara's middle name],

I have already given notice that this sheet which has been "rationed" to me, is to be used for "strictly personal" items, and that all of Christmas activities not related to me will have to be covered by someone else. You have certainly given us the "direst respect" I have ever seen given by any absent daughter, beginning with the huge box, including accurate daily accounts of you through correspondence, and ending with an all day attempt to reach us by phone. Our phone was out of order that day or I guess you would have reached us. Its being out of order also caused me to miss my Christmas day telegram from Herman, tho it was mailed out to me and I received it the day following Christmas. It said, quote: "Received your nice presents. I'm fine. Love, Pvt. Herman S." It was sent from Yuma, Arizona, the nearest town from his California desert maneuvers. I sent him a 4 lb. fruit cake, a Testament and Psalms ($3) from the M. Publishing House, which had his name on front and a knife which had a very clever combination of locking and releasing blades. He has not sent me a present yet as he has had no place to buy it. He wrote weeks back that he had something in mind but would have to wait until he got somewhere to buy it.

I'm glad you got so many good presents. I continue to feel sorry for [her Lynch admirer], *who deserves you, and wish you had D.A.C.* [Bud], *who doesn't deserve you. Tom makes a nice reliable reserve, who doesn't really expect to get the heroine (and won't). . . .*

Lots and lots and lots of love,

Eleanor

Oh, dear me. What has happened? What can Eleanor mean—"doesn't really expect to get the heroine, and won't"? Is it possible that in all the flurry of holiday communication, Sara has failed to

bring Eleanor up to date on her relationships? Or has something
between Tom and Sara gone awry? A responding letter clarifies
the situation to my relief.

February 1, 1943
Lynch, Kentucky

Dear Eleanor,

*I've been feeling the urge to write you lately—though why I know
not, since there's no news as far as S.B.B. is concerned. Maybe it's
because I haven't heard much definite about you and want to know.
How are you getting along without Herman? Is he at the same place,
same address? I still believe firmly that he will be a better person in
every way when he returns, and that the only thing you have to worry
about is just being separated for about another year, nor is that a
worry as I know he loves you. It's just a lonesomeness.*

*I'm so thrilled over your new fur coat? Is it loose or fitted?
3-quarter length or full length? Slick or fluffy or curly? I just don't
know my furs!! Mother said you looked beautiful at church last
Sunday. You're (but definitely, my dear) the type to wear a fur coat
and I feel tremendously proud to have one in the family.*

Eleanor, have you heard of the man who had 7 sons?

The First was a banker.

The Second stole money too.

The Third worked for the Government.

The Fourth didn't do anything either.

The Fifth was a preacher.

The Sixth chased after women too.

And the Seventh was a bachelor, just like his daddy.

*Also, puzzle on this and then see the postscript for the answer. If
Papa Bull eats green grass and Baby Bull eats green grass, what does
Mama Bull eat?*

I enjoyed your Christmas letter and want to see the picture of you and the Christmas tree on the front porch.

Everything with me is "status quo." One deduction you drew wrong though. Not only does Tom expect to get the "heroine" (if so she could possibly be called), but also does she expect it, and that in the not-too-far future. With him I could add 2 and 2 together and know the answer will come out 4 and that's what I want.

Love as always,

Sara

P.S. There aren't any Mama Bulls.

Tom may not be home free yet, but he is still very much in the running.

4.

Oak Ridge, Tennessee

June 1943–December 1943

In addition to information given on the attached
form would like to add a little information to
it. Miss Barnes was the most outstanding employee
that we have ever had with us during my 25 years
experience with this Company. We were not able
to give her the money she deserved. She not only
got along with our entire organization but was
well liked by the community as a whole. She was a
stranger when she came to Lynch but was as well
known in town when she left here as anyone that
lived in Lynch. . . . Above all, she was loyal,
honest and has a good personality. . . . She was so
far above average that I felt should give a little
more information than was asked for in the form.
M. L. McCorpin
(Manager The United Supply Co., Lynch, Ky.)

Approaching Oak Ridge from the southwest, Bob and I saw
signs directing travelers to the Y-12 security complex. We veered

off state Highway 95 and slowed for the guard station ahead. "I'm researching my mother's life and would like to see where she worked during World War II," I explained to the burly guard who greeted us cordially, but impassively. He appeared unimpressed. The facility is closed to the public in the wake of the World Trade Center terrorist attacks. Only workers with security badges are allowed on the premises, he explained.

Continuing down Highway 95, we saw another entrance to Y-12, this one apparently unguarded but with signs warning visitors away. I briefly contemplated seeing where the road led, then decided to make a second stab at entering through the first gate. Returning, I showed the guard my press badge and asked if a public relations officer might waive the entry ban. The question elevated me from a curiosity to an annoyance. No, he said, but now he'd like for me to park the car while he filled out a form about us. Moments later, a security patrol car drove up. A second guard emerged and asked me to face the camera while he snapped my picture.

This was as good an introduction as any, I suppose, to America's Secret City, one of three that helped launch the nuclear era. Oak Ridge combined with facilities in Hanford, Washington, and Los Alamos, New Mexico, to form the Manhattan Engineer District, later known as the Manhattan Project. Charged with constructing a nuclear bomb before Nazi Germany mastered the feat, the program was one of the most covert and consequential military initiatives in American history. Escalating from site acquisition in 1942 to seventy-five thousand residents three years later, Oak Ridge was so hidden that it did not appear on Tennessee maps until 1949. Sara's arrival there in June 1943 coincided almost exactly with the opening of the Y-12 plant, one of three Oak Ridge sites where scientists over the next two years raced against time to produce fissionable material to fuel the bomb under development at Los Alamos.

Barely anyone knew about that mission in the spring of 1943 when Tennessee Eastman, the manufacturing subsidiary of Eastman Kodak, began interviewing prospective employees for a work site somewhere in the ridges and valleys west of Knoxville. Certainly, a twenty-seven-year-old woman soon to become secretary to the superintendent of mechanical engineers at Y-12 had no clue as to the ultimate purpose of her employment. Harry Truman himself did not learn the full nature of activities at Oak Ridge, Hanford and Los Alamos until he assumed the presidency after the death of Franklin D. Roosevelt in April 1945.

Would Sara have agreed with Truman that the quick ending of World War II, perhaps saving thousands of American lives, justified the carnage wrought on Hiroshima, Japan, on August 6, 1945, by a nuclear bomb fueled with material developed at Oak Ridge? Or would she, over time, have experienced the moral ambivalence felt by Robert Oppenheimer, the theoretical physicist and scientific director of the Manhattan Project, who recognized the awesome— and awful—potential unleashed by his work? "I remembered the line from the Hindu scripture, the Bhagavad-Gita; Vishnu is trying to persuade the Prince that he should do his duty, and to impress him, takes on his multi-armed form and says, 'Now I am become death: the destroyer of worlds,'" Oppenheimer recalled in a 1965 television documentary, describing his thoughts during the first atomic test in the isolated New Mexico desert in the early morning of July 16, 1945.

Sara's postwar letters do not say. My guess is that she would have sided less with Isidor Rabi, a physicist skeptical of the Manhattan Project ("You drop a bomb and it falls on the just and the unjust"), and more with the pragmatism of Oppenheimer himself. At the time, his solitary focus was on beating the Nazis in developing an atomic weapon. Despite her periodic willingness to defy authority in her family or on the job, Sara gave no evidence of being a political renegade. In 1943 she, like most of America, was bent on defeating fascism and bringing the troops home. Discussing what she ultimately thought of Oak Ridge's mission is one of many conversations I wish we could have had.

No letter says exactly when or why Sara decided to leave Lynch, although a substantial pay hike factored in the move. At the time, she reported, her savings consisted of five $25 savings bonds. With my father in Texas and interest in her Lynch suitor dwindling, she may have welcomed a change of scene. She may also have preferred closer proximity to her family, a less remote setting (although it could be argued that Oak Ridge, given the tight security, was even less accessible than Lynch) or the opportunity to play a more direct role in the war effort. Word was abroad that the mission at Oak Ridge was extraordinarily important, even capable of helping end the war.

In April 1943, as Sara was beginning to contemplate a move, Tom returned to Lynch on furlough. It was their second meeting since he left his home in Virginia on Easter evening a year earlier and drove over Big Black Mountain to tell Sara good-bye. Once again, by coincidence, they were together on Easter Sunday, the day—my father told me years later—that he and Sara came to regard as their special holiday. Only now have I recognized the symbolism of that choice, given Easter's promise in the Christian faith of eternal life.

Despite his obvious interest in Sara, Tom traveled to see her only once during his furlough—for Easter day and the previous evening. How like him that he was busy helping with spring planting at home, and how lucky that she did not ditch him then and there. Tom, what were you thinking? If you want Sara to be anything more than the girl of your dreams, you have to spend a few waking hours in her presence. That myopia regarding work still plagued him decades later when he almost reneged on a long-planned trip with me because the store he managed was short-staffed. Maybe he recognized Sara in my outrage; in any event, he found a way to leave.

Given Sara's growing expectation of marriage, she was understandably surprised and a bit miffed at his lapse, although it's possible that his divided attention also whetted her interest. Several months later, she chided Tom in no uncertain terms. "Do as you like," she wrote, as they were planning for his next furlough, "only don't you dare do as you did last time and drift over to see me the last two days of your furlough only!! I was furious at you then, but that wouldn't be a candle to this time—I'm warning you!"

His May 1943 letter immediately upon returning to Texas indicates that their meeting, however brief, had elevated the relationship to a new plane. The topic of marriage arose during the April furlough, but just as he was leaving and without adequate time to consider pros and cons. Tom did not believe in wartime marriages. Sara disliked long engagements. "Tom, I'm not going to talk about us, as we said we'd just leave things 'status quo,'" she observed in her first post-furlough letter. Perhaps remembering Eleanor's and Herman's rocky romance, she added, "I still think indefinite promises, even in wartime, are unwise; and you still think war marriages are unwiser! But I will promise, that because you love me, I'll be a bigger and better person." A few days later, she added,

I feel that our chances of spending a lifetime together were lessened by our mutual agreement that wartime marriages are not desirable and that towns close to camps aren't the best place to live. One of the characteristics which you haven't mentioned (and thank you for the very flattering ones that you have) which I do possess is being pretty impulsive. And it's because of that, that I don't like promises or engagements or long view plans. So, dear, don't love me too much and if you should say, "She's not worth the bother," I'd agree with you heartily.

Was Sara being coy? Or was she rethinking her earlier statement to Eleanor regarding Tom's prospects? His first post-furlough letter, which probably crossed Sara's in the mail, took greater encouragement from their time together. A new phrase—"I love you"—had entered his lexicon.

> *May 2, 1943*
> *Majors Army Air Field*
> *Greenville, Texas*

Dear Miss Barnes,

The first weakly epistle of another four or five months period of correspondence finds the train of thoughts running backward despite the effort to think mostly of a "good morning and a clear dawn."

Sara, somehow, coming back this time was accompanied by a different feeling to any I had had before. Just to see the reaction of it, at times I tried to visualize the possibility of returning, not alone, but with someone who could easily mean as much to me as life itself. By dawn on Wednesday morning we were again in Texas, riding on the same train I had ridden before, passing through the same villages and towns I had gone through before, seeing the same pastures with the same herds of cattle, the same cultivated fields and the same wooded sections as I had seen before. It was the same Texas I left a few days before but in reality a different one.

The villages and towns gave off a more neighborly and friendly feeling, the cattle grazed more lazily and contentedly in a deeper and greener pasture, the plowed fields were more fertile and productive being cultivated with new vim and vigor, the wooded sections were more dense and enchanting.

Sometime soon you will be getting a vacation. Eventually I'll get another furlough. Whether they're at the same time or at different times, can't we look forward to that as a time when we may agree on things important to both of us and make plans for a mutual happiness?

Sara, I love you darling.

Sincerely,

Tom

A few days later, Sara reported that she had interviewed with the Tennessee Eastman Corporation in Kingsport and had decided to accept a job offer. Training would take place in Knoxville, beginning June 1. After that, she would be doing "war work" for the Clinton Engineering Works, a Tennessee Eastman subsidiary, at a job site about twenty-five miles outside Knoxville. Details to come.

Meanwhile, just as she was leaving Lynch, Sara witnessed her first UMW strike and offered her first ambivalent assessment of the organized labor movement. John L. Lewis's decision to call a nationwide coal miners' strike, closing more than three thousand mines and idling five thousand miners, evoked passionate dissent coast-to-coast. Supporters of a $2-per-day wage increase clashed with critics who thought it disgraceful to jeopardize steel production in wartime. As a United Supply Company employee, with little first-hand awareness of the dangers and depravations of life underground, Sara offered a perspective mirroring management's. "Everyone here is more or less holding their breath until April I to see just what materializes about a strike," she wrote in late March. "Mr. McCorpin says he believes the miners will get the $2.00 wage increase, but I don't know. Surely, surely, we can't have a strike now. . . . People have about stopped buying down at the store, just waiting to see what will happen. Is John L. Lewis crazy or am I and a lot of others? Is it possible that even yet we don't know we are at war?"

By late April, the unthinkable had happened.

You'll see newspaper accounts before you get this letter, so you already know that Lynch, as well as most of the other coal camps in Harlan County, and I know not how many elsewhere, is on strike. For us here it is the first day. Everything's quiet and peaceful enough on the surface, and even the store is not filled more than usual (11:45 a.m.). The most noticeable thing so far is that the telephone lines, long distance, are solidly busy. Since you've seen many strikes here, and this is my first, I can't tell you much about the tension of the whole atmosphere, except in war times it must be greater than in peace. It seems to be the general opinion among the people with whom I've talked . . . that Roosevelt will retract as gracefully as possible, and the miners will get their raise. Maybe I'm not a full-fledged miner yet, for I hope that will not happen. I feel if it does, the results will be catastrophe; and the lid will be off the inflation pot. . . . It is cruel and inhuman for us to be letting down all the boys on the front, while we argue over who shall receive what. I'm mad clear through.

As she typically did in the infrequent moments when she wrote about race or class, Sara followed that outburst a month later with a more temperate assessment—one that recognized the touch of hypocrisy in herself. "The miners, as you'll know, by this time, went back to work today, John L. Lewis having given them permission to do so. They've wanted to work and are of course no less patriotic and interested in the war's outcome than any other group of people. I suppose in all honestly I can't blame them for wanting higher wages, when I too want them and am willing to change positions to get them." She summed up by quoting poet Robert Burns: "O wad some pow'r the giftie gie us, to see ourselves as others see us."

Sara's boss graciously accepted her resignation. A joking reference ("What's the matter with you men anyway, don't you either want me? I gave both of you a chance to tell me to stay here and you both say do what I think best") triggered a spasm of anxiety in Tom. His next letter eliminated any doubt about his intentions.

May 10, 1943
Greenville, Texas

Dear Sara,

. . . Since your letter came yesterday at noon, it has been hardest for me to keep my chin up. It was sort of an accusation that I didn't want you. That I had let you down. If you didn't want to go or wanted me to tell you to stay, why didn't you say it? Rather than lose you, Sara, I would marry you tomorrow if it meant going AWOL to do it, and I could persuade you to have me. It will help a lot if you will promise to try to keep your love for me. We can make a few promises by mail can't we? . . .

I know it is absurd, but that doesn't keep me from wishing you would take enough time between positions to come to Greenville for just a little while anyway. You have an invitation to do so if you like.

*Remember you told me how old you are but not when your birthday is,
and also that your fingers are longer than mine but not the size ring
you wear. I couldn't buy you that kind of birthday present without the
size or any other without the date. . . . If you don't get enough time
or see fit to pay me a visit, can't we promise each other that on my
next furlough, that won't be making long promises, we'll weigh all
the evidence pro and con and lay plans, so much as conditions will
permit, that will last through eternity. . . .*

    I feel better now. . . .

    Love,

      Tom

Sara's last letter from Lynch was dated May 25 ("There never
was really another Lynch," she noted as her time there wound
down). After a weekend visit to Delina, she headed for Knoxville, where she and Mary Crockett—a Mississippi friend who
followed her from Bowling Green to Lynch and later became my
sister's godmother—had accepted Tennessee Eastman jobs. After
a "deadly dull" week spent filing, she marched into the personnel
manager's office and "just told him I wouldn't be willing to keep
up with that sort of work indefinitely, as I'd understood I was to
get secretarial work." Within a week, she began employment in the
administration building of the Y-12 plant at the yet-to-be-named
Oak Ridge, surrounded by oceans of mud and dust.

The birth of what Sara came to affectionately call "my
town" and "this crazy town," full of "noisy, bulldozering days,"
occurred a few years earlier and an ocean away. In January 1939
German scientists succeeded in splitting an atom of uranium
by bombarding it with neutrons. Aware of the development and
its military potential, U.S. émigré physicists Enrico Fermi and
Leo Szilard, among other scientists, frantically sought to alert

government officials to the danger of allowing the Nazis to use the discovery to build an atomic bomb.

Later that year, they persuaded the brilliant physicist Albert Einstein, a German Jew who immigrated to the United States in 1933, to sign a letter to President Roosevelt. Today, the American Museum of Science & Energy in Oak Ridge displays that historic letter, mailed from Long Island, New York, and dated August 2, 1939.

It reads in part:

```
    In the course of the last four months it has
been made probable--through the work of Joliot in
France as well as Fermi and Szilard in America--
that it may become possible to set up a nuclear
chain reaction in a large mass of uranium, by
which vast amounts of power and large quantities
of new radium-like elements would be generated.
Now it appears almost certain that this could be
achieved in the immediate future.

    This new phenomenon would also lead to the
construction of bombs, and it is conceivable--
though much less certain--that extremely powerful
bombs of a new type may thus be constructed. A
single bomb of this type, carried by boat and
exploded in a port, might very well destroy the
whole port together with some of the surrounding
territory.
```

Achieving only passing notice at the time, the concerned scientists persisted. By the summer of 1942, according to historians Charles W. Johnson and Charles O. Jackson's Oak Ridge study, *City Behind a Fence*, "American nuclear research had advanced sufficiently to insure that a full-scale bomb development program was feasible and advisable." On June 17, 1942, Roosevelt approved an initiative and shortly thereafter, the Manhattan Engineer District was organized within the U.S. Army Corps of Engineers. Colonel (later Major General) Leslie R. Groves, a jowly West Point graduate known for an abrasive manner and an incisive intellect, assumed direction of the project on September 17. Drawing on already completed research, he selected its East Tennessee site two days later. The location was sufficiently inland to protect against enemy attack. Also, a series of ridges formed natural barriers in case of explosions, nearby Knoxville offered a potential labor market, the Clinch River supplied water and hydroelectric plants at TVA's Norris and Watts Bar dams provided a major energy supply.

On October 6, the government filed a petition in U.S. District Court to seize some fifty-six thousand acres of land occupied by about one thousand families. Bulldozers erased stores and housing in four small communities—Elza, Scarboro, Wheat and Robertsville—to make way for a town site and three separate production facilities on a reservation averaging seven miles wide and about seventeen miles long, east to west. Beginning the following spring and over the next three years, the sounds of saws and hammers created a constant background din as a population originally envisioned as thirteen thousand residents soared to seventy-five thousand. By 1945 the new city had become Tennessee's fifth largest, consuming at peak one-seventh of all the energy then produced in the United States.

At Oak Ridge, as at Lynch, Sara moved to a city constructed from scratch. This time, she was in on the ground floor. At Y-12, which eventually exceeded the size of more than twenty football fields, scientists and engineers aimed to produce a critical mass of explosive material—highly enriched uranium, or uranium with a high concentration of the isotope U-235. To do so they built huge machines called calutrons, arranged around a giant electromagnet like an oval racetrack along which charged particles accelerated at incredible speed and could be separated out according to their mass. One former worker described the calutrons as "screeching like two powerful planes taking off." Another recalled that "the whole Y-12 valley was filled with a mighty roar that could be heard back in Oak Ridge, four miles away."

The workforce that monitored calutron operations would be mostly young women, hired and trained to sit at banks of control panels and read meters and adjust dials without asking why, told only that their work was vital to the war effort.

For thousands of workers, high national purpose entwined with the small but critical decisions of personal life. To a young, single woman, Oak Ridge presented in microcosm all the restless, rootless contingencies of the home-front in a time of war. A buzzing hive, the city swarmed with folk up from southern farms, down from northern cities, crammed into hastily constructed neighborhoods and dormitories, competing for groceries and cigarettes in lines that notoriously stretched for blocks, yearning for sweethearts far away, finding new ones in the clutter and clamor of Oak Ridge's barren, bustling nativity.

No feature defined the town more than security, which was as tight as feasible on a military reservation with a largely civilian workforce. Residents were instructed to "Keep Your Eyes Open and Your Mouths Shut." A February 12, 1943, letter on display at the American Museum of Science & Energy reflects the government's deliberate vagueness about even the plant location:

```
This will confirm the offer I made to you for
work in the new plant of the Tennessee Eastman
```

Corporation, which will be located somewhere in
Tennessee. Unfortunately I cannot tell you the
nature of the work . . .

Sara's correspondence underscores the confusion. Her early
mail is addressed to Clinton Engineer Works (the project's initial
name), Box 590, Knoxville. "I thought you were going to be located
in Kingsport," John C. Howard, the general superintendent of
the United Supply Company, wrote in a June letter complimenting
her work in Lynch. Even my father seemed unclear about her
destination, suggesting that she may have been as well. "Darling, I
am glad you are going to Knoxville," he wrote on May 21. Not until
August did the name "Oak Ridge" appear on envelopes.

Ed Wescott, official photographer for the Manhattan Project,
described the intensive security buildup in the spring and
summer of 1943. "Armed guards appeared at the seven defined
entry points to the reservation, fencing was erected at strategic
points on the exposed perimeter of the area, and mounted patrols
guarded the area that bordered the Clinch River," he wrote in a
photographic history of the project. Residents aged twelve and over
were expected to wear official badges at all times. Only special
visitor passes, often hard to come by, allowed others through the
heavily guarded gates. Large billboard messages, including one
with a swastika representing the pupil of a seeing eye, reminded
residents to zip their lips.

The Enemy

is

Looking

For Information

Guard Your Talk

So shielded were the identities of Oak Ridge workers that high school football players were identified only by their jersey numbers on rosters, and coaches scheduled nothing but away games. When the *Oak Ridge Journal* began publishing birth announcements in November 1943, only neighbors and friends were likely to recognize the new arrivals: "Elizabeth Ann, born Nov. 8 at 205 E. Tenn. Ave.; Robert William, Nov. 11 at Oak Ridge Hospital." On one occasion, the newspaper elected not to publish a picture of members of the Oak Ridge Women's Club for fear that someone might recognize the wife of a famous physicist then living in Oak Ridge under an assumed name. The newspaper, which largely restricted itself to noncontroversial matters such as event listings and announcements from base officials, poked fun at its plight: "We are unique. The only newspaper in the country without any news."

With so many eyes and ears, total secrecy was impossible. Johnson and Jackson describe as "perhaps apocryphal" but "widely accepted as true" the story that the Oak Ridge Library had to repeatedly replace the page in its dictionary on which the word "uranium" appeared. Meanwhile, spies and prominent physicists were said to have slipped in and out of town, at times equally undetected.

Sara's descriptions match those of historians. "Have I told you much about Clinton Engineer Works?" she asked Tom in late June, shortly before moving from Knoxville to an on-site dorm. "Not much I know, for I had to sign so many papers the 1st week that I've been wary of mentioning it verbally or written. It is a really tremendously large defense project, and I've heard there are only five men who really know what is being built. Every precaution is being taken." When she forgot her badge one day, "it took me till 9:30 to get myself cleared and I still quaked all day whenever a guard came near. It's the most guarded place I've ever been around."

Settling in at Oak Ridge, Sara chattily informed Eleanor about
the four-and-a-half-mile bus ride from the dormitory to the
Y-12 administration building, described her latest expedition to
Knoxville and announced the purchase of a grape-colored winter
coat. "The family may take one look and gasp for it's anything
but conservative—but a honey nevertheless." She joked about the
chaotic working conditions and contrasted herself with Eleanor in
two ways. First, Sara said, she preferred the stop-and-go nature
of clerical work to the pressured demands of the classroom, and
second, she claimed far more tolerance for barren settings than
her older sister:

> *It's 10:20, and no signs as yet of Mr. Rogers, and I've finished the
> work which was continued from yesterday. Another advantage of
> the "business world" over the academic one—in teaching you know
> daggoned good and well that every day will be packed to the brim,
> while here and similar places, some days we work hard, and some
> days are more or less breezes.*

As for the ambiance of Oak Ridge,

> *there's something about you that makes me unable to picture you in
> unlovely settings, maybe because you always do something about it.
> Now I'm perfectly satisfied for myself to be placed in a corner of a
> barn, with a slightly soiled typewriter—and that just about describes
> the office I had when I first came out here too—and either mud or
> dust a half foot thick on the outside, but not for you.*

On the love front, once again Sara consoled Eleanor, whose
long-running romance finally was collapsing for good. Sara spoke
from experience:

Time helps tremendously, although it never can erase completely memories of loving and being loved. The best and most effective cure is always someone else, and in your case there will be someone. You could never be a misfit, for always you've been a joy to those who know you. Just keep on being, and things must come out right in the end. I believe that with all my heart, however trite and old and untrue it may sound.

In 1942 Americans trooped to the marriage altar in record numbers. Defying wartime uncertainty and fears, some 1.8 million couples tied the knot. Many were young lovers determined to grasp a moment of happiness before fate cast them off an unknown precipice. The Rev. Rudolph Ray, rector of New York City's Little Church Around the Corner, one of the most famous Episcopal parishes in America, penned a warning. His volume, published in 1943 and entitled *Marriage Is a Serious Business*, cautioned against hasty wedlock dictated more by a draft card than considered thought. While Sara and Tom would ultimately contribute to that year's statistics, they came closer to following Ray's advice than many. At thirty-three, Tom was almost a decade older than the average male marrying for the first time in 1940–1944. Why had he waited so long? He simply was never sure until he met Sara, he said. In 1943 nothing was certain, but he appeared less likely to wind up in Europe or the Pacific than men in their twenties. "This is a young man's war," he observed in a letter just after Sara arrived at Oak Ridge. Sara's age, twenty-seven, exceeded that of the average wartime bride by about six years. Moreover, the gentle, gradual nature of their courtship allowed time for seriously contemplating such matters as finances and marital expectations, even as their love deepened. Sara's letters suggest as much admiration as passion for her future husband; his convey an adoration that never ebbed.

What led Sara to decide, finally and for sure, that Tom was the one?

In March 1943, before Tom's second furlough, she confided to Eleanor a lingering ambivalence. "Occasionally since Christmas I have doubts concerning whether I should marry him (if Barcus is willing of course being understood) and of course it's impossible even yet at times not to hurt over what has been," she wrote, "but most of the time I am happy clear through that someone as fine and worthwhile and to-be-trusted as Tom loves me, and I feel that way now."

My own experience suggests that people value in a second romance what was absent in a first. It is no accident, I suspect, that Sara emphasized Tom's trustworthiness. With him, she needed not fear reliving the heartbreak of her relationship with Bud. There was nothing false or inscrutable about Tom. As for my reticent father, I set off in quest of my mother but found an unexpected dimension of him as well. It is one thing to be told that your father loved your mother deeply, another to come face-to-face with his tenderness and ardor. I weep for a father who never expected life to be a bed of roses, almost miraculously found one and just as capriciously saw it slip away.

Throughout the spring and summer of 1943, Tom pressed his case for a postwar marriage with a blend of love and logic.

May 30, 1943
Greenville, Texas

Dear Sara,
    . . . Do you believe love is strong enough to hold people together until they can acquire the material things of life they have looked forward to having? Can you imagine yourself being married to a

pauper with a strong desire to spend every ounce of his energy and every minute of his life trying to make you happy? By the time a person reaches my age he should be better prepared for the making of a home than I am. I could have managed differently possibly, but that is too late to help now. Sara, I am selfish enough to want you still.

What kind of beginning could we make with thirteen hundred dollars? If you are superstitious, I can save another hundred before fall and make it fourteen. After all, that is a tenth of what you said would be enough for a person to retire with. All but about five hundred is in Postal Savings and War Bonds. The cashing of them now wouldn't be the most patriotic thing to do. How's this for a suggestion? At maturity value they total eleven twenty-five. We wouldn't have to add a great deal to them to make the cash value a thousand. We could then cash them in two hundred at a time, and at the rate of two hundred dollars per head that would buy the first five of a family of ten or twelve. Of course there would have to be something to live on between cashing periods. Uncle Sam might have to be responsible for a while. After that we will find something. The Supply Co. might consider taking me back. . . . We could go back until we could afford something better, like going to a farm and being the lowest paid workers in America or maybe some other kind of business of our own. Conditions will be different and we would have to work them out together.

. . . The next time I go home, I want you to go with me. The war plant can do without you long enough for that.

Love,

Tom

He remembered that, during his April furlough, "when I held you close and looked into your eyes, there were times I could have crushed every bone in your body. . . . Believe me, I adored you then as I never had before."

Finally, the ardor in Tom's writing rivals Bud's.

She worried that her love did not equal his. "Tom, I don't know whether I love you or not," Sara wrote with blunt honesty in late June.

Sometime I think I do, and other times I think I don't as much as you deserve to be. I even wonder how you can be sure that you do me. We've been together so little that we haven't had a chance to build up the comradeship and interdependence which I still think is a great part of love. Letters help, but we know each other more from letters than from being together. We can't help that, I know, but it's all part of what I mean when I say—I don't know.

Four days later, Sara wrote again. This time, she had not heard from Tom in more than a week, and she ruefully acknowledged the void. "Tom, I missed your letter which didn't come all last week. Sometimes perhaps there is more of that 'interdependence' than is realized. . . . 'Scuse me for writing, Mister. I meant to wait till I heard from you but tonight I just wanted to. OK?"

Her musings appear to have prompted a rare phone call—long to them but humorously short by modern standards. "How good it was to talk to you," she replied. "I'm scared to think how long it was but I know it was well over 3 minutes. . . . As is always the case, I couldn't think of all I wanted to tell you, but it was sweet to say good-night rather than write it." Throughout the summer, their letters continued to blend everyday events with intimations of a shared future.

July 4, 1943
Greenville, Texas

Dear Sara,

Of course you aren't entitled to another letter this soon, but today is one of our most cherished holidays and it's quite natural to associate special people with special occasions. If the people of 1776 were to come back today, I don't believe that we Americans are so different from them that they would declare their efforts were in vain.

This morning a much stronger wind than usual which was howling outside had its bearing on the restfulness of a late Sunday morning's sleep. When I get back home I'm going to sleep for a solid week or maybe a month. By 10:15 it was too late to go to church. That's a good feature of church services here. They are over early leaving plenty of time for other things just in case there is something else to do. In case we don't get up early it is too late to go and the same holds true—more time. This time I had an over-sized laundry that needed doing. Now half the joists in our barracks are hanging full of dripping wet clothes . . .

Dad and James [Tom's brother] have just finished harvesting their wheat. That is all except the threshing which comes later in the season. That is always hot work, and I am glad it is over. Two years ago Dad almost had a stroke from getting too hot while threshing, so it is always a relief to know when certain jobs are finished. They tell me all about their work as it progresses from one stage to another; in which field certain crops are being grown; how many tobacco plants have been set; and how many new pigs and calves they have. It seems that I could go back and find just anything without their showing me.

There's still an emptiness and a deeper craving for something they can't furnish. At times just a card has satisfied that wistfulness. Could that be a reason for being sure? Among the people we both

know, haven't we separately chosen the same ones as our best friends?
Since we have been together so little, could our mutual friendship
with others be a guide as to whether we would fit into the same social
world?

. . . Still I haven't written anything about Texas. When it comes
to writing I can usually think of things I like better, if you don't mind
too much.

Love,

Tom

Soon, they were planning for Tom's next furlough later that
fall. An early August letter affirmed his change of mind about
wartime marriages.

August 8, 1943
Greenville, Texas

Dear Sara,

. . . I had wondered if hotel accommodations in Knoxville were
as scarce in Knoxville as in Dallas and the other larger places around
here. I didn't have any trouble in April but that has been four months
ago. When you suggested that maybe two weekends might be spent in
Knoxville, I thought perhaps they were more fortunate in not being
so overcrowded. There's no point in defeating the purpose of anything
before it has begun. I've returned my furlough for this month and
consider the possibility of having more time with you well worth the
risk in being able to get one later.

Knoxville must be terribly hot now, anyway. I remember how
the candlestick on my mantle used to bow its head during just such
days as we are now having. Personally, the closer we can get to the
country the better I will like it. . . . Gatlinburg would be an ideal
place to spend a whole week during such days as we are now having.

Horseback riding in the fresh morning air over the mountain trails; fishing for trout in the afternoons and then maybe a Tennessee Fish Fry over a campfire at night. Do you suppose there'll be such things as vacations any more? Sure there will, but wonder if we can ever take one together. One that wouldn't require planning. Just steal away, leaving the whole world and all its cares behind.

Sara, maybe I shouldn't write this, but when I think of my last furlough (you furious woman, if you will remember, you will recall that I did tell you I wanted a couple of your evenings. Did I get any answer?) I would rather never see you again if it would be to leave you as I did then. Perhaps if we had known before how the other felt concerning certain things, it might have been different. Greenville is better than the average near-army camp town in that there are a smaller number here than at most camps. . . . On Staff pay, two people should be able to live and have a bit left for recreation. Maybe enough to keep life from being too deadly dull. . . . Then there is also the fact that you have no way of knowing that you can be sure. That, I consider more important than the other.

I used to think how different it would be when I went back to Lynch. Even if I did have to work half the nights and Sundays, we would have the others to develop that comradeship, to build up an understanding of relations which are essential to interdependence and to being sure. I can't think that way anymore.

Even when this war is over we might not have any better opportunity of being together than we now have. Waiting no longer seems to offer any solution to the problem; it is rather robbing us of time that might justly be ours. Sara, I do want the best for a wife—the very best. In you, I know I would have the best. On my next furlough I sincerely hope that we can reach a better understanding than we did on the last one. Goodnite darling. I won't take warnings. I still love you.

Tom

Sara replied with a demand for greater clarity. I empathize with her struggle. What young woman, heartbroken once, would not tremble as she stood on the brink of a lifetime commitment?

August 16, 1943
Knoxville, Tennessee

Dearest Tom,

It's Sunday afternoon, the before-sleeping period, and everything here is calm and quiet. As yet in midday or mid-afternoon there's not a great deal of beauty in the immediate setting here, but as seen by the light of the moon the buildings and surrounding vicinity become almost lovely.

Tom, your last letter is before me; and I have read and reread it. This afternoon I would give a great deal if you were here . . . so we could go walking and, more important, that we might have a long talk together.

We know each other well enough to recognize and love the qualities which are good in the other, but not well enough to say something and always have the other understand the thought or the desire which is back of it. For instance—your letter. It, you, and you and I have been on my mind most of the time since Wednesday. And yet I cannot read between the lines well enough to really interpret your feelings—other than that you do love me, the knowledge of which is always around me like an invisible cloak.

There are one or two—perhaps irrelevant, perhaps pertinent— ideas you seem to have concerning me which I believe are wrong. One is implied in your quoting the words deadly dull. I remember when I wrote them and concerning what. To me it would be deadly dull to be off to myself typing the live-long day. But it would never enter my mind at all to apply those words to a pattern of living which held love and understanding, no matter what the physical privations and

economies and lack of paid-for recreation might be. . . . True, I like
big houses, and lovely clothes, corsages, and many other things that
money can buy—but it's just as true that I also like single rooms, and
aprons, pear blossoms and the hundreds of joys which all the money
in the world couldn't purchase.

Another thing—if we were married and your salary were six times
what it is or more, do you think I could be content idle with our
country at war and the work and labor of every person needed? I
couldn't. . . . When all the victories are won, there'll be time for
relaxing.

Tom, I do love you—certainly not as much as your own unselfish-
ness and fineness deserve, perhaps because I cannot match them. Will
you write me again, this time more frankly, telling me what you want
from your own standpoint and not from your interpretation of my
own best interest.

Your picture of Gatlinburg is very enticing. It would be lovely
there in October, the "magic month."

    Sara

Regrettably, the letters do not include Tom's reply.

For the next month, letters dashed back and forth, consumed
with details of a furlough due to begin October 14. In one, a
barrage of questions underscored how many gaps remained in
Sara's knowledge of Tom.

At the time you finished in Athens, did you want to go on to U.T. [the
University of Tennessee]? I mean really want to? Was the business
school not a change of desire, but a secondary choice? Do you want
to be a dentist? Or a farmer? Or an USCO valued employee? Some-
times I get so angry with us; we almost wasted the little time we have
had together—no, that's not true either, as knowing little things about

a person is almost as important as knowing big things. Do you realize
that actually we've had 5 nights and 1 day, and that is all? I'll not
count the night that I begged to go along with you and Bill—and you
let me, but still brought me home first!

Did they know, when Tom arrived in Knoxville, that he would
return to Texas a married man? No saved letter even hints as much.
Remembering Sara's description of herself as "pretty impulsive"
and reconstructing a time line, I suspect that the decision to cast
aside doubts and caution was cemented in the romantic hours
after he arrived. I hope that those moments reverberated with
passion and glee and the inner certainty Sara sought.

On October 20, six days after Tom's furlough began, a special
delivery letter with a ten-cent stamp affixed to the usual three-cent
one sped from Fayetteville, Tennessee, where Eleanor was teaching,
to Oak Ridge. In it, Eleanor celebrated the announcement in a
telephone call the previous night that her baby sister would be
marrying three days later. Coincidentally, the family was expecting
the arrival of Johnny and Frances's first baby, Katherine had
just found a job and word had reached southern Tennessee that
Herman, Eleanor's former sweetheart, had shipped out overseas.
Focusing on Sara, Eleanor joyfully urged her to put aside any
apprehensions about the momentous step, to revel in the moment
and to trust that heartfelt commitment would see the couple
through.

October 20, 1943
Fayetteville, Tennessee

My dear Sara,
    If anyone had told me a year ago that I could receive the following
information: you getting married, John O. having a baby (figuratively),

Katherine having a job, H. having sailed, all in one night—and still be living to tell the tale, I would have doubted their veracity. . . . When I got your card this afternoon, and then mother told me tonight that you were going to Tom's, then he was coming on here, I suspected; when Central said "long distance" I was almost sure; when you said "Hello E" I was completely sure. So by the time you told me, I was prepared by the space of one minute, which kept it from being a shock!

Now, we shall take "you" up first, you being the most important of all items listed. I suppose Tom knows that he is getting the best we've got (or that anybody has for that matter). If he doesn't, tell him, but I have a feeling that he loves and appreciates you like I do—(well nearly as much). Also tell him that we are going to be glad to have him in the family for he comes to us highly recommended!!

After this takes place we shall be in a position to say whether or not it is wise to engage in war marriages. We can prepare an article "by Sara Barnes, who did" and "Eleanor Barnes, who didn't." We'll have all the arguments for and against right there in one issue. As to your feelings in the matter, I don't suppose anyone (and especially a Barnes) ever went into a new "field" without looking back into the previous "field" and wondering if they were making the right move. Now there is nobody that can see all the hills and dales of the field they are entering, but if they can see enough level, grassy land ahead to make them want to enter said field, I say go ahead through the gap and put the bars up behind you. You, being a farmer's daughter, probably follow me in all these ruralistic figures of speech. So when doubts arise squelch them, for all wise people doubt occasionally. "Only a fool is perpetually happy." Quote Elizabeth Mills.

But what I do want to say and impress upon you is this: For this brief period, forget the past and the future and make this the most perfect time of your life. Don't have one little worry about how the family is getting on, and what you want for each member of the family in the future. We'll work that out later. Forget every one of us for a few days (and then, my little lady, you had better remember us and get home). This is your time for happiness so make it perfect, and I have every reason to believe you will. I was sure that someday "if you'd watch and you'd wait you'd find the place where the four-leaf clovers grew" (quote Mrs. Altsletter with the tense changed) and sure enough, come to find out you did.

I'll bet that wedding dress is pretty and I know you are in it. Don't worry that you can't marry at home with accessories. I tried that and it didn't work. From now on I'm for these little "quick got up" ceremonies. It's the people that count anyway, and two perfect people equals a happy marriage, anyway you take it. It can't fail to work out when you put as much into it as both of you will.

I love you so,

Eleanor

No letter describes the actual ceremony, but it must have involved some chaos and a heap of laughter. Upon first reading the announcement that appeared in Sara's hometown newspaper, I thought there must have been a mistake. According to the article, the ceremony, conducted by the Methodist minister in Clinton, Tennessee, near Oak Ridge, occurred at 10:15 p.m. Even amid the craziness of war, that seemed unlikely. Surely, the Methodist parsonage had not taken on the aura of a Las Vegas wedding chapel, providing twenty-four-hour service. But no, in a letter a few weeks later, my father affirmed that "the hour 10:15 p.m. holds the sweetest and dearest of all [memories]." Something must have delayed their departure from Oak Ridge, and I can only imagine the gaiety as they sped through the night, accompanied by their attendants, the diminutive and loyal Mary Crockett and the boisterous Della Mae Hopper. The bride, as reported in

Sara's home paper a few weeks later under the headline "Social Happenings at Petersburg," wore a tailored suit of bride's blue wool with black accessories and a shoulder bouquet of white orchids.

Over the next week, Sara and Tom visited both of their homes, sharing their happiness and affirming the solid place of family in their lives. I savor the image of those light-dappled, halcyon days. From this vantage point, as my own children shape their futures and return home for ever briefer visits, I can relate also to the bittersweet restiveness experienced by Jennie May after her family gathered to meet the new addition and then dispersed.

November 1, 1943
Delina, Tennessee

Dear Sara:

Did you get back all right? I hope you don't feel so lost as I do. This was a busy morning with churning, washing dishes and etc. After John got home from Mrs. Hallie Dyer's funeral we ate dinner, then I lay in bed a long time feeling about worn out. I feel all right now but have wandered here and there looking for I don't know what. After feeding chickens I went out by the barn to hull a few walnuts. I hulled 6 and it hurt my hand and I missed Kay so much I came on to the house.

Last week was just about as perfect as a week can be, only it wasn't long enough. I wouldn't have a thing changed, even to the rain and certainly not Tom and you. Both of you are so lovable. The world will certainly be benefited by your both being in it and belonging to each other. Sometimes we grieve over things and wish for them when it isn't best for us. As Kay said, I'd give a million bucks to have another week as pleasant and I feel sure we shall have.

Something has been getting my hens. Last night John thought he heard one squall so got the poker and flashlight and went to the upper

*hen house where he spied a possum. He was about to get away but
John jerked him back by the tail and lashed him good with the iron
rod. He certainly wasn't playing possum as John finished him up good
and proper. I had found 2 chickens or hens that he had killed.*

*Eleanor grieves over H. but I know there must be something better
in store for her. The telephone is off again to my disgust. I want to
talk to her every night. She says she can hardly wait to hear my voice.
Now isn't she sweet. I've always wondered why I drew the sweetest
children in the world but have found out there were some just as fine
born in Virginia.*

*Begin to ask at once about coming with someone Christmas. I love
you so much.*

Love,

Mother

Come soon

Back in Texas a week after their wedding, Tom could hardly
have been happier.

"October with its bright blue weather and all its magic wonders
is swiftly passing to join the thousands of others that were once
just as real as today and every one of which holds secrets of its
own," he wrote on October 31. "No matter how fine, how noble,
or how great their combined secrets may be, October 23, 1943,
the hour 10:15 p.m., holds the sweetest and dearest of all. From
that hour on it has been and will continue to be a different life—
one worth living—a life based upon our love and devotion to each
other. . . . Darling, I have needed you so much."

For her part, Sara never again—at least in writing—suggested
any doubt that she had made the right choice. If her thoughts
ever drifted to Bud, her roguish and intense first love, she kept

the memories to herself. Instead, her letters convey appreciation and acceptance of her new husband and the family into which she had wed.

In early December she traveled alone by bus to visit Tom's family, unfazed by the rusticity of a four-room, three-porch mountaineer's cabin reached by a quarter-mile gravel road running through cow pastures. "I don't know how they managed to time it so well," she wrote appreciatively,

> but we had a delicious hot supper almost immediately. It was wonderful! Chicken and dressing, creamed potatoes, cucumber pickles, and your Mother's own delicious cake. Afterwards we made no effort at all to get to bed early. Jewell played the organ and James the violin, and we all sang, even me, who can't. It was well after 1 before any of us went to bed. . . . Then yesterday was a perfect day. After breakfast I walked out the way we went when we were there in October, down past the barn and over to the fence adjoining the corn field. That's a beautiful lot; I like all the trees and the rocks. The sun was so warm that I just wore a jacket and was comfortable. . . . When I came back, Jewell and Ruby went with me over to the cave, and we came back by the holly tree and gathered me some. Then we walked up on the hill in front of the house to see the view. Everything seemed so unhurried and peaceful and good. . . . Your family's so fine, Tom; and I love to visit them. There's such a sense of well-being there, and contentment, and love. I'm proud to be a part of them.

With their first Christmas as a married couple three days off, and her husband in an army barracks hundreds of miles away, Sara pulled out her best stationery and added a red poinsettia seal for a long-distance holiday embrace.

December 23, 1943
Oak Ridge, Tennessee

My dearest Tom,

What occasion more special is there than Christmas on which to use one's newest stationery or to tell one's deepest feelings? So, dear, here's the stationery; and here's the way I feel. It's easy for me to like and to love people and to enjoy their friendship and association. But I want you to know that now and always you are first in my heart, and that I love you dearly.

Christmas is a wonderful time of the year. It's a time when values can curiously become disentangled, and the best is on top. I appreciate deeply the kind of person you are, Tom. Your honesty and your sincerity, your deepness and your strength, your patience and calm, all intersprinkled with your sense of humor and your understanding.

I'm sorry I cannot be with you this Christmas—you will be much in my thoughts, you may be sure. And with the faith that your ever coming Christmases may each be happier and that we may be together for them, I'll say goodnight, my dear husband, and a Merry Christmas— and a happy New Year.

Sara

As 1944 began, she contemplated the mysteries of a two-year passage that had transformed her life. A month past her twenty-eighth birthday, she reveled in her good fortune. "I sometimes wonder if there is anyone else like you anywhere. . . . I am a girl whose luck surpasses all others."

5.

Oak Ridge, Tennessee

January 1944–September 1944

Tonight it's very good to be alive and young enough to have the best years of living and work and fun and joy to look forward to, yet old enough to weigh and evaluate and appreciate those years. I've much to learn about you, Tom, even as you have much to learn about me. We can't possibly as yet know all the characteristics and parts that make each person different and individual. Nor would we prefer to—there's too much adventure in the discovering of those traits. But what I do know of you, I love. —March 5, 1944

In due respects to being a married woman now, I've let out the hem of three dresses. But I've started going again without hose, and wearing ribbons in my hair—a sign of not being completely grown up, I fear. —May 1, 1944

My night's reading consisted of Drew Pearson, Dorothy Thompson and Walter Lippman and a more thorough perusal of Gasoline Alley, Harold Teen and Dagwood. Add the latter to the list of funnies that is consistently funny. Others rave of Dan Dunn and Dick Tracey, but toward them I remain only passive. —May 17, 1944

*Your fairness and constancy and poise make me ashamed at times
of my own hot-headedness.* —*June 23, 1944*

*I've had seven dips of ice cream today—two at dinner, a double cone
this afternoon, one at supper and a double dip since!!* —*July 3, 1944*

*Last night I was wild with loneliness. It seemed that ghosts were
walking and I couldn't stay in my room. So I went out to the Montgomery's. Seeing them brought me down to earth again.* . . . *I felt lots
better when I came home.* —*September 18, 1944*

*Virginia said tonight what a pity that no one but the family would
ever know how dumb I am. They all agreed, saying that probably even
Tom would never know. I think he probably will* . . . —*October 14,
1944*

So, who is my Sara? How does one reconstruct a life? Give an
apparition shape and heft? Memories serve as the usual starting
point, but mine of my mother are so fleeting.

Sara's letters, embellished and informed by conversations with
as many of her contemporaries as I can find, add brushstrokes to
the blank canvas in my mind. What have I learned? She was the
youngest, prettiest, most daring daughter of a family in which
life centered on education, the local Methodist church and a
host of relatives. Similar nutrients enriched much of the rural
South in the decades before television and fast-food homogenized
America. I think she sparkled. The parallels are not perfect,
but her vivid, high-tempered nature, leavened by strong ideals
and a deep capacity for friendship, summon up Lizzy in *Pride
and Prejudice* and a cross between Jo and Amy in *Little Women*. She
loved ice cream, smart fashion, Judy Garland, lyrical language
and anything that blossomed. She could be vivacious and funny,
impulsive, passionate in defense of those she loved, a tad vain,
occasionally melancholy, suspicious of narrow-mindedness

(especially in religion), quick to fire back at a perceived insult and conscientious about job and community commitments, though she jokingly feigned laziness at work and was surely less dutiful than my father. "She was opinionated, just like the rest of them [her siblings]," observed one acquaintance wryly. More than one male suitor complimented her soft voice, deep chuckle and dancing eyes. She elevated character over wealth, else she would not have married my father, who had an abundance of the former and precious little of the latter. Even allowing for the goodwill afforded the dead and the natural desire to please an inquiring daughter, I am struck by how many acquaintances said something along the order of Barbara Embree, the ninety-year-old widow of my father's first cousin: "I thought she was the most perfect person I have ever run across in my life."

Even so, Sara was less altruistic, more easily nettled and less embracing of all humanity than Eleanor, who thrived in a profession—teaching—that Sara found burdensome. Relating how, in annoyance, she once rejected an ice cream from a soldier who woke her up during a bus ride home, she added: "Mother and Eleanor felt bad about the soldier wasting a nickel on me. You see, Tom, I'm not as sweet as you thought me, but I come from a family that is." Nor was Sara as observant or as critical of society's flaws as Virginia, who challenged my sister and me to envision a world without wars and racial strife. Virginia ignored put-downs and even ostracism in her pursuit of political and social causes she found just. Sara never hesitated to battle for a friend, but she rarely challenged the larger status quo.

My biggest disappointment lies in the fact that Sara's racial attitudes reflected her time and place. I detect nothing overtly malicious in her words or actions; she simply appears oblivious to—or, at worst, accepting of—the disparities at her doorstep, particularly in Oak Ridge. In Sara's absence, Eleanor and Virginia became my strongest female role models. Would I have paid as much attention to their attributes had Sara lived? Inevitably, our losses redirect our gaze, inviting, allowing, unanticipated gains. Then, too, Sara would have developed as her life matured. She wrote the bulk of her letters when she was in her twenties; Eleanor and Virginia were many decades older, and the beneficiaries of profound societal changes, when I knew them best.

The letters that pre-date Sara and Tom's wedding on October 23, 1943, create an outline of their relationship; those from the following year provide a far more explicit record of intimate thoughts and mundane moments. As a new bride, there is a sugar-coated quality to the writing. But as the weeks wear on, interspersed with furloughs and monthly "anniversary" presents, dented fenders and disappointments, dorm-room bridge parties and news of distant deaths, an ease settles into a relationship still remarkably new on their wedding day. Sara and Tom occupied common geographic space in Lynch for about five weeks in the spring of 1942. Their first date occurred a week before he left town. They saw each other, briefly, during two furloughs, that autumn and the following spring. And then, they married. In the letters of the next year, as she remained at her secretarial duties in Oak Ridge and he with an Army Air Forces personnel unit in Texas, their discovery of each other grew.

"I've just reread your last letter and it seemed to me, as it did the first time I read it, that you were not feeling very happy when you wrote it," Sara wrote in February 1944. "At times I feel very inadequate. Undoubtedly, we have had too little time together and I was more or less a spoiled brat during the time we were. But will you please not be sorry that you took me 'for better or for worse.'"

Tom and Sara, in their twenties, before they met.

(Left) Sara's high school graduation photo, 1932. *Courtesy of Hue Counts Photo/ Lifetouch, Fayetteville, TN.*

(Below) The Barnes siblings at Hilltop View, Delina, TN. From left, Katherine (kneeling), Johnny, Sara, Eleanor and Virginia.

Furlough, Easter 1943, Lynch, Kentucky.

(Above, at left) Front of the Lynch Hotel. *Courtesy of the Southeast Kentucky Community & Technical College Appalachian Archives.* (At right) Tom (far right) and friends outside the Lynch post office.

Lynch's "Big Store." *Courtesy of the Southeast Kentucky Community & Technical College Appalachian Archives.*

Sara and Eleanor in Delina.

Oak Ridge days. From left,
Virginia Black, Sara and
Mary Crockett.

Eleanor, fourth grade
teacher in Petersburg,
TN, 1941.

(Above) Lynch, August 24, 1947: Coming home after Margaret's birth.

(Right) Lynch, October 23, 1948: Sara's and Tom's fifth wedding anniversary.

Rachel and Margaret, June 1950.

Lynch Hospital.

Sara, 1943. *Courtesy of Thompson Photo Products, Knoxville.*

At other moments, they dreamed and planned for the normalcy of a postwar future. "I'm entirely in accord with you about our emphasizing quality instead of quantity when we buy anything," she wrote.

Let's never load ourselves down with a lot of possessions for which we care nothing. Money is so much better spent for beautiful and ageless things, a few good pieces of furniture, maybe a picture or two of the masters', books whose worth have been proved by their never-ending popularity, that trip to the West to enjoy the wonders that God has so lavishly provided, an educational start for our children (and of course a well-pedigreed mare for me to ride!). We'll accumulate those things one by one, enjoying and reveling in them to their full worth, and forgetting about fancy doo-dads.

Anticipating a furlough the spring after their marriage, Sara wrote happily, "We've a completely new experience ahead of us as we've never known each other at all in the space between early April and late October." Later the same week, however, responding to Tom's apparent suggestion that she seemed less upbeat than usual in a recent letter, she sounded irked: "I cannot at all times have a super-abundance of it [vitality]." She worried aloud that "you might not like the everyday me as well as you thought. (I can always say though that it's your own fault that you didn't know me better for you only came to see me once during your second furlough.)"

As the weeks passed, the doubts settled. "You're becoming a part of me," she wrote. She no longer found composing long letters a strain, Sara said. Now, both idle chit-chat and her deepest thoughts flowed from the pen.

Tom and Sara fought World War II from the home trenches,

an arena where a sense of high purpose mingled with the tedium, the triumphs and the setbacks of daily life. Sara quipped about her lackadaisical commitment to bandage rolling. Reporting that she was making Red Cross bandages for the first time since Lynch, she added: "The trouble about good deeds is that they have to be kept up, just like insurance (so I never took out insurance)." But when it came to making genuine plans, she remained in Oak Ridge, rather than join Tom immediately in Texas, in order to fulfill her personal commitment to the war effort. As they contemplated her moving to Greenville in time for their first anniversary, she rejected the idea of a weekend meeting in Memphis—both because she thought such a short visit would be more unsettling than satisfying ("We do so very much need a long uninterrupted stretch of time together") and because she did not want to shirk her responsibilities in Oak Ridge. "In spite of the fact that my reason for leaving in the fall seems justifiable to me, it remains that I accepted a job in a defense plant, have stayed long enough that I know I can do more here than I could any other place for the duration, and now I intend to quit in the fall. Therefore, I think the very least I can do is to not ask time off even a day before that time."

Millions of Americans, including Sara's siblings, were equally committed to using their skills in any way helpful to winning the war. The military assignments of various cousins and friends stretched from England and Italy to Africa and the Pacific; others served stateside, both inside and outside the military. Virginia spent her school break in the summer of 1944 working at the Navy Department in Washington, D.C., exciting the family when she glimpsed Charles de Gaulle, the visiting leader of the Free French movement and later president of France. Eleanor contemplated and then rejected a job offer teaching in Oak Ridge, even with a

$1,000 raise. "I'm not sure she would like this crazy town as much as I do," Sara correctly forecast. But Eleanor fulfilled her patriotic duty by accepting a one-month summer stint teaching thirty-five Oak Ridge fifth graders. Katherine, who had never worked away from home, wound up briefly at a factory job in Chattanooga. And Johnny, forced to forgo military service because of his childhood leg injury, headed up scrap rubber drives and performed other community services at home in Middle Tennessee. "Wherever I can do the most good is the place I want to be, let it be teaching school or whatever else I may be called upon to do," he wrote Sara in 1942 while still waiting to hear from the army.

As an early arrival in Oak Ridge, Sara was an active observer of the town's fevered, haphazard pace and the day-to-day patterns of its residents. She rose each morning at 7:15 a.m., left the dormitory at 7:35 a.m. and boarded a smoky and crowded bus to the Y-12 site, where she arrived at 8:00. After grabbing breakfast in the cafeteria, she was at work by 8:20, five minutes late. "Even at that," she wrote, "I'm the first one in our offices, and am able to give the appearance of having been here a long, long time when the others come in at around 8:30 or a quarter to 9." Work progressed in fits and starts. "I, Sara Edds, have worked today and it Sunday too. I really felt like Honest Abe when I got home this afternoon for it's the first completely full day's work I've done in a week or so. It was old blueprints, a hundred and fifty-seven of them to be indexed and filed and what not," she wrote on February 14. A few days later, she reported that the unusual burst of activity continued: "This is one of the few weeks when I've been worth my salt (maybe), as I've been busy during the day and have worked two nights. Aren't you proud of me?"

A typical workweek provided plenty of interludes for both letter writing and reading:

You'd have got a kick out of what happened today. We've an official down from Eastman Kodak at Rochester and a day-long conference was held in Mr. R's office. But he, the visiting gentleman, came in my office to take a telephone call, and happened to see lying open a book of Plato and Aristotle and what not. It seemed to amaze him so that he had to ask all about why I was reading that and one topic of conversation led to another and so on until finally the waiting conferees in the next office got impatient and the superintendent came in to get him. Five to one I get fired yet before I resign.

On another occasion, Sara reflected on the much-publicized surprise visit of Treasury Secretary Henry Morganthau to an agency office in Washington, D.C. "I couldn't help but grin," she said. "He found one girl reading a book, another a magazine, a third eating an ice-cream cone and the fourth with her shapely legs on the radiator while she day-dreamed. I'm afraid Oak Ridge couldn't stand too many surprise visits without somebody getting stirred up." She recorded, as well, the reply of a prominent Tennessee Eastman official when asked how many people worked at Oak Ridge. "About half," he reportedly replied.

Some other observations were less humorous, but equally on point:

This is a strange place here, better I imagine than most defense-plant towns, but still strange. The people are real, and kind, and interesting, but nobody really has roots here. It's almost like a huge group of totally strange people with diversified tastes and interests being marooned on a desert island. The rules and laws of conduct are no longer the same as they were at home or in any strange but established town. For some it's good; for others bad. I don't know which predominates, but I've an uneasy notion that it's not the first.

With Y-12 located one ridge to the south of the town proper, Sara found herself in the "riding-a-bus to business category" most days. The Oak Ridge fleet of more than eight hundred buses rivaled that of a major city. Off-site buses carried residents to Knoxville and other nearby towns. After her marriage, Sara kept Tom's car for a while, enjoying the freedom to escort friends to Knoxville for an event or shopping spree, although gasoline shortages and worries about worn tires kept pleasure rides to a minimum. "Your car is a sight, but I can't help either the mud or the dust," she reported.

Sara learned firsthand the pitfalls of venturing outside the perimeter of a facility protected by scores of armed guards. Every exit and entrance of a guest or employee was subject to careful screening. "Are you interested in hearing a tale of woe?" she inquired after a troublesome trip into Knoxville. "Of course I shouldn't tell you, for any lingering doubts you may have cherished of my sanity may alas go out the window with the telling. But I need sympathy so much that I'll risk the former."

Mary and I'd been looking forward with glee to going into Knoxville some pretty afternoon, in which we'd window shop and gaze and I'd leave the car for the proper alignment and balancing. So we chose today, perfect because her boss was out of town and mine was pinchhitting in another building. A heavy rain though held us up, so it was well along in the afternoon before we got started. I'll skip the events of the afternoon for the present up to the coming home time. Mary was spending the night in town, so I went down to the bus station at 5:30 to be sure and get a seat on the 6:00 bus. I did, well and good, but we'd not much sooner than got well on our way toward Clinton before the bus broke down. We all waited fairly contentedly until a different one was sent out from the bus station. We came via Clinton and Elza Gate. The latter was my Waterloo. I reached into the purse to get my badge and after a futile search for it, I remembered sadly but too late that on going out of the Area I'd put it in my lap and that it was no doubt reposing at the moment at the back of red leather seats in an auto at Knoxville Buick Company.

Well, out I crawled and after trying three offices finally located the Sergeant who could write me up a temporary pass, provided the badge number I gave him as mine corresponded with the number which the T.E.C. officials that he would phone gave him. But when he called in first they couldn't locate a Sara Edds' name. The second trial was for Sara Bruce Barnes. That didn't work either. At this point I took my seat in the far corner of the room, just washing my hands daintily of the whole affair and leaving it to the Sergeant and the officials. They finally located me as Sara Barnes Edds, and I was issued a temporary pass and started thankfully toward home.

But all was not won, for when we came to the next gate they wouldn't let me in on my pass—said I'd have to have a badge to go with it. So out of the bus I got again and trekked back in the rain to the first gate where they gave me a numbered badge. So you see when I finally got home after three hours on the road I wasn't in a mood to care when I discovered that I'd left the key to my room, the key to my desk and to Mr. R.'s desk, and to the two files in our office, and to my suitcases on the key ring in the car!!

But all wasn't a failure for I found the cutest animated picture edition of my old time favorite of Flopsy, Mopsy, Cotton-tail and Peter, complete with Mr. McGregor, for Sandra [Thomas's niece] and also "Lassie Come Home" for Sonny [a nephew] and a book of Will Alexander Percy's poems for myself—and I got something for you too, but it's a surprise and I had "size" trouble for it.

Across Oak Ridge, construction continued apace, often twenty-four hours a day. Entire neighborhoods sprang up almost overnight. Aerial shots show row upon row of postage-stamp houses plopped on naked lots ornamented only by telephone poles. "Our town is still growing, though I don't guess I'm supposed to say so, even to my husband," Sara wrote in February. "There is a new recreation hall, although I haven't seen it inside and new grocery and drug stores are going up at various locations throughout the townsite."

On a drive through Oak Ridge today, flowerbeds and hillsides wooded with sixty-year-old trees soften flat, utilitarian bungalows, public buildings and commercial strips constructed during the war. In 1943 and 1944, there was no such buffer. Most wartime residents lived on treeless lots in one of a half-dozen styles of single-family homes, known as cemesto houses because their exterior walls consisted of thin sheets of cement and asbestos. Visiting one of her former pupils and his parents in a cemesto house, Sara reported:

It was really pretty cute. From the outside those houses look as though there wouldn't be space to turn around in. But somehow or other, there's a good-sized living room, a small kitchen (and even a tiny pantry), two fair bedrooms and a bath—not to mention five or six closets stuck around at odd intervals. Since you were here last October those houses have been "pitched" everywhere, including in the already small yards belonging to the permanent type houses.

Trailers, dormitories and substandard hovels aptly called "hutments," reserved for African American laborers, expanded the housing stock. The latter were sixteen-foot-square, olive-drab boxes, each housing four to six workers, set flush on the ground and ventilated by four openings, unglassed and unscreened. Hutments were segregated not only by race, but by gender.

Men and women, even married couples, were forced to live in separate areas, divided by a high wooden fence. Original Oak Ridge plans called for a "Negro village" with housing comparable to that for whites. In the frenzied building boom, those plans never materialized. White housing took precedence. A postwar investigation by the *Chicago Defender* newspaper described Oak Ridge as the rare community where slums were deliberately planned. "The concept back of the planning and operation of this small city is as backward sociologically as the atomic bomb is advanced scientifically," wrote Enoc P. Waters on December 29, 1945.

Did Sara notice or lament that abysmal double standard? Not that her letters mention, I regret to say.

In March, five months into their marriage, Sara and Tom debated making their first post-wedding meeting a furlough that would include visits with their families, but elected for Sara to come to Greenville instead. The priority was uninterrupted time together. In their entire relationship, they had been apart from family or close friends no more than a day or two. Once again, they would manage to share Easter Sunday. As the trip approached, Sara described her mounting excitement amid the passing of the second anniversary of their first date.

> *March 31, 1944*
> *Oak Ridge, Tennessee*

Dear Tom:

The last week or so I've had a guilty feeling that I've been pretty selfish. It's mostly concerned about next week. Tom, can you under-stand that as much as I love my family and yours that I still didn't want them mixed in at all with the next time I saw you? I guess that's the real reason for my deciding to come to Texas and see you

rather than insisting on your coming home, as I probably should've.
Here out of two weeks we wouldn't have had two whole days to have
really learned each other better or been together. I hope you're not
disappointed. Anyway I'm excited about coming.

The reservations are all made, both for coming and going. I'll leave
Knoxville at 8:05 Thursday night, April 6; get to Memphis around
7:00 a.m. Friday, leave Memphis at 8:00, and get to Greenville
about 9:30 p.m. that night. From Knoxville to Memphis I have a
Pullman, my first time for one—in fact my third time to ride on a
train, as far as I can recall. I'm so glad that the part from Memphis
on is in the daytime, for it's all new country to me, and I'm interested
in seeing all of it.

Now I don't know whether I'll ever stay with you or not; you make
it too much fun for me to come home and find surprise packages when
I'm not with you! And yesterday's candy was such a complete and
delightful example of what I'm talking about. Two years since you
took me driving over to Norton and we discovered that we both like
sweet things to eat, and riding in a car with the radio playing, and
Lynch! I have to rub my eyes in amazement to remember that it's been
that long . . .

Love,

Sara

Simultaneously, Tom was in Texas composing an "anniversary"
message to her.

March 31, 1944
Greenville, Texas

Dear Sara,

D'ye remember tonight two years ago? It's now 9:20 which would
be 10:20 eastern standard time. Perhaps we were riding along

somewhere between Norton and Big Stone Gap at this very hour.
That night I learned the first of your likes. Were there any dislikes?
I don't remember one. Chocolate pie (when we stopped, for that is
when I forgot to turn off the lights, so you see you've always attracted
all my attention when you've been present), music, dancing, large
homes located on big hills are among the things you told me you like.

That night I liked to hear you laugh, to listen to you talk. Your
voice was so soft and pleasant. Your accent was different and I liked
that too. Even then I realized how very nearly I had come to missing
something that was promising of what I had almost decided didn't
exist.

These have been a short two years and different in practically every
respect from any two previous ones I've known. The next two—what
do you suppose they hold for us? If they are as short and all the others
following are as short in comparison, we'll have a brief life together
even if both of us live to be eighty. As for that we'll have to make each
one of them count. None can be wasted. They are already too few.

With each passing year, March 31st will have a deeper and richer
meaning because through them I'll continue to learn more and more
about you. Each year I'll be just a little prouder of you. It will take
years for me to appreciate all of your courage, your sincerity, and
your goodness.

Good night and love,
Tom

How thrilled and nervous Sara must have felt, setting off
for her farthest trip west and farthest away from home, moving
toward the arms of a husband she had not seen for five months
and with whom she had spent only four previous nights alone. I
hope the reality matched her dreams.

Once back in Oak Ridge, her letters suggest it did. Sara reveled in the memories of a visit to Dallas, where she and Tom strolled the campus of Southern Methodist University on Easter Sunday; a shoe-purchasing trip to Neiman Marcus and the opportunity to meet his friends and see his surroundings. "The corner room at the Washington was beginning to seem suspiciously like home by the time we left. You'd made it so pretty for me, and every hour I was there you were doing something sweet—except you were horrible to beat me at pingpong and to remind me that Evelyn wrote 'for hours' to Chick (Will you swap with him, even for the letters? OK, then if you won't, you have no kick a-coming)." Her references to sexual intimacy and the newness of the experience shall remain their private domain. "Tom, I had such a good time, and I enjoyed being with you both night and day more than I can say. . . . P.S. Nope, you're not scheduled to be a pappy in the near future; so it was excitement after all."

A few days after her return, Sara basked in the "magic" of an anniversary bouquet, wired by Tom each month of their year apart. In February, Sara reported a corsage of "the palest, most delicate pink carnations." In March, a floral box arrived filled with "the essence of spring—lively deep pink carnations, velvety peach-colored gladioli, fuzzy little yellow something-or-other, dewy fern. They're too beautiful to describe. You know without my telling you which ones I'm wearing today." The April present stirred a flood of memories:

I came home to find flowers from you. They always have the power of transforming my dormitory bedroom into a lady's boudoir. Especially lovely are the snow white carnations with the background of deep green fern. There are colored carnations too and stately gladioli. But the white carnations take me back a year and a half (lacking two months only). It was two nights before Christmas and the [Lynch] "store" was a busy place, teeming with last minute shoppers, and dripping with those huge fat Christmas bows. Someone put a box in my hand and said, "These are for you," and there were my first flowers (in a box—I've not forgotten the pear blossoms) from you. They were white carnations—there must have been a dozen of them and they were tied with red ribbon. And they made me glad.

Soon, they were planning for a fifteen-day June furlough. Anticipating that event, Sara queued up with the rest of Oak Ridge to arrange for the necessary supplies.

Guess what—I can get enough gas coupons for 900 miles! That plus your five gallons should be far more than we'll need while you're here. So our only worries along that score will be tires, and I think they're still pretty good. The gas is the amount that the Rationing Board here grants residents with cards every three months. That custom was started back when the project was new and people had to go to Knoxville for everything from a handkerchief and a nail on up.

As June approached, Sara and Eleanor consulted on summer plans. Advising Eleanor on whether to spend the summer working in Washington, D.C., or at a summer camp (eventually she settled on teaching at Oak Ridge), Sara exposed her renegade streak:

I'd do just whatever I wanted to do most and not be worried at all about what I should do or what would be best for me or best for my family! That's maybe poor advice, but nevertheless the course I'd follow. Personally I'd welcome two months in Washington much more than I would three weeks at the camp, but I've a sneaking feeling that you would feel just exactly the opposite (You know in spite of the many ways we're like, there are quite a few ways in which we're unlike).

Sara was as deeply invested as Eleanor in their family. But it was no fluke, years earlier, when she defied her father to quit teaching and leave home. As a daughter, I cherish the realization that Sara found the courage to follow her inner leadings and urged Eleanor to do the same.

The countdown to Tom's June visit included a one-page letter that Sara termed "the sweetest and most wonderful you've ever written me." Far less religious than Tom about preserving every piece of their correspondence, she vowed to keep that particular message. "'Spite of what I said, I don't destroy all my letters and this shall be one that I will keep a long, long time." How glad I am.

May 4, 1944
Greenville, Texas

Dear Sara,

Fifteen minutes past midnight and it's still too early to go to bed without taking time to remember the thoughtful and understanding wife that you are. Does it mean anything to you to know that you more than everything else combined give me a real happiness. Tonight as I sit here in the day room trying to think of a way to tell you the kind of person you are, how much I love you, and how thankful I am that you are my wife, time and time again I have dipped my pen in the ink only to let it dry without writing a single word but each time realizing more and more how incapable I am. Words won't come to express the satisfaction you give me, or the challenge I feel to make myself worthy of your love. My aim is to strive to meet as much as possible the type of person you would have me be. Regardless of the number of hours I spend or pages I fill writing, the thought could best be expressed by the simple phrase, I love you and in doing so I am happy.

Goodnight darling,

Tom

Two years and three months after they met, seven months after they married, Sara and Tom prepared to spend a fortnight in each other's company—longer than any previous, shared rendezvous. Both could hardly wait.

Sara wrote:

From all sides, with emphasis on the Virginia and Tennessee sides but with strong support from Kentucky also, I'm getting returns on how glad people are going to be to see a Staff Sergeant from Texas come sauntering (Texas influence) home for a 15-day period. Don't let cadet graduations, Texas winds, dust storms, or nothing keep you from "carrying through" on those plans either. 'Cause a girl from none (all) of those places (just a government-leased nook) is going to be gladdest of all. . . . We've a room reserved at the A. Johnson for next Thursday night. If something happens that you miss the train in Memphis, send me a wire so I'll know not to go in. (But don't you dare miss it!)

Her letter, arranging their meeting at the Andrew Johnson hotel in Knoxville, passed his in the mail:

Just remember, Lady, that tonight (It will be tonight when you read this) you've a date with your husband. He's a very ordinary kind of person, this man of yours, but he loves you in a very special way. . . . If someday he's no longer just a paper husband, don't be surprised if that same phrase is nightly whispered in your ear.

Foolish for me to have questioned Tom's courting skills. Genuine devotion outshines Bud's glib tongue.

Over the course of the next two weeks, they traveled to both of their family homes. Along the way, they collected wedding presents from aunts, cousins and church ladies; dined on early garden fare and fried chicken fresh from the henhouse; played countless games of croquet, helped with house and yard work and whiled away hours on porch swings and rock fences. If Sara regarded Tom's letter just prior to their visit as his sweetest, my favorite from her to him was written on the day he left Delina to return to Greenville. I can feel the languid heat of late afternoon and envision the slanted streams of sunlight filtering through maple branches onto the green-and-white, front-porch glider where she might have sat, telling family members about the two-hour drive to and from the train station in Huntsville, Alabama. As evening came on and a new moon rose, she wrote, half-hollow, half-full with memories of a husband speeding now through the night, farther and farther with each lonesome whistle and revolution of the train wheels. Sara's usually playful tone sounds pensive and I glimpse an awakening maturity, reminding me of what I easily forget—how young she was, still half a year shy of her twenty-ninth birthday.

> *June 23, 1944*
> *Delina, Tennessee*

Dear Tom,

Right now you're out of Memphis about two hours—over in Arkansas, but when you read this you'll already be back at work on Monday morning and with Saturday's work to your credit too.

All is very calm and quiet here tonight. There's a new silvery crescent in the west sky. A house can be very empty even with six people in it, if the night before there were eleven.

We didn't stop again in Huntsville after leaving the depot—came straight on to Fayetteville and were there only long enough to make the swap of the "left front" with the "right rear." We were home by three-thirty.

Tonight, after a desultory game of croquet with Virginia and Katherine, I sat in the cool, close-cropped back yard and washed clothes—mine this time, and there were no uniforms or shorts or socks, so I got your towel you'd used and washed it along with my things.

Tom, you're becoming very much a part of me. And this time we had two weeks together. A little hard to grasp at their close that, though this was our first such fortnight, we'll have more of them together from now on than we've each had previously apart, God willing.

You were so dear to me these two weeks, and so sweet. You imbue me with confidence and trust for our future. Your fairness and constancy and poise make me ashamed at times of my own hot-headedness and too quick temper—yet you always praise me, never blame. Victor Hugo said "To pay compliments to a woman we love is the first way of caressing her. A compliment is like kissing her through a veil." I cannot but like the beginnings of your caresses, however unfounded they may be.

A cool breeze has started up now, and I hope that somehow it's reaching you too and that you're not uncomfortable on a hot, crowded train. You do too much for me, and too little for yourself, and never, never say again that you do nothing for me. For if you do, I shall cry with hurt.

Goodnight dear,
Sara

In subsequent letters Sara relived other moments and recalled other details of the two weeks.

Didn't we have a good time—I loved hiding in the tree while the rain came and your bringing me an armful of chiggarweed (Indian paint brush!), and our washing dishes together, and playing croquet—and other more personal things too, the nice, clean smell of you when we'd

*go to bed, and people saying Sara and Tom as though the two names
had always gone together, and bringing Nancy Ann [Johnny and
Frances's baby] in to wake you up. You were so sweet to all of them at
home, beginning with taking their trunks and boxes home, and then
just taking over the yard (didn't it make a difference in the looks of it
though), and too, remembering to take Mother the lovely towels. But
they all like you and appreciate your being what you are almost as
much as you deserve—and that's a tremendous lot.*

No babies of their own were yet on the way, she reported as
she headed back to Oak Ridge. "To tell the truth, I was almost
disappointed . . . although cold logic says it's best." Had she been
pregnant, Sara suggested, it might have been harder to follow
through on their next plan: she intended to be living with him,
in Texas, before their first anniversary. "When October 23 comes
I shall either be with you for good, or awaiting your furlough so
that I may go back with you for that purpose, or remaining here
only because you expressly tell me that you want it that way. . . . I
think a year of separated marriage is long enough, too long, and
I want to be with you."

Back on their respective bases, as the pivotal war summer of
1944 evolved, Sara's letters offered a running commentary on
the news accounts from Europe. "I just don't see how Germany
can keep taking those air beatings if they're as fierce as is told in
the newspapers. But however much they're weakened by those,
we can't realize yet how awful and numerous the casualties will
be when the march on land inevitably comes. I don't want to be
selfish, but I hope you will not have to go across, for there's danger
there in all the Divisions," Sara had written on April 25. "We, the
Allies, certainly seem to be giving the Germans an air lashing. I
hope it means that lives will be saved in the long run," she added

two weeks later. By mid-July, with the D-day invasion over, her tone shifted from one of anxious anticipation to optimism that victory was within grasp:

> *Last night on a radio program I heard the boys in Normandy singing "Pistol Packin' Mama." There was nothing depressed in its sound. Though we must have lost a great number of men, we've certainly made a secure place for the Allies on that peninsula. Hope is soaring high around here. Eisenhower says before Christmas, and so does* [newscaster H.V.] *Kaltenborn, a born pessimist.*

Mounting confidence collided with sadness as the names of the Normandy dead began sifting back to the homeland. Sara observed on July 17:

> *It looks like the Russians are going to beat the American doughboys to Berlin. I'm afraid the Americans would actually be disappointed if they're beaten there, though onlookers like me would be glad. The casualty list leaking back now is beginning to include more and more that we know or know of. Brothers of a boy who works three doors down from me, and of a girl who also works near have been reported killed and missing in action respectively. Uncle Monroe and Aunt Nannie heard from Frank* [a cousin who landed at Normandy] *for the first time since the Invasion. Others haven't heard at all yet. But progress is being made on all fronts now. My belief that it will be over by late summer or early fall of this year doesn't seem too impossible now—especially in Europe.*

That prediction was overly optimistic, but a bet placed by Sara a month later was not. The wager—her largest ever, Sara declared—was recorded on official Tennessee Eastman stationery.

*I, Sara Edds, do hereby wager the amount of five dollars ($5.00)
to Paul E. that the present wars with the Axis Powers and with Japan
shall be terminated and the American boys and men returned to their
respective homes, with the exception of those who remain in foreign
posts to maintain a permanent peace-time standing army, by or
before February 1, 1946.*

> *Signed—Sara Edds*
> *Signed—Paul E.*

As Sara and Tom waited for October, when they would be together for good, day-to-day life resumed its mundane pace. A year after Sara's arrival, Oak Ridge seemed far more civilized, less a frontier town. "The dust is bad here but doesn't compare to last summer. But nothing is quite the same this summer. Oak Ridge doesn't seem quite as much 'my town' since it's become so grown up," she wrote.

When a huge swimming pool, billed as the largest in the eastern United States, opened, Sara traipsed with scores of other walkers to the site.

*Last night when we got home from work Mary and I decided that the
lure of the swimming pool was stronger by far than hunger pangs, so we
set out for the new pool on the Area. But it was a disappointment. It's
nothing more than a big mud hole. There's no concrete sides or bottom,
just mud, and only a few people had dared in. We looked the situation
over and decided that hunger now had more lure than swimming, so
away we went again, this time to our favorite New York Avenue drug
store for ice cream, which, though vanilla, tastes like caramel.*

So little foliage brightened the landscape that any hint of green caused celebration. "The dorm has two trees in front—one split for electrical wire and one 'dwarfish.' Nonetheless there is a certain elegance and debonairness (yes, it's a word for I looked it up) in having any trees here," she wrote. In contrast, the view from her office window at Y-12 consisted of "a steep clay bank and two telephone poles, and that's absolutely all. It would take a person with greater imagination than I to see much beauty in it."

However raw the physical exterior, life in Oak Ridge hummed. Bridge parties, Tennessee Eastman "teas," tennis-court dances, dinner invitations, movie dates with Ginger Rogers or Humphrey Bogart, subscriptions to *Life* and *Reader's Digest*, borrowed books, church at the nondenominational Chapel on the Hill and late-night listening to distant bands filled the hours away from work. "The music is really smooth after midnight, and we were getting some keen orchestras," Sara explained her sleepiness at the office one day. And again, "listening to the Hit Parade has been another important feature of the evening. It's pleasuresome that both first and second choices tonight are particularly lovely, 'Wherever You Are' and 'Long Ago and Far Away.' Later, there was a good program of Irving Berlin's." While writing, the sky had turned from dusk to dark, she said in one letter. Out of the twilight, "a group of boys and girls are singing on the steps of the next dormitory, 'Strumming on the Old Banjo.'"

In a pre-television age, reading was a mainstay, and Sara filled her letters with references to both books and magazine articles. "Maybe we should decide to go to Alaska to live for a few years. It might be pretty much of an adventure at that," she suggested after consuming a *Reader's Digest* article on postwar possibilities in Alaska. "Today I amused myself by rereading the old classic myths," she reported. "Mortals have no troubles in proportion to the ones Juno, Jupiter and the other gods had. Neither do we have as simple solutions to problems. Venus is my favorite of the lot, although there's a bright spot for Diana and her bright-winged brother, Apollo." She described *The Timeless Land*, a book about the early settlement of Australia, as musically written but boring: "I found myself reading aloud just for the sound of the words. That's the reason I love poetry, not for what it says, but how it says it." Nor did she neglect the comics. *Little Orphan Annie*—"Little Orph"—prompted regular comment.

Life among a host of female friends seldom dragged. "Hopper's latest antic is to take a Du Barry Beauty and Reducing Course. She lasted for three weeks on it, but then broke over. After all we tempted her by having peanut butter Saturday night," Sara wrote after a dorm-room "picnic" supper.

When Virginia Black, a dormitory neighbor and one of Sara's closest friends, received word that her husband was about to ship out overseas, Sara and others rallied to get Virginia onto an airplane to Washington, D.C., that very night.

During the evening Jim called, and this time he is leaving the States— leaves Washington Saturday for his port of embarkation—and he wanted Virginia to come up. This makes about the 4th time they've said good-bye for the duration. But anyway we all bustled around considerably and in an hour's time got Virginia packed and ready and off to the airport to catch the 1:35 (a.m.) plane—luckily there had been a last minute cancellation. She was to get to Washington by 5:00 a.m. this morning—just four hours by plane and almost a whole day by train. I fixed her a corsage of flowers to wear, and she did look lovely. She's very beautiful to me most anytime, but she's really glamorous looking when she's all dressed in black, with a veil, and flowers.

In closer proximity Sara and Tom surely would have had disagreements and arguments, but at long-distance, their most serious tiff involved a stretch of time when he wrote too infrequently to suit her. Even her decision to vote for Democrat Franklin D. Roosevelt for reelection in 1944 and his to support Republican Tom Dewey prompted mention, but no prolonged debate. Both seemed primarily concerned that each take part in civic life. "I want our hometown to be a better place because we live there. And I want all who in any way come in contact with us to have reason to believe in the integrity of our ideals and the sincerity of our actions, whether they agree at all with our ideas and our actions," Sara wrote.

She was less amiable about his failure to keep up his end of correspondence for a few weeks.

I appreciated the long letter, air mail edition, and the enclosure; although I think what I'd said about writing had made no impression, or rather maybe not the impression I meant. If you don't understand without words that waiting eight days and receiving a one-page letter and then waiting nine days for another is a kindly lonesome arrangement, even when I know without a doubt that you love me and that I am in your thoughts, then you can go on with the arrangement of writing only when you feel an urge to write. Only when it comes to the point of "monthly" you can make it the "not at all." [A note penned into the margins the next morning apologized: "Correction: I don't mean that of course."] *And this, Sergeant Edds is the very last time I'll ever mention this writing business, other than to tell you I'm glad when I hear from you, which I always am. I promised myself that last fall after another similar interval, but this time I promise you to make it more binding.* [Here, the script slips into the margins, encircling the letter's final page.] *So I apologize sincerely for increasing temperament and though "yours sincerely" and "yours truly" can be pretty clear in meaning, they are accompanied by I love you.*

Meanwhile, dinner dates, chance encounters with old acquaintances and home-front pursuits filled the calendar. "Everybody here is Victory Garden minded, which seems funny as all the yard space is already taken up with little houses." Amid a shortage of "soap flakes" for laundry, she and Mary were delighted to purchase two boxes apiece at the grocery store, then unexpectedly received gift boxes from Tom's mother, Katherine, and Frances (Johnny's wife). "Mary says I have entirely too many people looking out for me." A "marvelous supper" at the home of a friend included

roast beef cooked with carrots and potatoes, Brussels sprouts, hot corn bread and tangy jelly—coffee and chocolate soufflé. The last was my first, but it shain't be the last for I'm going to practice till I can make them as good as the one we had, then probably feed you one a week for the rest of our lives. Sometimes I can hardly wait for the days when we can have a house or an apartment or something. We'll make it a good one and a gay one, won't we?

As she took dictation, answered telephones and filed blueprints at Y-12 administration headquarters, Sara had no inkling of the intense pressures and high-level debates riveting Gen. Leslie Groves, Robert Oppenheimer and others of the Manhattan Project's military and scientific elite in the summer and fall of 1944. Those architects remained anxious and uncertain about how far German scientists had advanced in developing a nuclear weapon. Neither of the two techniques for enriching uranium being developed at Oak Ridge—the Y-12 electromagnetic separation method and a gaseous diffusion process underway at a separate location known as K-25—was working out as hoped. Midway through the year, doubts remained about the ability to produce enough enriched uranium by 1945 to support even one bomb. At Oppenheimer's suggestion, Groves added yet a third enrichment facility at Oak Ridge, a thermal diffusion plant. On September 27 he awarded a contract for construction of the plant within a mere ninety days. Adding to the frustration, as prospects built for an end to the war in Europe, a handful of scientists began to question whether the United States should proceed with developing so cataclysmic a weapon. The conflicting concerns about the failure to crack the uranium-enrichment code, and about whether such a bomb should even be built, intensified as the war approached its fourth year.

Smaller, less momentous personal dramas tested legions of Oak Ridgers, including Sara. One episode illuminated what she referred to as her "hot-headedness," as well as her passion for fair play, her deep loyalties and her regional bias in an era when the South was regarded by many as an underdeveloped, wayward cousin to the more advanced North.

August 16, 1944
Oak Ridge, Tennessee

Dear Tom,

Fraid you're not going to get the good letter promised tonight, as it's already midnight. I'm very worried tonight for a devilish situation has arisen, which seems to promise a good deal of hurt to the two people I like best on the Area, Mary and Virginia.

Here it is: Virginia has had seven or eight years secretarial experience and is a very capable and desirable employee in every sense of the word. But the secretarial job which she's had here is definitely not one of the top ones. She has after serious thought decided that there was no point in her sticking around longer and has made known her intentions to leave in a couple of weeks.

On the other hand Mary has not had very much secretarial background at all; her position at Lynch with Mr. K. was more as typist and her job before that partly clerical. Here she's secretary to one of the very top men and probably the most demanding as he's the lawyer for this whole big outfit.

And here's the situation: The authorities have offered Virginia Mary's job. They have told her that Mr. B. [Mary's boss] has asked for another girl to be his secretary and whether or not she accepts it, a new girl will be secured for the position. For Virginia it would mean a substantial salary increase as well as a much higher rating.

As yet Mary knows nothing about it. And it's going to well nigh break her heart and spirit when she does know. Whether Virginia takes it or not, it will be the same blow to her. And Virginia is sick over it, for it's a big chance for her, but it's bitter to rise at the expense of a friend. Of course Mary will still have a job here, although I don't think she'll stay. I don't think I could if I were in her place.

Tom, in comparison to a war, this sounds trivial enough. But wherever the happiness of a person is at stake, it's really not trivial. I'm pretty worried. Mary hasn't had an easy time; I've seen her cry her heart out night after night over her marriage and now this. Virginia realizes some of the unhappiness she's had and being an extremely sensitive and sympathetic person herself, realizes what a tough situation this is.

So tonight it can't be much of a good letter.

Love,

Sara

The episode accelerated over the next few days.

August 18, 1944
Oak Ridge, Tennessee

Dear Tom,

I intended to write you last night but yesterday became very complicated before it was over—so much so that last night I postponed all that I should have done and dropped into bed, thankful to be there.

In fact the last two days have been very strained. Mary was "fired" (not technically so of course, as she was offered another position with T.E.C. at Nashville) late Wednesday afternoon. Now I realize that instead of writing you Tuesday night when I found out about it, I should have waked Mary and told her. I thought I couldn't and that Mr. B., the ex-employer, could do it much more smoothly than I. But he simply butchered the telling—just another damn Yankee who should have stayed up North. There's no place for him down here. (My opinion, of course).

Mary has taken it very hard and that's a very conservative statement. She resigned this morning. She hadn't been back to work since Wednesday afternoon. Virginia, as I didn't say, accepted the job. Technically there was not a reason in the world why she shouldn't, but emotionally I don't think I can ever like her as sincerely and wholeheartedly as I did before. I wanted Mary to take my job, but she wouldn't consider it.

We went into Knoxville yesterday afternoon to go to the employment offices of the other companies that work out here, as Mary thinks she might be interested in working for one of them. We couldn't get very far of course since she didn't have her release and letter of availability at the time. She won't have any trouble of course in getting a job here or elsewhere, for she is good. I believe she's right in saying the reason for Mr. B.'s decision was not that she couldn't do the work, but rather a clashing of personalities.

Coming back from Knoxville we were caught in a heavy down-

pour, so dense that it was impossible to see more than a few feet ahead. Then Mary slept with me last night and she was of course very restless and we didn't either sleep much. And then this morning I've been over to Mr. B.'s office to make the termination arrangements, etc. That was difficult. So now, I feel very much like a washed-out dishrag.

I don't know what you meant about my weight? I haven't lost any, nor had you asked me anything about it before. I feel fine, except that all the happenings of this week have given me a don't-much-care-for-anything feeling. That will pass.

Love,

Sara

. . .

Sunday afternoon
August 21, 1944
Oak Ridge, Tennessee

Dear Tom,

It's 7:15, cool by now, and I've just finished eating supper, alone for once. I'm sitting by my window, from which it's easy to see all of Oak Ridge strolling by.

Today I've done something I don't remember doing in a long, long time—and that is I've slept the day away. The past week has literally worn me out; so I had no trouble at all sleeping until 12:00 this morning, getting up and going over to dinner, came back and lay on a pallet in the sun for an hour, then came in and right back to sleep till going on 5:00. As a result I feel like a million dollars now; think I shall go to church tonight, since it's been three weeks. Besides I think I need to go to get my sins forgiven.

For I have raised merry hell this week. Not that I have any regrets

*along that score. I intend to continue it as far as Mr. Edgar P.B.
and his office is concerned. I'll probably be fired for insubordination
before October 23. But Tom, he was so unfair to Mary and she's
taken it so hard. She didn't go back to work at all after Wednesday,
but I resigned for her. Friday morning when I wrote you I'd just been
through a round in his office, and as a consequence I really don't
know what I did write you. It was probably a devilish one for I was
still simply consumed with anger at his insufferable smugness, his
Machiavellian cunning. Just because he makes $15,000 a year I
suppose he thinks he can come down from his Northern domain and
lord it over all he meets in the poor unenlightened South. (Time out
for some friends from Petersburg came by—the couple we went by to
see there but didn't find at home. I was so glad to see them. However,
it's too late to go to church now.)*

*Mary doesn't know yet what she is going to do. She went into
Knoxville tonight to spend the night with a friend and she'll get
an early start in the morning, seeing about several jobs with other
companies. I do hope she finds something well suited for her and
don't feel she will have difficulty in doing so. Tom, do you think I'm
a mean shrew for getting so angry over it all? I know I should watch
my temper more closely, but it does something to me to see someone I
love mistreated. If you're ever dealt with unfairly by anyone, you can
know you'll have a staunch supporter anyway!! (One of the men in
Mr. B.'s office, for I included them all, told his secretary that he didn't
feel that he deserved what I said, but gee, wasn't I gorgeous when I
was mad!!)*

*My room and my clothes are in a mess, but my disposition is fine
by now. I do hope you've had a pleasant weekend. Will try to bring
some order to this chaos.*

Love,

Sara

Tom responded appreciatively to Sara's tirade. He also reported that he had begun taking concrete steps to ensure that their hopes of living together, come October, turned into reality.

August 23, 1944
Greenville, Texas

Dear Sara,

An interesting and amusing letter I received from you today. Not in subject matter of course but it revealed so clearly a side of your nature I haven't thus far discovered myself. Mind you, I have no desire ever to discover it if it should be by way of having such rage directed at me.

Just now I've reread that letter and with the same sense of pride as the first reading—perhaps a little greater for this time I didn't have to stop to figure out the meaning of a single word. Do you speak as fluently when you are angry as you write about it afterwards? Sara, your convictions are high and noble ones and the beauty of it is you have the stamina and courage to defend your beliefs against those who consider themselves in the upper brackets. . . . Time and again I've thought how easily you could have chosen a partner with a financial income sufficient to provide untold luxuries of material things. Of those you are deserving, but you must not have wanted them or you wouldn't have chosen me as your companion. Now I realize that by such thinking I was doing you an injustice for you are much bigger than that. Never again shall I harbor such small thinking.

. . . Our tenth anniversary tonight. Has it been a long time. Yes, long in separation but short together—much briefer than the actual time. I've celebrated by making a search for an apartment. I am not too well satisfied with what I found. The first place [has] three rooms and private bath in a little square bungalow on the corner of Henry and Langford Sts. It has a private front entrance and includes the

north side of the building. It's not a first class place. The living room suit is good enough, the bedroom not as good. It has one chest of drawers and a tiny dresser both of which are old. The bed is not a fancy one but better than G.I. Closet space is roomy. The kitchen has lots of cabinet space, a gas stove, a frigidaire, table and chairs. In general paper and paint are both old; however, they say they intend to have both renewed and if we don't use it until October, they will have a better chance to have the work done. They are an elderly couple of common people. The price is $30 plus half the light, gas and water bill. I think the rate is reasonable enough . . .

Even though I got hot and worn out walking, and am now sleepy, it was fun looking for a house for you and me. It will be more exciting living in it with you.

I am glad you are again in your own sweet disposition.

Are you as happy as you were ten months ago tonight? I love you equally as well.

Goodnight sweetheart,

Tom

Over the next few days, Sara reported that Mary had found a job with another company working in the Area, as the locals referred to Oak Ridge; that Virginia was back in Sara's good graces ("She's too nice a person for me to stay angry with. As far as that goes I wasn't ever angry exactly with her, just somewhat disappointed. She was hurt too at the way it all came about, though not as much affected of course as Mary, or I either."), and that Tom's latest "anniversary" present—"long, green stalks of pink and white asters"—had arrived. "The flowers tonight make me feel better than I have the last week." The tempest had passed.

Incensed as Sara was by personal injustices, I find myself surprised and disappointed that she was not similarly offended by the racial inequity then rampant in Oak Ridge and elsewhere across America. Had she been, that would have put her well ahead of the time and place in which she lived, I know. It may be unfair to hold her to account for what most of her society ignored. I would like to think that she—like her brother and sisters, who helped dismantle segregated schools and political organizations in their small Tennessee towns in the 1960s and 1970s—would have adapted to and encouraged a changed South. Still, no doubt because so much of my work as a southern journalist over three decades has centered on exposing racial injustice, I cannot help but feel let down that someone as spunky and idealistic as she failed to see beyond stereotype.

In December 1943 Sara reported on a disturbing, late-night ride home from Knoxville in which she and a few white friends wound up on the bus usually reserved for blacks. Her discomfort surely reflected the strangeness of finding herself, probably for the first time, in a racial minority. Her reaction was vaguely empathetic. Even so, I cringe at Sara's acceptance of the superior status afforded whites.

"Saturday night, I was almost frightened," she acknowledged in relaying the tale.

We came back on the 11 o'clock bus and it was filled with negroes with the exception of us four and possibly about 4 or 5 other white people. There was another bus of white people but it was loaded to capacity when we got to the station. The negroes were quite opposed, and volubly so, to our being on the bus, for it meant that some of them had to stand. Virginia wanted us to get off, but there was nothing else to do. The driver actually had to talk to them in sort of a cajoling way to soothe them down. The negro situation is getting worse here than I've ever seen it. We have only a few rather scattered families around home, and never see anything like this. At Lynch sometimes they were pretty rowdy, but lots of things cause them to be worse here. One thing they're more in demand and at good wages than ever before; another is of course that they're fighting for the same things the white people are, and yet their status is much lower. I guess it would be natural to resent it. I can understand their situation and yet be irritated by their attitude.

Her concluding preference for chivalry over justice seems astonishingly, even humorously—were it not for the seriousness of the matter—myopic, illuminating the narrowness of her experience and her world: "But even for a white man, I think it's very rude to sit on a bus or anywhere else and let a woman stand. I'd rank courtesy to women, even when they don't especially deserve it, as one of the most desirable characteristics a man can have."

I hope also that the rose-colored glasses through which Sara viewed her native South also might have cleared with time. She bestowed higher praise on William Alexander Percy's *Lanterns on the Levee: Recollections of a Planter's Son* (1941), an elegantly written apologia for the Old South aristocracy, than on any other book read during 1944. "The most exhilarating book adventure I've had in a long time is now in reading 'Lanterns on the Levee.' You've probably read it but whether or no it will have to be a 'must' for our library. . . . I've lived it for the last two days and nights."

I can only speculate as to what Sara found most appealing in the autobiography of the lawyer-poet. The cousin and adoptive father of existentialist novelist Walker Percy, Will Percy was the son of a U.S. senator who bravely fought the Ku Klux Klan but also helped preserve white rule. Percy brought mesmerizing language, wit and a probing intellect to problems of politics and human nature. Metaphors for the human condition patterned on gardening would have spoken to a lover of flowers, such as Sara. His embrace of timeless virtues—good manners, protection of the defenseless, wry humor, appreciation for the arts—fit Sara's general philosophy and temperament. Still, from a twenty-first-century perspective, there is no escaping Percy's paternalistic attitude toward blacks. In an era when Charles Hamilton Houston, William Hastie, Thurgood Marshall and other brilliant black attorneys and activists were plotting the dismantling of segregation, and scores of black artists were flowering, Percy was stuck on black inadequacy. "The black man is our brother, a younger brother, not adult, not disciplined, but tragic, pitiful, and lovable; act as his brother and be patient," he counseled.

Meanwhile, Lillian Smith's seminal southern novel *Strange Fruit*, a searing story about the lynching of a black man falsely suspected of killing a white man in a mythical Georgia town, left Sara dubious. The interracial relationship at the heart of the book, as well as several vulgarities (tame by today's standards), raised a scandal across the South when the book appeared in 1944. "I've been reading a strange book, 'Strange Fruit,'" she wrote. "I haven't made up my mind yet whether it's very fine and sensitive, or just plain trashy. Same old problem—race question. Book reviewers and newspapers and book guilds, etc., have rated it highly, but the U.S. Government won't let it go through the mails anymore. The town described, a small one in Georgia, may be true of that state and maybe Mississippi, but I don't believe it's representative of any place I've known, in Tennessee anyway."

Forgive me, Sara. If I have a tendency to question assumptions, it may well arise from the genes you gave me. In any event, had Sara not died, had I not spent so many hours alone as a child, I might not have steered toward such an ornery, independent profession as journalism. I cannot now undo what is done. My fingers gravitate to Google, where they type in the words "lynching" and "Marshall County, Tennessee." Here is the search result, a report from *The Tennessee Encyclopedia of History and Culture*. Sara might have thought lynching was confined to the deep South; the encyclopedia says it occurred at her family's doorstep. "Little research has been undertaken about the county's black history," goes the report. "During the 1920s the Rosenwald Fund's school building program constructed new black schools at Farmington, Chapel Hill, and Lewisburg. This positive development, however, occurred within a context of four verified lynchings in the county from 1900–1931, one of the highest numbers in a Tennessee county for those years."

If it helps, Sara, I hold no illusion that my own worldview will survive the test of time intact in every particular. Even now, my offspring root out misconceptions and prejudices of which I am unaware. Such is the impertinent, evolutionary nature of children, yours and mine.

So what would Sara and I have clashed over? Boundaries, philosophies, hemlines? Something. Mothers and daughters, I am led to believe, almost always do clash, and the generation that came of age in the 1960s—mine—found more ways than most to contest the attitudes and authority of its parents. Rachel challenged convention more than I, but neither of us copied Tom's views on religion, politics and social mores wholesale. At the same time, each of us took care not to dishonor a father whose steadfastness we valued. Having lost one parent, we were loathe to unhinge the second. We did not serve alcohol in his presence; we did not expect to sleep in his home with unmarried mates. My guess is that, with Sara, there would have been freer discussion of such issues and, given her own mildly rebellious streak, more tolerance. Her skepticism about organized religion, for instance, peeked through in a late August letter.

Sunday night
August 28, 1944
Oak Ridge, Tennessee

Dear Tom,

Today has been wonderful from a weather standpoint. After the bright, hot, shimmering Sundays of the last three months, visualize one that was dark, and moist, and heavy-lidded. At ten I opened one eye and decided that if I did get up I had absolutely nothing suitable for wearing to church. If such reasoning was specious, it didn't disturb my conscience, for I went right back to sleep until about a quarter till 12:00.

Tonight though I did go to church, in my green wool suit, made gay and sassy with your red cherries. They must have attracted the attention of the little 7 or 8 year old boy, black haired, and tender-eyed, across the aisle, just as his flaming red sweater attracted me. We fell into step coming out of church and I told him how much I liked his sweater. He didn't, it developed, because it was too scratchy. The sermon was on "Is There a Hell." Sometimes it bothers me because so many sermon topics have lost their importance to me. I'm afraid I'm not as deeply religious as I ought to be or would like to be. But I'm mainly afraid I guess of narrow-mindedness which seems to sometimes accompany doctrines of religion.

After church I met Mary and Elizabeth in the cafeteria for a late supper of bacon, eggs, coffee, and a thick wedge of raisin pie. How good it all tasted. It's only after 8:00 p.m. that you can get eggs cooked as ordered and while you wait.

You're very domestic, going house hunting. You mean you're going to be an exception to that universal characteristic of which

I've endowed all men concerning their participation, or lack of it, in moving. I really hate to rent an apartment two months before we'll need it, for we don't have enough money to use it foolishly. Maybe I'm too much of a Mr. Micawber in my belief that "something will turn up." . . . *Nonetheless, you do what you think best and want to. It's fun to start thinking of an apartment.*

My flowers are still beautiful. You are considerate of my every desire and so mindful of my pleasure. Again thank you, good night, and love,

> Sara

With September came the news that their living arrangements in Greenville were settled. "So we have a house! The Edds of Greenville, Texas. I'm sure it's most charming and I know I shall like it," Sara wrote. Farewells and travel plans consumed Sara's final month in Oak Ridge. Two of her chief worries—leaving Mary and leaving her boss stranded—converged for a happy solution, as Mary was hired as Sara's replacement. With an 850-mile trip pending in wartime, gas and tires were major concerns.

What does perplex me at the moment is [how] I'm going to get gas to come out. The 50 gallons which we'd been being able to get here for a 3-month supply is being done away with. If I'd known that in time I wouldn't have used the coupons we had at all, but I didn't. So at present I have enough for 20 gallons, plus what I can get on an A Book for Sept., Oct., and Nov. which will be about 30 more. I don't believe we're getting over 12 miles per gallon, which is about 600 miles accounted for. Since there will be a good deal to bring in the way of linens, things we'll need, etc. I just don't see how I'd manage without the car. Do you know how I could go about getting more?

A few days later, she provided an update and a new plan: "I've decided that I should be able to talk the Ration Board here into giving me 'Change of Address' gasoline. I'm not sure how sympathetic they will be, since I'm leaving a defense area, but it's one thing certain, they wouldn't grant me parking space to leave it [the car] here."

Tires demanded attention as well. After a pre-trip inspection, Sara reported,

The front left tire and the back right tire are in A condition; the back left, the inspector said, should be used for a spare, and the front right should be taken off entirely as it was practically shot. So, although I knew our chances for Grade I's were much better in Greenville, still it seemed best to get fixed up before I left. So the rationing board here gave me certificates for two Grade III's and Mary and I went into Knoxville Wed. night to Tinsleys and found two.

Sara's explanation to her parents of the decision to leave Oak Ridge makes me wistful for the less work-focused life Tom might have lived had she not died. "Tom needs someone out there to keep him from working so hard," she wrote, adding a description that fits perfectly my childhood memories of my father. "He would work just as hard on a 96-dollar a month job as a 500 one, and do it just as thoroughly. He works the regular eight hours, then goes back after supper till about 11 or 12 o'clock. He's lost ten pounds doing that since he was home in June, and he doesn't have that much to lose. It's nonsense for him to think he has to work so hard. I'll put an end to the overtime, I betcha!"

Writing to Tom, she asserted her independence and her entrepreneurial spirit, sparking my curiosity about how she would have received the Women's Movement. "Now, Sir, when did you start that masterful 'If I decide to let you work' business? You'd better make up your mind in a hurry, for I'd rightly feel like a criminal to be doing nothing while the war lasts. So if you want me, guess you'll have to accept the working too for awhile." In another letter, she observed:

> *Sometimes I think strongly that immediately after the war is the time for us to get into something of our own, rather than to continue working for other people. We'll have roughly a capital of $2500, which isn't too bad. Businesses have certainly been started on less. Of course when I get out there, we'll have plenty of time to talk and make plans. It can't be denied that the United Supply Company is mighty nice to work for, but I firmly believe there'll be a world of unexplored opportunity after the war.*

In mid-September Sara let slip a rare note of restless melancholy. "Last night I was wild with loneliness. It seemed that ghosts were walking and I couldn't stay in my room." Something has gone awry that Sara is not sharing. What can it be? Memories of her childhood friend Elizabeth? Of Bud? What ghosts wandered her soul? What secrets did she harbor that all the letters in the world will not reveal? A sentence later, the protective shield of rationality returned. "So I went out to the Montgomery's. Seeing them brought me down to earth. . . . I felt lots better when I came home."

The dawning reality of a life together sparked a touch of nervousness. "I'm scared, scared that you won't be as happy as you think with me out there, scared that I'm not big enough a person to have ever become a wife in the first place. Please don't answer me with compliments. They are partly what make me scared, for sometimes I think that you think of me as a person entirely different from what I am," she wrote on September 26. Two days later, the doubts had eased. "Well, our days are getting numbered until we can really start housekeeping. Don't take to heart too much my last letter. I'm sure we can solve any problems that I think up! At times I let my imagination depict troubles which don't really exist, or if they do, which we can handle."

On one of her last days in Oak Ridge, before heading to Jonesville and Delina for farewell visits and then meeting Tom in Memphis for the drive to Greenville, she pondered their future.

September 29, 1943
Oak Ridge, Tennessee

Dearest Tom,

It's 12:15 and tonight has been full. I could almost wish tonight that the next two or three were past and we were safely and securely "at home" in Greenville. However, they will pass in a hurry, and then we'll be together for always and always.

Tom, I hope I can make you as happy as I want to. You deserve the very best in everything, and it will be my first aim that you get it. You've been sweeter than I can express to me the last year, in words, in gifts, in understanding, in dreams. I realize anew all the time that I have the best the world has in a husband and that I am fortunate beyond my ability to say.

I'm packed and ready to go up to your home tomorrow. It doesn't really seem right that you're not going with me, and I realize again the unselfishness which prompted you to give up your trip home in order that I could have a few days longer at my former home.

For my present home, from now on, is with you. You know without

my telling you that you are the most important person in my life
by far and that however dear any others may be—my family, yours,
Mary, anyone I know and love—they're only a poor second to you.
  I love you,
  Sara

On a bright June day, sixty-three years later, Bob and I visited
the American Museum of Science & Energy, lingered in the
"Oak Ridge" room in the public library and followed a compact-
disc driving tour invoking images of the city as it existed during
World War II. We paused at the location of Elza Gate, now a
nondescript crossroads, where Sara waited after losing her
badge. We peered into the giant, spring-fed swimming pool
that she described as a "big mud hole" and imagined it filled
with hundreds of revelers, escaping sweltering heat as Glenn
Miller or Duke Ellington streamed from the jukebox. Our tour
wound past street upon street of cemesto houses, now updated
with carports and sunrooms, but still bearing traces of the era
when Sara played bridge and tasted chocolate souffle there. In
the evening, we strolled past Big Ed's, a popular modern-day
pizza place, at the edge of what was once Oak Ridge's principal
shopping area. Walking on, past empty storefronts and silent
sidewalks, I tried to conjure the ghosts of the street's frenetic
past. Up the hillside stood the Chapel on the Hill, the church
Sara attended when she did not oversleep, a simple, white plank
structure now festooned with lilies and flowering shrubs. Just
down the way, the guesthouse that was once a stopover for the
world's most famous scientists sat crumbling under decades of
decay. At Jackson Square, where Sara once queued up for ice
cream and Little Theater productions, a series of 1940s pictures
reminded visitors of the once-bustling scene. I scanned them

fruitlessly for a familiar face. Closing my eyes, I tried to feel Sara's presence, tried to summon up a spiritual connection, longed to transport myself to an earlier time, and could not.

Grateful that modern communication does not require a four-day, return-trip letter, I picked up my cellphone and dialed Rachel.

"Here's the damned thing," I said. "You collate and index all these letters. You talk to all these people, visit all these places. You read books and go to museums and study photographs. You do all that. And when all is said and done, she's still dead."

Did I expect something else? That letters typed with her fingers could substitute for an embrace? That reading her words would equate to hearing them? That knowing what lay behind her smile would be the same as having her step out of a photograph?

I imagined nothing of the sort. I knew letters could bring me closer, much closer to the person who gave me life, but could not ultimately give her life. I knew that from the start.

Be honest, now.

Did I expect something more? Hope for it? Long for it?

Expect it? No.

Wish for it? Long to slip through that impenetrable veil?

The emptiness answers for me. Yes.

6.

Greenville, Texas

October 1944–October 1945

October 27, 1944, 10:30 p.m.
2202 Langford Street
Greenville, Texas

Dearest Eleanor:

*You'd appreciate this little "homey scene:" the gas heater sputtering
like an iron tea kettle, the flame looking like a deep-seated bed of red
coals; Tom sitting at the kitchen table which he's plunked squarely in
the middle of the living room, with his Golden Delicious apple almost
eaten, and his correspondence accounting course from U.T., on which
he's made 5 A's and two B's on the seven lessons already submitted,
spread out before him open at the 8th lesson; me in the easy chair in
front of the fire, disregarding the white crocheted runners on back
and arms, with shoes on the floor and feet in chair, having in easy
reaching distance two pairs of Tom's shorts, minus one button each,
nail file, "Good Housekeeping Cook Book," brush, comb, and bobby
pins, new "Life Magazine" and today's "Dallas Morning News," the
last two being pro-Dewey, with my Golden Delicious apple completely
eaten and core deposited on anti-Roosevelt paper; small table in easy*

stepping distance containing more white crocheted affairs, a fat-bellied, maroon colored lamp, and a box of chocolates of nuts and assorted fruits; sofa in far corner completely nude except for white crocheted runners; little bookcase on opposite wall containing Tom's newest book-of-the-month additions, "Now Is the Time for Action," "Der Fuhrer," "Literary England," "So Little Time," "Jane Eyre," "Wuthering Heights," "Blessed are the Meek," "Tales of Edgar Allan Poe," and dictionary, and My Mama's "Bible," "Emily Post," and "Heritage in World Literature." And that's all one sentence and "a cross section of our typical night."

We're now in the ready-to-be visited category, having labored diligently (Tom helped me some) on floors, fixtures, shelves, drawers, unpacking, rearranging and so forth. Yesterday we put out a good-sized "wash" and today I stood and ironed it in one breath except for one shirt and one blouse—total expenditure of time, 3 hours, longevity being caused mostly by three khaki shirts and three khaki pants, but partly by several little ole blouses and dresses and slips of my own. Nevertheless at four I "stirred up" a little ole lunch in a hurry (yes, we'd breakfasted between 10 & 11) and we got dressed and were ready to go play golf at five—Tom being mighty good but me being a dud at it. We got home at 7:30 and pitched together a "quick meal," us listening to President Roosevelt all the way through it on his eight o-clock broadcast.

I enjoyed my visit with you, at school and Mrs. Towny's, more than I can say. . . . And you'd better be planning on skedaddling out here to see us as soon as you are able. . . . Your eighth graders are cute little tykes, and they've the best teacher there is. Have you taught them to write or have you gone from "primary objective" to "secondary" one.

Thank you for being such a sweet sister.

I loves you,

Sara

A woman of Sara's talents might have taken a different path had she come of age a few decades later. But in 1944 wartime America, her primary goals were to begin keeping house and to replace her defense-related Oak Ridge job with a similar one in Greenville, at least until embarking on an even more patriotic cause—starting a family.

After an eleven-day, post-Oak Ridge respite in Delina, she set out with sister Virginia in a car packed with jams, jellies, pickles, linens and towels, driving through autumnal splendor across southern Tennessee to a Memphis rendezvous with Tom. "This will probably be my last letter that I will write you for some time to come," she wrote on October 17, just before starting. "In answer to your last paragraph today, don't you be scared!! If I've been at times, that's a feminine trait, but I'm counting on your calmness and strength, for those are masculine ones. 'Rich living' isn't set down before anyone or served to them—it's a concomitant of useful living." After two days of Memphis visiting and sight-seeing ("It seemed enchanting to wander through the well-stocked department stores and shops") and three nights at the Peabody Hotel, the couple headed for Texas. They celebrated their first wedding anniversary along the way. With typical precision and enthusiasm, Sara detailed her first days as a housewife. Reflecting the times, cleaning and meals took center stage.

October 26, 1944
Greenville, Texas

Dearest Mother,

Tom and I got to Greenville 8:00 o'clock Monday night and found the apartment looking very lovely. All three of the rooms are nice and adequately furnished, but the kitchen is my pride and joy. It's about 12 ft. by 12 ft., which may be a little smaller than yours

but much larger than most. It's newly papered, overhead white and
walls a white background with a neat little red and black blocked
figure on it. The curtains are white and pale blue and all the built-
in cabinets are also white, freshly painted. It had a new-looking
Frigidaire, also gas stove, breakfast table and four chairs. There is
a drain board across one whole side, with a sink in the middle, with
built-in cabinet shelves under the drain board to the floor and above
it to the ceiling. There's a pretty linoleum rug on the floor with small
ones around at strategic points. I don't think cooking can be much
of a problem in it.

Although the apartment was cleaner than most, we still wanted
to take advantage of this week off from work to get it in jim-dandy
shape, so Tom and I have both worked like beavers (especially him)
yesterday and today. We washed out all drawers in the kitchen and
bedroom and bathroom and put the detachable ones out in the hot
sun. Then we cut up old cedarized storage bags which he had and put
them in the drawers instead of the discarded newspapers. So tonight
(we finished up about nine) everything is unpacked and in its place,
and a clean, sweet-smelling place at that. Tom cleaned out all the
windows, inside and out and washed the entire closet, shelves, walls,
floor and all, and also did the doors and floor boards.

[Need I say that their daughter has never had anywhere near
so spotless a house?]

My anniversary present was about the nicest yet. Two sheets, and
pillow cases, a fluffy all-wool rose blanket, and the most beautiful
white chenille bedspread I've ever seen. The bedspread has a little
pale pink around the edges and a little of the same color and lavender
in the center. They were all on the bed when we got here Sunday
night; Tom had come out Thursday night and fixed it up.

I know you wonder how I've come out on my first meals. O.K.,
I guess, since I've stuck to standard pretty completely on what I've

undertaken. Breakfast is simple of course, and we've had so much to do each midday that we ate mainly soup yesterday and sandwiches today. Last night for supper I had creamed potatoes, green peas, pickles (brought from the Edds'), iced tea, toast and jelly; tonight I had green beans and whole potatoes, tomato and lettuce and onion salad, turnip greens, cornbread and tea. Simple enough. Tomorrow I'm going to make a banana pudding.

You were all so sweet to me that it makes it that much harder to leave home. Try to take care of yourselves, all of you; and Mother, don't try so much canning in one day.

Lots of love to all,

Sara

P.S. Tom said he thought he was going to get by in the Army without K.P. duty, but I "wearned" him.

Sara's new hometown, Greenville, was a product of its soil, rich black dirt that gushed not oil but cotton. The town boasted "the world's largest inland cotton compress" and six rail lines to speed the product to manufacturing sites across the nation. "During the harvest season," according to a Chamber of Commerce report, "cotton brought a 'snowfall' to the downtown square as tufts of white pulled from bales for examination by cotton buyers floated into drifts around the courthouse." The adjacent Majors Field Army Air Corps base, where now-T/Sgt. Tom worked in personnel, was one of sixty-five army airfields and some 175 major military installations located in Texas during the war. Photographs of Sara's and Tom's first home, on Langford Street, show a classic, square frame house with a wide front porch and latticework for rambling roses.

Explosive weather and varmints embellished daily life. Months earlier, Tom had described the fickle climate.

Within the last two weeks we have had all kinds of weather ranging from cool, balmy days that make you feel the world isn't big enough for the things you want to do to days that are memorable only for their blinding dust storms followed by a near hurricane. Wednesday we almost had to shovel the dirt out of our barracks when we came home at night. Then Friday night came the most excitement ever. A storm had been threatening since about seven o'clock. Just before ten, time for lights out, word came for everyone to report to the flying line. Our orders were, three men to a plane or as many more as possible and in case the storm hit, hold down the ship. By one o'clock the worst had passed without damage. Not much rain, a lot of thunder and lightning, and considerable wind. For a while it blew at about the rate of fifty miles with gusts up to sixty miles an hour.

Sara's letters home recorded other sorts of pestilence—paralyzing heat and bugs. "The official weather temperature for yesterday was 98 degrees, but unofficially it was from 113 degrees to 116 degrees in the afternoon sun," Sara reported in June. As for insects, "after a week's constant effort I've got rid of the ants for the time being at least. But there's no complete obstruction of pests in Greenville looks like. For Sunday night Tom killed three more stinging scorpions—two on our front porch and one in the bedroom. I know I shouldn't tell you all this, but it's partly so you can know 'all' and back out of coming in August if it's too bad." A month later, she upped the scorpion count while scoffing at her family's escapade with a single snake.

Has Sammy Snake yet been captured and dealt justly with? I do hope so, but am afraid I can't be properly sympathetic over the appearance of just one reptile. I'm expecting to be a connoisseur of crawling and flying invaders by the time my Texas lease is up. Last night we

"laid to rest" our eleventh stinging scorpion in the apartment. No
stings received as yet, though some of our neighbors haven't been so
fortunate. And yesterday morning while we waited on the front porch
for Tom's ride to come by, I idly counted the mosquito bites on my
left leg. There were only 50. But the ants, thank goodness, we have
conquered, at least momentarily.

Throughout the winter and spring Audie Murphy, a Greenville–
Hunt County boy destined to become the most decorated U.S.
soldier of World War II, made local news by receiving the
Congressional Medal of Honor. Rumors about base closings and
mass transfers spread, then evaporated as they proved false. Even
as Allied offensives in the Pacific and on German soil pressed
forward, fueling expectations for a return to normalcy, the nation
mourned its losses—including the president. "[War correspondent]
Ernie Pyle's death yesterday was a shock. He was killed on the same
island where [cousin] Bob Downing is, as you know," Sara wrote to
Eleanor in April 1945. "I know how grieved and stunned you felt
about President Roosevelt, because I did too, and I'd never been
as whole-heartedly Roosevelt as you. I guess one of the reasons I
like you is that you're never lukewarm, you're either hot or cold."
Domestic chores—meals cooked, sewing projects begun, floors
polished—dominated accounts of daily life. Reading, both serious
and light, riveted Sara for hours. "Ever since little Orphan Annie's
dramatic escape, I've been hankering to write you to see if you
didn't think Little Orph handled that situation pretty well," Sara
began one letter to her sister. "My nomination for the two best
scenes are: (1) Little Orph hunched on hands and knees, curls
sticking up to high heaven, saying 'No-o-o- M-m-mamm' to Mrs.
B.H.'s honey sweet query, 'Aren't you going to let me in, Annie?'
and (2) Annie poised for escape by the door telling Mrs. Bleating

to knock the door down if she wanted to, since it was her door. Of course the 'chase through the night' wasn't bad either, especially when Orph couldn't find that loose board in the fence. It was nice of Sandy to just happen by."

Only a dozen or so letters remain from Sara's and Tom's year in Texas. In them, dramatic war news—Adolf Hitler's April suicide, Germany's unconditional surrender on May 7, and the Japanese surrender three months later—played second fiddle to the domestic front and its most momentous development, Rachel's pending August arrival. A joke related to Eleanor in a post-Christmas letter provided the first hint that Tom's and Sara's family would soon be expanding.

This may be a not-so-new one, for methinks I may have heard it before, but it still strikes me as right amusing. It's about a little six-year-old whose Mother was expecting a baby. She didn't know in what way to break the tidings to him, so detailed his teacher with the task. The teacher explained to him that he was to expect a baby brother or baby sister, and that a great bird called a stork would bring him, probably coming down the chimney.

"Well!" said Mr. Big. "I hope he doesn't scare Mother, 'cause she's pregnant."

Whether by choice or 1940s convention, Sara quit the job recently taken at Majors Field and devoted her pregnancy to housekeeping and anticipating motherhood. Worried about her own mother's deteriorating heart condition, she traveled back to Tennessee for a visit that spring and, at a distance, conferred with Eleanor, the family mainstay who continued both teaching and monitoring conditions at Hilltop View. "I still feel good when weekends come and I know you're safely home taking over," Sara wrote.

Heaven only knows how hard it is on you to do all your school work and then come home every weekend and pitch in, but I don't know how they would have got on at all without you. They just go from one crisis to the next at home. Now I have no idea what arrangements can be made since the Negro changed her mind at the last minute. I think Daddy should maybe have got the woman Johnny had—$2 or no a day. I don't know yet whether I'm glad or sorry I came on back. Tom was kindly lean and lank from subsisting on a glass of milk for breakfast and two fried eggs at night and he was just pitifully glad to get me back. (He just thought while I was gone that if he ever got me back, he'd never let me go again!) Nevertheless, I never hated to leave home and all of you more.

In May, Sara reported "a full day," including a sewing session with a friend who stitched a dress while Sara made "little outing blankets," plus the arrival of a windfall box of hand-me-downs from another friend: twenty-nine baby dresses, five gowns, ten slips, six diapers, three pillowcases, a sunsuit, rompers, two bibs, fifteen pairs of socks and "one of those zippered baby bags to put the baby in with matching cap. . . . I wish I could show you the dresses, the finest white material, dainty tatting and embroidery, the tiniest of stitches."

Late June found Greenville awash with rumors that Majors Field would soon close and a large portion of its personnel would be reassigned to monitoring the peace in Europe. A recent age ruling assured them that Tom, then thirty-five, would probably not be sent overseas, but a transfer—possibly to Galveston—prior to the anticipated arrival date of August 9 seemed likely.

Already, Sara and Tom were referring to the baby as a girl named Rachel. "I would most likely stay on here now until after Rachel's arrival no matter what Majors Field arrangements turn out to be. And it's likely that Tom could be here at the time as he could probably get a 15-day emergency furlough," Sara wrote home. A week later she reported that the "tempest in the teacup has blown over" and thanked Eleanor for a special delivery letter urging her to come to Delina if Tom left. "It was so sweet that I had to kindly cry," Sara said. "It wasn't that I was worried last week, but everything was upset and everybody excited, and I wanted to come home and didn't think I should." Soon, arrangements were complete for Eleanor to arrive in Greenville on August 13, "D-Day plus four." She planned to remain for two weeks, returning to Tennessee just in time for a new school year to begin.

Eleanor's long wait in Greenville and near-miss of Rachel's arrival is a staple of family lore. The baby emerged less than twelve hours before her aunt's scheduled departure on August 27. Eleanor described the events in a letter to Tom's mother later the same day. How many women would take the time to write in such detail to their sister's mother-in-law? Or be so foresighted as to reclaim the letter at some point and store it away for future generations? Without Eleanor, I shudder to think how much of Sara's life history could never have been reclaimed.

> *August 27, 1945*
> *Greenville, Texas*

My dear Mrs. Edds,

Since neither of the proud parents is in a condition to write the good news, that job is left to Aunt Eleanor. Your namesake, Rachel Forester Edds, arrived this morning at 9:30. She sent out her first "wail" soon thereafter. That was mighty welcome news to Tom and me who had been standing just outside the delivery room for an hour and a half. Both Rachel and Sara are in wonderful condition so all of the Tennessee and Virginia kin may breathe a sigh of relief. I know all of you, as have we, have been on edge since Aug. 9. The baby (if one should call her such) weighs nine pounds and five ounces!

My visit was almost at an end, so we had all despaired of my being here for the occasion. I had my ticket and reservation for tonight, Aug. 27, and you may believe that I was going to leave reluctantly. Very early this morning, however, (about 4:30) Sara woke Tom and me saying that maybe we had better dress. She wasn't feeling very bad so took her bath and finished her last minute packing. She had been so afraid of getting there too far ahead of time so she had us wait until nearly six o'clock. By that time the three of us were pretty well assured that "Today was the Day." Luckily the doctor had a similar case, that had arrived earlier in the morning, so he was already at the hospital. He assured Sara that she had not come too soon, so they put her to bed and she was only there two hours until they moved her into the delivery room.

During the time she was waiting the other baby, (also a little girl) whose mother had arrived before us, was born. The hospital was certainly in a bustle. Sara was brought back to her room about 10:30 and she came grinning. They had given her gas on the last, but she says she never quite lost consciousness. With the baby's being so large she naturally had a hard time but now that that is in the background the hard part is fading out and she is so relieved and happy.

I should say "they" instead of "she" for Sara's relief and happiness is no greater than Tom's. The broad smile that came over his face with the realization that "all was well" was a joy to see. . . .

The way flowers and cards and visitors are coming in one would think that Sara and Tom had lived in Greenville all their lives. They really have some wonderful friends here all of whom are so anxious to do something for them and Rachel. Of course Tom, himself, had white asters sent over. The florist herself brought them remarking to Sara about what a wonderful person Tom must be. . . . It has been

*such a relief to us that Tom has been able to be with Sara all the way
through when so many "war wives" have to have their babies with
their husbands even too far away to know about it.*

*I do hope that you continue to stay well. Sara, Tom and Rachel
send love to the grandparents, aunts, uncles and cousins.*

With kindest regards to you and the family, I am,

Yours very sincerely,

Eleanor Barnes

Ten days into motherhood, Sara updated her Tennessee family
on the transition. She lamented, as well, the death of her Uncle
Monroe Downing, announced by Eleanor in a special delivery
letter. Monroe's passing, with three of his four boys still overseas,
brought home to the Barnes-Downing clan the experience of so
many World War II families forced to endure tragedy with loved
ones far away.

September 6, 1945
Greenville, Texas

Dearest Eleanor:

*Your special delivery letter came Sunday morning about 10:00.
Tom hadn't gone to Sunday School and had not yet left for church.
Your letters, even of bad news, are always so sweet and comforting.
All the family and all Uncle Monroe's friends probably thought the
same thing—about how much easier it would have been to accept
his death if he could just have seen the three boys again. Yet it's true
he must have been happier this last month than he's been in years,
knowing they were safe and would not have to fight in another war in
the Pacific. He's always been the dearest of our uncles and seemed to
love each one of us almost as much as if we were his daughters. . . .*

Back to your visit, how bof' Tom and I did enjoy it. And I just wouldn't change the timing of events one bit—the conclusion being what it was. It surely was a comfort while in D-room to know you and Tom were in the hall close by. That was worth more than your being here a week or more afterwards would have been. I hereby promise to "reciprocate in kind" when the occasion demands if it's at all possible. I do appreciate more than I can ever say your braving almost 1,500 miles, two buses, and two trains (one without Pullman) just because I needed and wanted you.

Rachel and I came home Friday as we were getting along splendidly and also each additional day after Thursday morning was $7.00 ($5.00 for me and $2.00 for cute little her.) Annie [a friend and helper] rode home in the ambulance with us. The apartment looked just lovely, all cleaned and spic span, with furniture rearranged and bouquet from Mrs. Yates in her black vase on the chest of drawers. Bugs Bunny was just glad to move over and make room for his little mistress. . . .

Now more about "Her." She's a far cry (and a many a one) from the little red-faced, squint-eyed baby brought to my bed last Monday a week ago. She's just a doll. She lives in her bi-poos, as the little gowns make her so hot. She can wiggle and crawl around so that Annie says I'll never keep her covered in winter. She's sweetest when she cuddles up to me and nurses (still eagerly) but she's cutest when she screws up on Tom's shoulder and looks (as he phrased it) like the pictures of "See no evil, Speak no evil, Hear no evil."

I've got along quite well. Sunday was kindly a bad day, as I expect I was worrying a good deal about Tom's having to leave and then I heard about Uncle Monroe. I cried most of the time Tom was gone to church, but Annie was so sweet and petted me. Too I was constipated mostly because I couldn't get adjusted to a bedpan, I guess. Enemas didn't produce any results and I wasn't supposed to take laxatives on account of the baby. Then in the afternoon we had company. By late afternoon I was menstruating so profusely and sorta in clots that we called Annie home. She latched the door and wouldn't let me have more company and the next day they had Dr. B. come by. But I was already O.K. by then. Last night I finally got the "bowel situation" straightened out so I'm really feeling good now. Tomorrow I can sit up 15–20 minutes every two hours and Monday we go back to see the Dr.

"They" are through supper and I'm going to sit up a few minutes.
Much love,
Sara

Amid anticipation of the baby's arrival, World War II reached its dramatic climax. Back in Oak Ridge, residents learned for the first time the true nature of their mission. A combination of the three methods for enriching uranium had produced enough fuel to power the nuclear bomb dropped on Hiroshima, Japan, on August 6. Nicknamed "Little Boy," the bomb's explosive power equaled twenty thousand tons of TNT. "Oak Ridge Attacks Japanese," boasted a banner headline in the *Oak Ridge Journal* on August 9. Spurred by the devastation, the Japanese surrendered on August 14, just as Eleanor arrived in Greenville. No letter preserves the family's reaction to the cataclysmic events, perhaps because the sisters were together and had no need to write. Only Sara's elderly Aunt Lillie made passing reference to the bomb in a congratulatory letter welcoming the new baby: "Do you think Atomic Bomb will be used for practical purposes? Bo Brown said we were afraid of electricity when Franklin first learned that it could be controlled."

Over the next six weeks, Sara and Tom endured a roller coaster of uncertainty about their future. Just as it seemed settled that Tom was being transferred to an airfield in Salina, Kansas, new orders came through. Rather than Kansas, Tom's next destination would be the Army Air Forces Separation Base in Sioux City, Iowa. There on October 15, 1945, he was discharged from active duty. Sometime over the next two months, the couple resolved the debate over whether to return to a Kentucky coal town or find employment elsewhere. The next letter in my stash is dated January 7, 1946, and postmarked, Lynch, Kentucky.

7.

Lynch, Kentucky

January 1946–June 1948

January 7, 1946
Lynch, Kentucky

Dearest Eleanor,

I 'lieve you've been neglected by me, but no doubt you've been too busy to notice. . . .

I'd been planning to come home in January since Virginia wrote the first letter about Mother's last heart attack. But after Tom's trip to Chicago was canceled I decided to wait until I might be needed worse—although I know Katherine does need help now. Unless mother gets worse again, I'll wait until March as I'd first planned. If you think I should come before, you let me know. I did want Mother, as well as all of you, to see Rachel in her present "little stage" before she got much bigger.

Have you seen Herman yet? You will sooner or later. Mighty "thoughty" of him to inquire about all the relations. I hope his being at home isn't upsetting you—I want you to have what you want, but I hope you don't want him now. He just made me so mad that it would be hard for me to really like him again. Nonetheless, 'taint whether I'd like him or not that matters a'tall.

We are still amassing furnishings. Our latest (& most thrilling) buy is a 1946 Frigidaire. It's beautiful, inside and out, and the book of recipes that accompany it makes your mouth water—ice creams, mousses, parfaits, congealed salads, ices, and all. No ice cream could surpass your summer peach. I haven't tried it yet for any frozen dessert. We are just before buying, I think, a pressure cooker. It would can 14 quarts at once, at a great saving in time and effort. What I want most of all is a washing machine right now. We just don't have a reliable means of getting clothes washed yet. We've sent three fairly small washings to the laundry and I've done the rest. Evidently this laundry has already about all the customers they want, or else the driver is so trifling that he won't be bothered with new customers.

Rachel does seem awfully cute to us. She has such a big time when Tom comes home at night. She seems to like her Mummy and her Daddy pretty much these days. Sunday we were at the Edds and she stayed just about two points above crying all day—then we got into the car to come home and such an agreeable, merry little miss you never saw. I do want her to like everybody else almost as good as us.

We've had a deluge of rain yesterday and last night. All day yesterday the street in front of our house (Lynch's main street) flowed like a swift creek. I expect you all have had a good deal too.

Mary is working in Memphis with a company commercializing DDT. Virginia Black is back in New York in her old apartment. Hopper (I'll be daggoned) still at Oak Ridge I guess.

When are you going to come up and look over Uncle Tom's store— well it doesn't exactly belong to him but he's the best in it.

I can't help but stay pretty uneasy about Mother—especially on long stretches when none of you are home. Do you think she's much weaker now than before Christmas?

Now don't you work too hard. I might as well not say it though.
Much, much love,
      Sara

A mere fifteen months after leaving Oak Ridge, Sara had embarked on a new decade of life—her thirties—and a new phase of maturity and responsibility. Gone were girlish hair ribbons (unless for her daughter), midnight jam sessions and mad dashes to movie matinees. She had become a married woman in the fullest sense, focused on making a home, raising a child, partnering with a husband and bolstering both an ailing mother and unmarried sisters, who viewed her settled contentment as a source of comfort and strength.

I wish Sara might still have spun around a dance floor now and again, escaped on a romantic junket or allowed her dab of naughtiness to peep through, but that probably was not part of the bargain with my more sedate father. What she got instead was dependability, devotion and shared pleasure in mutual friendships and simple living. From a feminist perspective, her ambitions seem slight. But as a daughter, how can I fault a cosmos with me—or at least, the future me—at its core?

Reading between the lines of her letters, I think what Sara wanted most was a family patterned on her own, with multiple children arriving in rapid succession. Would that have sufficed through a long life? At some point, I expect, she might have put aside her reservations and returned to teaching, or resumed clerical work, especially if they became a farm family needing two incomes. But perhaps not. She gives no hint of missing the work world. My choices are mine, not hers. Their ideal, my father once told me, was two girls and two boys. They got halfway to perfection.

Postwar Lynch offered a unique backdrop for the transition—extraordinarily communal, upscale for the region, yet hostage to the ever-present threats of labor strife and mining disasters. An instant job offer for Tom, as manager of the furniture department at the Big Store, doubtless headed the lures. Lynch's neighborliness and relative security held powerful attraction as well. Sara's writings over the next few years portray a world in which women sewed outfits for each other's children, met a neighbor returning from a family funeral with a full spread of food and shared each other's burdens. Rachel's baby book records how "six kind neighbors (Sally, Pauline, Mrs. Beets, Mrs. Shipley, Mrs. Hyde, and Mrs. Kelly)" put on a third-birthday party for Rachel, including "about 45 little boys, girls, and Mamas," during the first summer of Sara's illness.

Photographs of the era capture an appealing, leafy main street in Lynch. Everyone walked. Scores of people passed daily up and down the sidewalks, and neighbors separated by postage-stamp yards chatted across clotheslines and flowerbeds. Ladies paid visits, politely sipping tea and munching pound cake while their children learned to sit without fidgeting. A night out meant dinner at the hotel or a movie in Benham. Summer holidays featured picnics or a trip across Big Black Mountain to the swimming pool in Big Stone Gap. Pauline Nunn, the former neighbor, now in her late eighties and living in Corbin, Kentucky, told me that she never locked doors in Lynch. The sense of safety extended well beyond that conventional measure, however. Neighbors also went out of their way to announce when their houses were empty. "When you went on vacation, you'd put the porch light on saying you were gone," she said.

People from every ethnic group and station of life felt an uncommon affection for the town. Frank Vincini, whose deceased wife, Lizette, was one of Sara's closest Lynch friends, grew up in the town in the 1920s and 1930s in an Italian family with a dozen children. "It's a place I'm really proud of; I love it," he told me after I tracked him down by telephone. Frank praised a school district considered one of Kentucky's finest and the town's progressive— for the times—attitudes on race and ethnicity. Frank remembered ethnic slurs when the football team traveled away from Lynch but only modest friction at home. "You knew everyone in Lynch . . . I had friends on both sides" of the black-white divide, he said.

High wages and the town's friendly atmosphere also attracted Mattye Knight, a teacher at the Lynch Colored Public School who moved to town in 1945, the year of Sara and Tom's return. The "sense of neighborliness was unbelievable," she told Thomas Wagner and Phillip Obermiller, authors of *African American Miners and Migrants*. The book describes the Eastern Kentucky Social Club, a remarkable organization of black citizens with roots in the Appalachian coal fields. EKSC chapters stretch from New York to Atlanta to Los Angeles, but the annual homecoming occurs—no accident—at a spot that taps a deep well of regard, Lynch's former Colored Public School building.

For all the camaraderie and warm memories, however, Lynch was no perfect world. Our across-the-street neighbor, Barbara Tiabian, who still lives in Lynch, recalled a 1940s incident in which the family of a white girl, caught in a romantic tryst with a black boy, was told by town authorities that either the family or the girl had to go. "Next thing I knew, the girl was gone; she never came back," she said. "The good ol' days wasn't all good," agreed Ronnie Hampton, the state mining inspector who grew up in segregated Lynch and still pastors an African American church there. As Sara was leaving the town in 1943, Tom addressed a portion of her decision, then ended: "Labor conditions, housing conditions, living standards, and etc. can wait until next time." Clearly, those were problems to be weighed against the warmth the couple felt toward former employers and a host of friends.

While Lynch was a safe haven compared to much of Harlan County, the rowdy ethos and disturbing social disintegration in nearby hollows and ridges could not be ignored. In the 1930s in Harlan County, according to historian Hevener, "one of every four local marriages ended in divorce, a situation almost unknown in the preindustrial era, and child desertion had emerged as a social problem of serious proportions." Several dozen roadside taverns dotted the Harlan County landscape offering "liquor, dancing, gambling, prostitution, and brawling. These taverns quickly emerged as the county's major crime centers," he wrote. Progress surely had been made by the mid-1940s, but at a minimum, anyone driving into and out of the region had to confront images of striking poverty. Such conditions were not tolerated in Lynch. A cerebromeningitis epidemic that struck the area in 1936 demonstrated the far superior circumstances. As the death rate among patients in nearby communities soared to 85–90 percent, Lynch reported only six deaths out of one hundred patients treated at its hospital.

Labor disputes added an edge of chronic discomfort. Even during the war, wildcat walkouts plagued Lynch mining operations. Resulting unrest, combined with production changes, cut the January 1942 payroll of almost 4,100 employees to under 2,000 at the end of World War II, according to company documents. During Sara's and Tom's early days in Lynch, United Supply workers—such as themselves—who staffed the Big Store and other commercial enterprises were not unionized. During the couple's absence, the United Construction Workers, a UMWA affiliate, won the right to represent store employees. Just prior to Sara and

Tom's return, store workers staged a thirty-five-day strike, and miners walked out in support. The strike ended only after U.S. Coal & Coke officials threatened to shut down the Lynch mines altogether unless the miners honored their contract.

Trusting in corporate goodwill and convinced that the top echelons of union leadership were largely corrupt, Tom had little sympathy for organized labor. In his mind, the role of unions in improving working conditions and mine safety did not outweigh the liabilities. "I realize they have no other way of earning a living except by the sale of their time and that their present wage scale is due largely to labor unions. I also know the type leaders they have and what they stand for," he once wrote to Sara. "Under proper leadership, unions would be a blessing to the individual laborers as well as the nation as a whole."

Never personally motivated by material wealth, Tom without a hint of irony suggested that the cost of living should be reduced to fit the wage scale, rather than vice versa. How he expected to achieve such a result, minus a recession, large-scale government intervention, or unlikely corporate concessions, mystifies me. Divided union loyalties split an otherwise homogeneous community. Pauline Nunn, who clerked at the main store before her daughter's birth, recalled that some union members refused to trade with her until she began wearing a union badge. Tension from the strike lingered as Tom, Sara and Rachel arrived in Lynch in late 1945, and Tom took over a management role at the Big Store.

I can envision that store—which figured prominently in my parents' lives—before its decay. An imposing, four-level, glass-fronted, cut-sandstone building, it offered a dazzling array of products far beyond those associated with the typical mining town. Shoppers could purchase meat and groceries, fill a prescription, furnish their home, carpet their floor, pick up a block of ice, clothe their entire family, meet a friend for an ice cream soda and eye a mouthwatering array of sweets, all under a single roof. "You could smell that bakery all over town," recalled Bob Lunsford. "Cakes, bread, pies—buddy—we had it." An elegant stairway with polished wooden banisters greeted customers on the first level and led to the mezzanine. Company buyers, including my father in the late 1940s, traveled to New York and Chicago regularly to stock the store with up-to-date fashions and products.

As Sara and Tom settled into a married life free of the back-drop of war, both deepened their commitments to extended family, particularly aging parents. Reflecting simpler and more communal times, they resolved to ease the burdens on stay-at-home siblings, even at a distance. On days off, Tom traveled regularly over Big Black Mountain to help plant and harvest crops. Sara reported spending about one-seventh of 1946 in Delina. Even that did not fully satisfy her father, as Jennie May gently observed after her hospitalization brought Sara and Rachel to Tennessee for several weeks in early 1947. "How did you find Tom," Jennie May wrote after their return. "It was certainly sweet of him to do without you 3 weeks. I never spent a week or half week at home after I left, yet John couldn't see why you couldn't stay on. He wanted you and Rachel so bad."

Despite dismay over her mother's declining health, Sara found delight in Eleanor's dawning romance with Charles Murray, an Indiana farmer with roots in East Tennessee. The couple had met years earlier when Charles visited Delina relatives, but mutual interest kindled only after other attachments faded. Just before the opening of a new school year in August 1946, Eleanor traveled to Indiana for a fateful visit. In Kentucky Sara dashed off a postcard urging a full report.

August 31, 1946
Lynch, Kentucky

Dearest Eleanor,

Happy Beginning-of-School-Year. Are you as close to school as the past three years? . . . How many pupils do you have, and how many classes? Schools here start the day after Labor Day. We hope to move [to another Lynch house] last of next week. Tom is working too hard and too long, but I can't deter him. He's at the store tonight working. His help is half sick and half on vacation. Littluns is learning new things every day. She trots all over the kitchen, busily putting her toys in a box, then taking them out, moving to a new place and starting all over again. She says Chicken in a high-pitched tone as though she were calling them . . .

I'm still waiting to hear all about Indiana people and places—am so glad you enjoyed it. Have you written your thank you letters?

Love,

Sara

Eleanor's ecstatic reply was on the way even before the postcard reached its destination.

September 1, 1946
Fayetteville, Tennessee

My dear Bruce,

I know I have neglected you. . . . It hasn't been from lack of interest but, I suppose I was waiting until I got "set up" so to speak. Neither has it been from lack of news and I have not been entirely deaf to your pleas for "details." Maybe it's been that I had too much to tell for a short letter and I didn't have time for a long one. . . .

There is a long story connected with my "new home" and I am here only for a month—unless they reconsider, but I wish you could see me now. I feel like Cinderella after the fairy godmother touched the pumpkin! It is the most beautiful room I have ever had access to, a corner front one with double windows across the front and one on the side. The house faces west, so I have the northwest room. There are Priscilla crisscross curtains at the windows which also have venetian blinds. There is a soft moss green wool rug on the floor, with matching wall paper of green with rather large pink roses shading from pale to dark. The bedroom suit is walnut with a 4 poster bed with pinkish peach chenille spread. The woodwork is white and while the house is heated by furnace there is also a fireplace and fireboard for looks. There are little pink hurricane lights on that. The floors are light hardwood and are lovely. The whole house is in keeping with this room, though I won't take you on a tour of it now! . . .

Well, I won't tantalize you any longer but I knew I'd better get the other out of the way or I'd never get to it! Complete details will have to be given at intervals—over a lifetime—but I can say that in all my life I have never been so happy and so thrilled as I am every minute of every day as a result of my visit! (So maybe the roses on the wall paper aren't so rosy as they appear to me to be!) Of course you can make "general guesses" from that much information—which has only gone (so far) to you, Mother and Stammer (the 3 who have seen me the most miserable.) In due time it will be known to all but this is far too soon to give it out.

Sara, it is just as if I'd found a new person for I had really known so little about Charles and I found him so different from anything I had dared hope or expect. As I told him I hadn't thought we had anything in common and found that we had everything—On top of that, he is just the sweetest thing in the world to me, treating me as if I were so extra special. As I told Stammer, I had thought they lost the pattern when they made her Cecil and your Tom but that they made one more before it was done away with.

We just enjoyed every minute of every day and we really were together most of the time. When we left home the last morning to go to Indianapolis to the train Charles said he never hated to do anything as bad in his life as to take me away from there—and I never hated to leave anywhere so much! We had already changed the leaving from Friday until Monday, then from Monday until Tuesday and I thought they would think "wolf, wolf" at home and not meet me at all. They did however. . . .

Charles worked a little bit while I was there—but not a lot. He has a lovely farm so we walked over most of that enjoying the woods lot in particular. I'd go with him after the cows and sit in the door while he milked. We gathered big blue plums from the garden, then cut them up while Mrs. Murray canned them. We went a lot of places until Mrs. Murray accused us of just "cooking up" places to go (which we did—like to town for nails or something). . . . I never knew that just doing everyday things could be so much fun but I see now it all depends on who you are doing them with.

Charles is coming down here in September—in fact he said he was going to try to be here by the time school was out on Sept. 20. When I asked him if he knew what day that was he said, "Sure—your birthday—that's the reason I've planned to be there then." He is going to look about a farm down here also in east Tennessee where he and his mother plan to visit before coming on here. They both want to move back. . . .

Well, this isn't the details but at least it is a bird's eye view. I should have written you sooner for I know how happy you'll be over it all. I'm really not supposed to tell all of this but how could I keep from it—to you? And I haven't told you anything except that I'm very happy—have I?

Sara this place is wonderful. Keep your fingers crossed for my staying on after the month is up. We had waffles, melted butter,

*syrup, sausage and bacon for supper. The whole set up is perfect and
the people are lovely.*

> *Lots of Love,*
> *Eleanor*

Sara answered with an equally detailed word-picture of their
new home at 503 Lynch Road. She elaborated on her domestic
routine, rued the fact that Tom's tendency to overwork seemed to
be winning out and excitedly detailed their plans for an upcoming
trip to Greenville, Texas, and Delina.

> *October 5, 1946*
> *Lynch, Kentucky*

Dearest Eleanor,

*'Course I'm going to see you in a little more than a week;
nonetheless, it popped into my mind a while ago that I'd enjoy
writing you a letter tonight. 'Achel Edds sleeps happily away in her
little white, paint-eaten bed, and the head of the home is working
at the store as usual.*

*"He" is leaving tomorrow for three or four days at High Point,
North Carolina, to attend a furniture exhibit of some kind or other.
Rachel and I will stay alone. I really don't relish doing it, but . . . I
really need to take advantage of the extra time I'll have as a result
of fewer dishes and less cooking. My sewing basket is long past
overflowing. And the curtains and pillows for our new home are
still unmade, and Rachel's pictures and cards need assembling and
put into her book, and my church correspondence needs attending
to. (Did mother tell you I'm treasurer of the church now—and that
entails a good bit of time to keep the financial record of 500 people
when I never had my own bankbook to check.) So all in all I can find
more than plenty to do to keep me out of mischief.*

My canning record has soared to 102 up, but with about 40 of said number already down. I'm really dazzled with my 42 quarts of apples—really 39, as I gave away 3 yesterday in exuberance over being done. I "placed" them piece by piece in the cans just as though I were going to enter them in the Colts Show, and Tom and I have loudly and long sung their praises.

We're just delighted with our new home. You'll enjoy visiting us in it more than you would have the other. The floors of the living room and our bedroom are especially pretty. Since we still have no real living-room furniture, we've made this room into a combination living-dining quarters (although we dine in it only on special occasions, that being once since down here). We use our birch breakfast table, folded, (or rather the extra leaves pull out, then slide back under the main leaf) as a center table, with a white crocheted "runner" and Bud's lamp (sparkling white by the very simple process of making up a tub of Lux water and giving it an out-and-out dunking) and the Masonic Bible and a magazine or two on it. Then the birch china closet is in the corner, with my Ladies-of-the-Methodist-Church china and Spode demitasse cups and saucers and other sundries showing through its glass door. We have a bookcase in here too with Tom's Harvard Classics and three chairs (one of the breakfast set and two rockers) and a floor lamp. We already have big, glowing fires in the grate. The mantle is white and has Miss Mary Dee's pitcher vases of dull blue and pink, with tall pink candles in my silver candlestick holders back of them. [A picture of] Washington's Monument is over the bookcase, and a spray of roses and mixed flowers is centered above the mantle. All in all I think the room is pretty, though it probably sounds like a hodge-podge. I'm eager to get the curtains up.

While I'm on furniture and furnishings, Tom and I have decided to furnish our whole house in the same style and period of our breakfast set and bedroom suite. They're both Old Colony style, made of solid

*birch, very simple lines, and will fit just right in a country home!
Tom can only get a small allotment from the company that sells this
particular line of furniture, but we'll just take up the whole allotment
in things we want.*

*Your birthday sounded like a good one from the Mother-Katherine-
Virginia reports. Virginia said she'd never seen you prettier than the
Sunday of it, wearing a rose gabardine dress and black hat. (Is it the
black hat with rose trim or another? That was straw, though, wasn't
it?) I guess Charles was re-carried away. How is he, and has he made
any farm transactions? It's such a good feeling to think of you and
know that you're happy when you go to bed and wake up ('course you
never gave up being happy in the daytime).*

*All the good news about Mother has just been almost too good
to believe, so I wasn't really surprised to learn that she had the bad
Saturday night. Did you think she seemed weaker this weekend? I
think Aunt Lillie must be about as frail as ever, too.*

*I want to get my Saturday bath before Tom comes. We have a pint
of ice cream a-waiting him. That's a Saturday night ritual. Rachel
just grins happily at the mere mention of ice cream.*

*I've saved your "Indiana" letter. It's good that your moving is
over. That's trouble, whether it's individual or a household.*

    Lots of love,

    Sara

Illuminating as letters may be, they are not a crystal clear window to a life. Few correspondents, certainly not Sara, record every
irritation, every annoyance. After observing scores of marriages—
Charles and Eleanor's, those of other relatives, my friends', my
own—I have shed any juvenile illusion that my parents' marriage
was or would always have been idyllic. Reality and imperfection
coexist; adapting is part of the challenge and the mystery. That is

a lesson it took me a while to learn. When your model of marriage
is a fantasy of perfection, then it takes time to understand that
real-world messiness and commitment can trump illusion. Still,
I come away from Sara's letters confident that she and Tom were
building a union destined to thrive through a lifetime. She disliked
the long hours Tom devoted to work, and when after my divorce I
pressed my father for details of their marriage, he summoned up
a few minor arguments—mostly eliciting chuckles. Sara's temper,
I happily report, did not go into mothballs quite so quickly as
her taste for an occasional scotch and soda. Even so, her writings
contain nary a hint of disappointment in her choice of a mate.
To the contrary, a letter advising Eleanor on the pros and cons of
marriage is as poignant a love letter to Tom as any addressed in his
name. Eleanor's second visit to Indiana, just after Christmas in
1946, prompted the thoughts. The Tennessee portion of Eleanor's
family had a mixed reaction to her trip. ("Where's Eleanor chasing
down Murray this time?" my grandfather famously asked before
one such visit.) Sara voiced only enthusiasm.

January 15, 1947
Lynch, Kentucky

Dearest Eleanor,

 *. . . We were so glad to be communicated with both on your way
to and back from Indiana. We were two members of the family who
were glad you went! As for that matter, I don't think it was that the
others disapproved as much as that they just downright hated to miss
a day of you themselves.*

 *I know how happy your going made Charles, and you, and Mrs.
Murray too. Your presents were nice. The Eastern Star pins which I have
seen are beautiful. How did Charles like his shirts and accessories?
Did they have a Christmas tree? Did he, Charles, think you looked*

*pretty in your green suit and off-the-fore hat and "scalloped oysters"?
I'm sure you did and I'm sure he said so.*

*I do, indeed, think there are more reasons "to" than "not to."
Having ever pressed on (one might say) and reached that stage myself,
I'll "make so bold" as to say that married blessedness beats single
blessedness by a whole heap. Illustration, please: well, a week or so
ago I heard someone say that she had been so depressed lately. That
started me to thinking whenever I'd been depressed and I just couldn't
remember when—grief and worry when Mother was so sick, concern
over Katherine and Virginia (not much over you anymore!), pity for
Aunt Lillie. Yes, lots of emotions that are wholly or partly sad—but
no "depression" that I used to feel recurrently (I'm trying to say every
now and then) from high school days right on through Oak Ridge. For
every hour I know that Tom loves me devotedly, and every hour I love
him more completely, and there's no room left for depression (and, of
course, there's "little oyster" too). And that doesn't mean that we had
just everything perfect to begin with either. I think you and Charles
would have a better beginning than we did. For we were both pretty
miserable the first year of our marriage.*

*I know at home that your not being at Fayetteville and home in
summers and on weekends would be hard for all of them. But you
wouldn't be leaving "for ever and ever," for even I spend a good
percentage of a year's time at home and I imagine you would too.
Even if you couldn't, you still shouldn't stand back on the family.
Now, I'm not urging you to marry Charles. Don't if you don't want
to, but do if you do! But I gather the latter is the case, since you've set
your face toward Rome.*

*I heard from Tom today. He's staying at the Stevens Hotel in
Chicago, which I guess is about the biggest in the world—least that's
what I've heard. He is planning to be home tomorrow night, and I do
hope nothing changes his plans, as it's pretty lonesome here without*

him. Little Rachel went to the window last night and poked her head around the shade and called plaintively "Da Da, Da Da, Da Da."

In every letter and card Mother continues to say how much better she feels than formerly. It's all miraculous and wonderful.

It has rained almost steadily the last two days and nights. I went out in it to the P.O. this afternoon while Rachel took her nap. . . . I hope all goes well at school. Am so thankful you have a good place to board. That means so much.

Love,

Sara

A postcard three days later recorded Tom's happy homecoming.

January 18, 1947

Lynch, Kentucky

Dear Eleanor,

Rachel and I walked to the P.O. yesterday to mail your letter, so she got to carry her pkg. from you home. She is carried away with the book; I read it to her twice, then started to put it up as it was time for her nap'. She cried so pitifully that we read it again and of course she still cried at the close of that reading. Then last night after her bath she even relegated her beloved Mother Goose book . . . to second place and put "I See a Kitty" first. Tom came home last night—to a clean house, us, and a banana pie. Guess which he liked the best. My Bendix is doing a washing for us while I do the breakfast dishes and odds and ends. It's a wonder. Are you swamped with work?

Love,

Sara

Although Sara did not say so, and possibly did not know for sure, she may have had an extra reason for blissful contentment.

She was already two months pregnant with her second little oyster—me. As a new life began, in time's unending cycle, others in Sara's constellation waned.

> April 1, 1947
> Lynch, Kentucky
>
> *Dearest Eleanor,*
>
> *We were just sick that Mother had to return to the hospital so soon . . . . She hasn't missed her letters and cards to us, even writing from the hospital. Aunt Lillie [visiting in Lynch] doesn't seem to worry any more about her here than at home—maybe not quite as much as she isn't there to see every time Mother feels bad.*
>
> *Tom is home today, as a result of the celebrating of the founding of the Union here. I'm glad to have him for whatever reason. He is working in the kitchen with nails and lumber and square and what not, and Rachel is utterly entranced with each move. She could eat him up, if possible and says she's his "peet'art" and Mama's "pecious" and Aunt Lillie's "woommate."*
>
> *Are you coming, rather going, home this weekend? With all you have to do, I really hate to ask you to tend to something else, but we'd like Mother to have some flowers from us for this Easter, and Tom had such a time getting them delivered the time he sent in the order to the florist that it didn't seem worthwhile to fool with that.*
>
> *I'm sending $4.00, which probably won't buy much with flowers as high as they are. You use your own discretion in choosing, although if Mother were to be well enough to dress for Sunday, we'd really like her to have a corsage, as I'm not sure she's ever had that and she has had an abundance of cut flowers and potted plants. Gardenias are always a pretty corsage, also roses. If you don't think she will be up that day, cut carnations are colorful, or an Easter lily is all right. Let them be from you, Aunt Lillie, Tom, little Rachel and me.*

The other night at 3:00 a.m. I heard a little voice saying, "Pot, Pot, 'mode,'mode, Mama's coming, Mama's coming." When Mama got there, the little girl was standing up in bed, confidently waiting for her Mama and dry as a powder house. . . .

It's nap time for Rachel and time for me to put the dinner pintos on.
Much love,
    Sara

The death of Tom's father in July 1947—a month before my expected arrival—shadowed Sara's and Tom's anticipation. As parental deaths will, it elevated Tom to a new level of responsibility to his mother and siblings, just as his own family was expanding.

July 9, 1947
Lynch, Kentucky

Dear Eleanor,

Technically "my day" has been a "burnt run." I had two things to accomplish—to go to the doctor for the monthly check-up and go to Cumberland to the bank. The doctor told me to come back another day without Rachel as he wanted to give me a physical examination; and I'd waited so long to see him that it was a minute past closing time when I got to the bank. So I might as well have slept the afternoon away.

We got home Sunday night about dark. Though they'd had late dinner at the Edds, we were still ravenous; and the supper that Pauline, our next-door neighbor, brought over was surely quite timely, as well as delicious. She brought us meat loaf, potato salad, green beans, tomatoes and little new onions, and pineapple upside-down cake. I was glad to be back home, as were Tom and Rachel. Tom was pretty well worn out, though he hasn't admitted it, as there was so much on his shoulders last week, and so little rest, even at night.

The funeral was Friday afternoon. . . . Mr. Edds looked so young, handsome, and so much at peace that I couldn't wish for him to be back suffering as he was the last few weeks of his life. Tom said he couldn't either. He had a beautiful cherry casket and steel vault. The flowers were very beautiful, and there was a room full of them. There were a number of wreaths and sprays from Lynch.

Mrs. Edds seemed to be doing fairly well when we left Sunday. She is and will be very lonely, I know; but there won't have to be any drastic change in her home, as is true in some families when there is a death. . . . Although Jewell could still come to be with us in August, it would be hard on the rest for her and Ruby [Tom's older sisters] both to be gone, so we are trying to get someone here, and I think we will be able to do so all right. I don't really want any of you to come at that time, for it would be nothing but hard work. . . . It's a long, hard trip up here from home; and I think with Mother and Aunt Lillie both being in the condition they are that all the "helping out" should be for them and not us. Nevertheless, I do appreciate very, very much your being willing to come if I need you . . .

[Rachel] talks all the time. Last night while Tom was at a Board Meeting she and I were going up to Sally Delph's. I sat down at the dresser to comb my hair and she said, "Going to put on a little lipstick, Mummy?"

Down at Tom's home Saturday, he was cutting down some bushes around the front gate with an axe, and he commented to me that an axe wasn't what he needed. Rachel heard him and asked, "What you need, Daddy?" He told her a saw, so she said, "I'll go get you a little saw, honey." Away she flew around the house, and in a minute was back to tell him that "the saw's gone."

Tom's home from the store now (it's about 10:30) so I'm ready to retire.

I enjoyed your letter so much, and was very glad to get Mother's and Aunt Lillie's today.

Love to all,

Sara

Before Sara's next letter, the family of three had become four. My baby book reports the 1:12 p.m. arrival of an eight-pound, four-ounce girl on August 18 after an uncomplicated four-hour labor. In contrast to the two-day hospital turnaround when my own children arrived, Sara spent a then-standard six days at the Lynch Community Hospital. Even after returning home, she enjoyed being waited on for a few more days—a soothing, humane and now obsolete entry to a hectic phase of life.

September 11, 1947

Lynch, Kentucky

Dearest Eleanor,

The biggest little girl at our house got into my stationery box, hence all the wrinkles. Of course "family" gets the messed up sheets. A few minutes later I found the same little girl out on the back porch sucking on Baby Sister's water bottle for all she was worth. The fact that the bottle is forbidden fruit makes it all the more tasty to her.

How are you and your new eighth grade? Now loyalty to past classes should prohibit you from saying this soon that it's the best you ever had—though I'm sure that will be forthcoming before commencement. So I won't bother to hope you have a good class, but will hope you have a smaller one, for it's fun to grade fewer of even good papers!

We're getting along just real well with our newest member. She's a sweet little boneless-feeling thing, who just sleeps and sleeps—she

*hasn't been nearly as tempestuous as Rachel was her first 3½ weeks.
I can't tell that she looks much like Rachel—she had much more of
a "new baby" appearance than Rachel ever had—hence wasn't as
pretty—but she has a lovely shaped head and a dear little nose. Her
eyes have watered a lot, and aren't too accustomed to much light yet.
She's long, but when she sleeps, she draws her knees up to her tummy
and takes on the appearance of a pink and white ball.*

*Jewell was just wonderful, and was as careful about not letting
me do things as one of you would have been. Rachel lived in a state
of rebellion for the week I was away ("Don't help yourself, Aunt
Jewell," at the table, etc.) but soon got back to normal. She renigged
on morning nap, afternoon playpen, milk, staying in her own yard
and most of the rest of her little rules and regulations. But now she's
playing with dominoes in her playpen as happily as if she'd never
scorned it. "Littlest One" is sleeping.*

*We were glad our Texas company came, even it if did seem like
a bad time. They stayed such a short time that it didn't run into any
hardship much. For a while after I came home, we had company
pretty steadily at night, so much so that one night after her bath
Rachel calmly announced, "I'm not going to bed; I'm going to wait
till the people come." Margaret Ellen has had a number of nice gifts,
including six lovely little dainty dresses.*

*Tom woke up last night with his right side hurting badly. It had
stopped by morning, but was still sore. It alarms me for anything to
be wrong with him. In fact, it has to be real wrong before he would
even mention it. I'm afraid of appendicitis, but he thinks it might
just be gas. . . .*

*Aunt Lillie must not be doing much good, from what Mother
writes. And poor Mummy, to have to fall and suffer more than she
already does . . .*

I wish you could have come this summer. Maybe you can next one.

Write, when you can. I enjoyed your 'specially long letter which you
wrote after your Morristown visit.

 Love,

  Sara

A letter to Virginia written the same day added a few details
about the family transition and Lynch.

September 11, 1947

Lynch, Kentucky

Dearest Virginia,

 It's "Back to School" in Lynch this week, and Rachel is thoroughly
enjoying the droves of boys and girls that swarm by in the mornings
and afternoons. Lynch was a week later in starting than most schools.
One of the teachers (Mrs. Metcalfe—alias Aunt) came by to see me
this afternoon, and she said they had quite a few new teachers. There
are five on the faculty that she had taught in the 4th grade, so she's
beginning to feel she's taught long enough.

 How was your opening? And how and who are your faculty co-
members this year? I hope you have some competent library helpers
for the year.

 We are getting along fine with four members instead of three. It
surely feels fine to be less bulky and cumbersome. Little Margaret has
seemed exceptionally good so far. She wakes for one night feeding
(after her ten o'clock feed) and usually goes right back to sleep. . . .

 Rachel is ready for bed having been bathed by her Daddy. I told
her I was writing to you and what did she want to tell you. She smiled
and said, "I love her." She sleeps in the single bed now—has fallen out
one time. That little Margaret Ellen crawled off the bed yesterday. I
heard her crying and went in to see about her. She wasn't on the bed,
but was looking up at me from the floor! It didn't appear to hurt

her, but I've started keeping her in the baby bed all the time since then. . . . I could hardly stand it about [Mother's] *fall.*

After starting "This Side of Innocence" it was easy enough to finish it. As you said, it was quite "readable."

I won't do much, if any, visiting for awhile; and am not going to Sunday School and church either until the baby gets "firmly established." She seems to be gaining and progressing quite nicely.

The geranium has a beautiful red bloom, and the pink lily three. Tom reset the plants (geraniums, coleus, begonia, and fern) from the box the Sunday School class sent me in the hospital.

Our football games have already started and we lost the first game. Tom and I could go separately, but it's not much fun to go alone.

Love,

Sara

I am thrilled by Sara's joyful embrace of me, watery eyes and all. I may have no conscious memory of her. But I cannot read the letters of the next three years without knowing that, if I have a confidence toward life, a resiliency and a sense of self-worth, it was planted and tended by her.

In 1947 the U.S. birthrate soared to just under twenty-seven births per one thousand Americans, the highest since 1921 and higher than in any year since. A year earlier Dr. Benjamin Spock released the first edition of the *Common Sense Book of Baby and Child Care*, liberating generations of parents with the friendly adage, "Trust yourself. You know more than you think you do." I don't recall a copy in the family bookcase, but Sara read voluminously. Through magazines, at least, she must have known of Spock's general philosophy. As a new mother, I pored over parenting books, anxious to fill the gaps of a childhood without mothering.

Sara and Tom—with models and confidence aplenty—charted their own rules. They seem to have settled on a course of parenting that was friendly but firm, devoted but not permissive. My information comes primarily from Pauline Nunn, mother's letters and her careful notations in our baby books—a wealth of detail that stops abruptly as Rachel and I reached ages five and three. From those, I know that potty training began at nine months (almost laughable by today's standards, but more lenient than the four months recommended by the popular Dr. L. Emmett Holt earlier in the twentieth century), we spent far more time confined to a playpen than I would have considered for my children (to no discernible ill effect, I admit) and undesirable behavior was tackled, not tolerated. "Here's one of Margaret's latest," Sara reported when I was a little under fourteen months old.

You remember how she used small sheets to wrap around her finger and put in her mouth. Tom wanted to break her of dragging a little sheet around after her, so yesterday morning he hung it high enough on the bed (he thought) so she couldn't get it. We could hear her crying and fussing and trying to get it. Then a slight pause, followed by little joyful noises and Margaret appeared with the sheet, saying "Oh, doody" (goody)!

After several weeks of fruitlessly trying to reach the Corbin home of Pauline Nunn and her husband, Clayton, whom I'd not seen in over a decade, I was delighted when Pauline's cheery voice finally answered. Clayton was suffering from Alzheimer's disease and Pauline's days were spent in nursing home visits and care. But she took time out to sort through her memories, and she greeted me at her front door several weeks later with a pad full of notes. Still petite and pretty, Pauline launched into recollections I probably could have gleaned from no one else. She had a front-row seat to my life with Sara. "Mother had her own way of doing things. Every day she had a plan," said Pauline, who was about ten years younger and whose daughter, Linda Joyce, was my beloved early playmate. "They were more educated [than many Lynch residents], and time was always planned. She had lunch at a certain time. She read to you. She wanted you to have fresh air every day. Even in the winter, she'd set you outside in your snow suits." Later, when Sara had to take regular naps in the afternoons, "she'd set you on the front porch steps with your crayons. It's amazing you wouldn't leave. But somehow you understood that Mother needed rest." Once, Rachel and I deviated from the norm long enough to fill a basket with every blossom in Pauline's flower bed. "Here came your mother. 'I'm so sorry.' . . . She carried herself graceful and had a kind, soft voice." Another time, Pauline recalled, the two mothers and three girls were at a store when I cried for a ball. "She wouldn't let the man give it to you . . . . She said, 'We can't buy a ball today because we didn't come for one.' She was very calm with it—teaching you couldn't have something when you cried for it."

Along with strict rules, Sara and Tom also set higher expectations and allowed more freedom at an earlier age than is common for children a half century later. The latter may have been dictated in part by her illness. "[Margaret's] utterly untrustworthy as far as staying in the yard is concerned, and strikes a beeline for Linda Joyce's or Carol Jo's the moment she's outdoors, peering around the coalhouse back to see if I'm noticing," Sara lamented in a twist on Pauline's recollections. For goodness' sake, Sara, I was twenty-two months old at the time. What did you expect? I'm astonished to realize that Rachel began walking alone to the Little Store, a small neighborhood grocery out of sight and at the far end of the long block, when she was three years and nine months old. For an attentive parent to grant such freedom would scarcely be imaginable today, but for a child, the sense of mastery must have been exhilarating. "Rachel is growing up to the extent that I sent her to the store by herself last week," Sara reported matter-of-factly. "She was so thrilled."

In the cocoon that was Lynch, no day exceeded Christmas as a respite from the daily rush. As usual, Sara's letter home following my first Christmas was a detailed recital of events and expressions of gratitude for what now sound like exceedingly modest gifts.

December 29, 1947
Lynch, Kentucky

Dearest Mother,

I hardly know where to start as there's a lot to cover in Christmas week. . . . Your letter, and Eleanor's, came today; and how much I did enjoy them at both readings.

There are so many presents to thank you for, I'm afraid I'll leave some out. If so, I'll "cover" them later. Anyway thanks to each for all. The four dollars, one apiece, from Daddy, and the one from Aunt Lillie are very nice gifts, as anyone knows! Ours came right at the most appropriate time—between Christmas and the 1st of the year. And the sausage is another big item. It came Friday, in good condition. The biscuits disappear for breakfast with it and the gravy around. I don't know who did the wrapping and getting off of it, but that was a big job.

Mother, imagine my getting a slip which you've helped make. It will make me feel good in two ways whenever I wear it—of its nice warmth and because you made it for me. I'm sure Kay helped on it too. Your dollars and short little letters to the girls are appreciated too, and the latter will be saved long after the former is spent.

Virginia, Tom likes his shampoo—and the two little Golden Books are just right for one little girl and soon will be for another little girl.

Eleanor, the napkins (which I just out and out said I wanted) are exactly right. I still didn't have any solid white ones, and need them so often. I've already "torn into" use of the Handy Wax too. She and I like Rachel's little "Sunday white panties" and her Mother Goose soap. And what a lovely soft pink blanket for little Margaret. When she's dressed in Aunt Kay's little handmade white dress, or Aunt Frances' dainty pink one, with the blanket tucked about her, she'll be the sweetest baby in Lynch—which she is anyway though. She's been her most adorable today in her new snowy white knit gown and Auntie's pink outing kimono over it.

Kay, you sent such nice presents to the four of us—the Yardley shaving soap to Tom, the tea set to Rachel, that sweet dress to Margaret and a boxful of things to me. I like the vanity set—am always proud of the things you make—they're so much better and nicer than bought ones—and I'm almost out of stove rags. Rachel plays daily with the set, makes tea for all of us, drinks her own daily orange juice from the little cup "that Aunt Kay gave to me."

We just had one marring of Christmas, and that's most over now. Both the little girls up and took colds—the 1st Margaret had ever had. She'd look at me with reproachful, puzzled eyes. Nose drops kept her from suffering much though, I think. As a result of the colds, they and I didn't go out for Christmas Day. Tom went over home for the afternoon—leaving at noon and getting back at 8:00. We all slept till 9:00 Christmas morning, then had a leisurely holiday breakfast of grapes, tenderloin, biscuits, and gravy and damson preserves. Then the stockings. We didn't want to rush Rachel on that or mar her pleasure of each thing, so we waited till Christmas night to open the tree packages, except for the tea set and a kitchen utensil set, both of which she needed for her Christmas Day play. . . .

We had our own turkey Christmas dinner Friday night. We had guests—Virginia and Harley Mays, who have eaten Christmas dinner with us ever since we came back to Lynch. I had the turkey and dressing and gravy, creamed potatoes, cranberry sauce, cucumber pickles, a pear and cheese salad, hot rolls, ambrosia and John O and Frances' fruit cake and coffee. We ate by candlelight, to Rachel's amazement. The turkey was a very nice 13-lb. frozen one.

Sunday we had the most leisurely day I remember our ever having. We didn't go anywhere all day, not even to Sunday School or church. Tom made fires then went back to bed until a 12 o'clock breakfast—then took a nap on the sofa until a 4 o'clock dinner (which didn't have to be cooked). After dinner we looked at our Christmas cards and letters (around 100) and read a little. I didn't even have a guilty conscience about church, as the two babies didn't need to get out, Tom definitely needed the rest, and it felt pretty good to me too. I guess that about covers Christmas. . . . [Rachel] accepts "Santa Sous" as a matter to be expected for a little girl.

Love to each,

Sara

P.S. Tom had a $50,000 month which beat by $15,000 anything that dept. had done before. It also was more than any other department in the store. He had a nice letter of appreciation from Mr. Kirby.

I relish for them, for us, the normalcy and happiness of that Christmas season. The coming year—1948—would spell tragedy on two counts, Jennie May's death and the advent of Sara's illness. For a moment, time stood suspended in the quietude of a crackling fire and a napping family, at home in a small mining town deep in the Appalachian Mountains. I wish in some ways that the letters ended there, though I would not have come to know the depth of Sara's spirit if they did.

The first glimmer of what lay ahead emerged in Sara's sorrow following her mother's death on March 12, 1948. Her next letter grieved that loss, found comfort in the announcement of Eleanor and Charles's pending marriage and ominously reported a tiredness that did not go away.

March 28, 1948
Lynch, Kentucky

Dear Eleanor,

Your letter yesterday was a comfort. Even if the going is long and hard for a long time—which it will be—still it's good to know that at times they are getting along pretty good at home. Kay, bless her heart, wrote me the weekly letter from home, and then hearing from you and Virginia both all together kept me from missing Mother's usual letter as much as I might have.

I am getting along pretty good, as I should with Tom to give me all attention and love and the two girls to keep me entertained and amused. But still I miss her so much. There is the consciousness always with me that she is gone. I appreciate the friends who have come to see me, because I want to talk about her and tell them about her. I don't think I ever realized so much how it relieves the pent-up emotions inside to talk about what is troubling you. Today's Easter sermon, too, was a real solace. It was just as though it were for me—"Let not your heart be troubled."

I've been a little slow, physically, to getting back to where I was before Mother's death. I've just wondered how you and Johnny and Virginia have gone back to your jobs and been able to do them. The first week back I was so tired I didn't do anything, except the simplest meals and care for the children, but rest. This past week I've been some better, but still not too good. Tom has wanted and urged me to see a doctor; but I have felt that it was just the normal reaction after a period of emotional tension. Today is the first time I have felt good the whole day. I believe from now on I will be all right.

Of course I told Tom right away about you and Charles, and he—like me—is so very glad for you and for him. It means so much too that Mother knew. I'm selfish enough to know that it will be hard to come home and not have you belonging there completely, and I know too that Daddy and Katherine and Virginia cannot but feel a natural reluctance to share you. But soon they will know that in Charles, as in Tom, we have a new member of the family which enriches it. He is so fine, and I can rest secure in the feeling that he will never hurt you in any way that can be avoided possibly, but that your happiness will be his chief goal. . . .

Two pages was my limit, but I cannot stop without telling you of Margaret's christening. As I wrote Kay, she looked like a tiny and exquisite jewel, with her pink dress bringing out rosy tints in her bright little face and bare arms. She lay in the preacher's arms so contentedly while he placed his hand on her head. She seemed as fresh and new as morning dew. Tom and I both had our blue suits newly pressed and I had a corsage of the loveliest pink rosebuds I've ever seen. Rachel's little green suit was just back from the cleaners for her to wear, but it was so cold this morning (snow until after noon) that she got to use the usual blue overalls.

Ruby came over yesterday morning to be here for the christening and all of James' family came up too. I fixed a half of the ham shoulder, boiled till tender then baked with sugar and cloves. It was really good. Then I had potato salad, sweet pickles, tomatoes, lettuce, bread, iced tea, dressed eggs and fruit Jello and cookies for dessert—much that could be bought outright or easily fixed, so I didn't have a hard time getting it ready—and Helen and Ruby did the dishes.

Tom took Ruby home and will be gone till Thursday night. He's taking part of his vacation to do it, but he feels they need him especially this week. I'm letting Rachel sleep with me while he's gone so it won't be so lonesome.

    Good night—and I love you,
      Sara

Three months later, a one-page letter, addressed to the newly wed Mrs. Charles Murray and written by Sara during her first visit to Delina following Jennie May's death, confirms what the family must have feared. A visit to the longtime family physician, Dr. Gordon, had produced a diagnosis—a frightening, forbidding one—of tiredness and its now accompanying fever and aches. Still, Sara adopted an upbeat tone.

                                June 1948
                           Delina, Tennessee

Dearest Eleanor,

    We enjoyed your and Charles' two visits and are looking forward to the Friday one and also the Sunday one. We'd like night visits too but those cows do have to be milked and chores done.

    E., I hope this will get there before you go to the hospital Wednesday, but do doubt it. Now you're not to be alarmed by this. I was pretty well prepared for it when he told me today that I do have an acute case of rheumatic fever and am going to have to stay in bed 3 months. Now Tom and I will work it out so it will be possible and nobody is to worry. Hear!

    I tried to ask Dr. Gordon everything I needed to know but omitted 3 things which I badly want to know: (1) Am I to continue the two daily douches which he had told me earlier to take (2) If so, might I take a tub bath as often as every other day and (3) could I have a copy of the sedimentation (blood activity) chart he has, to show to a

Lynch doctor when I do go for a check up. I'd be real glad to get an answer to those questions.

Virginia picked beans while we were gone and they strung them tonight for canning tomorrow. Rachel went with Daddy and me today and was a darling—slept in the car the hour and half we waited to see the Doctor. Isn't he sweet!! I do believe he's the next most lovable man I ever saw, or should I say "next, next."

See you Friday or Thursday.

Love,

Sara

At least so far as her sister was allowed to know, tears and self-pity were not part of the equation as Sara braced for the challenges ahead.

8.

Lynch, Kentucky

Summer 1948–March 1950

> May 26, 1948
> Lynch, Kentucky

Dear Virginia,

Eleanor wrote she would like to be like Mother but that she was too concerned with details to be. I guess we would all like to be, and I guess we all fall short. You are prone to worry more than she, and Kay doesn't have the emotional control that she did over her own self, but I sometimes feel that I am the most lacking, as I don't have the genuine love and interest in just everybody like she did. . . . What future life there is I do not know—that it is a continuation of this one, in that it's similar to it, I don't believe is probable; but that Mother's bright spirit exists somewhere, somehow, I do believe—and I can believe too that it is growing in wisdom and understanding of all mysteries and in happiness. I can tell a great difference in my feeling about death since Mother died. It doesn't have the horror and sting that I always felt before. . . .

Sara

Now comes the hard part.

In the months after unearthing Sara's letters, I read the cache through several times, immersing myself at every opportunity in her distant but increasingly familiar world. After work and dinners, I rushed through evening dishes and phone calls, then escaped to the bedroom, curling myself into an armchair and the luxury of a thick packet. I chuckled anew at Sara's jokes, felt her heartbreak with Bud, grew misty-eyed at my father's declarations of love, and reveled in her delight in friends, family—and me. With the omniscience of a reader privileged to track her quarry through years of correspondence, I saw personality traits come full circle. "Mother wrote that she had 104 blooms on the jonquils in front of our rock fence, and I had a good laugh. Who but Mother would go down and count her flowers?" Sara joked in 1944. Yet, five years later, as a young homemaker in Lynch, she herself reported, "Our iris—the dark purple—have been blooming prolifically, sometimes having between 100 and 200 blooms." Who was counting now?

The death of her mother marked a milestone in Sara's quest for deeper meaning in life. "I miss Mother so much. We always will. Sometimes I can hardly bear to think of that last day," she grieved eighteen months later. Perhaps imitating her mother, but perhaps because she found genuine solace there, she spent far more time in church than in earlier years. "Our revival is just over. The gals and I went to 4 of the 6 weekday services (mornings) and twice at night—not nearly as high a proportion as Mama used to manage, but even that kept us right busy," she wrote in May 1949. Who knows how fully Jennie May and Sara would have entwined as the daughter aged? Or Sara and I, had fate allowed?

On each reading of the letters, my joy ebbed as the stack dwindled. With the diagnosis of Sara's acute rheumatic fever in June 1948, I felt gripped by an almost physical pain. Not only was

Sara's story taking its final, dark turn, but the magic of recapturing her through letters had nearly run its course. Soon, she would be leaving me again. I forced myself through the sadness, parceling the final four dozen letters out over several days. Slower reading prolonged the sorrow, but it kept Sara alive a trifle longer. I accepted the price.

As the summer of 1948 passed, weeks of doctor-ordered bed rest took their toll on a young, active family. Sara seldom allowed what must have been both emotional and physical fatigue to sap the spirited optimism of her letters. Yet anyone who has mothered young children could ache over her inability to perform the simplest of tasks. I wince at the regimen of more than 223 penicillin shots ("already 123 shots and more than a hundred more to go") prescribed during a four-week period after persistent fever forced her into a hospital bed that summer. I experience her yearning for three-year-old Rachel, shipped off to Tennessee for a six-week visit. ("I've feasted and feasted my eyes upon her," Sara wrote upon Rachel's return.) And I am sobered by a new idea—the suggestion in both a letter from Virginia after Sara's death and in several conversations with her acquaintances, though never in Sara's writings or by my father, that my birth might somehow have contributed to her illness. "As for me, even if the children did help to bring on the fever, which they might not have done, I would prefer that she have her 7 years of happiness than many more years of less completeness," Virginia wrote. What can she mean?

As I sat in Barbara Tiabian's comfortable, enclosed front-porch, directly across the street from 503 Lynch Road, the idea surfaced again. A teenager at the time of Sara's death, now a retired nurse, Barbara remembered the event and the neighborhood scuttlebutt about it. "People said your mother never should have had children, but she did it anyway because she wanted you," Barbara recalled. I shuddered, struck both by a jolt of grief and an odd hint of solace. Had I stumbled into a bitter discovery? Did I play an unwitting role in our family tragedy? Yet, if my mother wanted children badly enough to jeopardize her own health, was that not proof of the enormous love at my core? I resolved to present all the medical details in the letters to an expert—to better understand Sara's illness. What role, if any, did my birth play in her death? If the onset of the rheumatic fever had come years or decades later, would she have lived?

Sara's final odyssey commenced with fever, aches and exhaustion in the spring of 1948, wound through a partial recovery in 1949, and arrived at a fatal precipice in 1950. Her determined cheerfulness throughout that span cannot mask the hardship of the journey. Only twice did she mention being "blue," the 1940s term for depression. Never once did she allow herself to dwell in print on the fear and anger that surely surfaced. But unless she was superhuman, the determination to spare her family grief and worry could not possibly have extended to herself in every moment. How helpless she must have felt at times in the sterile, late-night stillness of a lonely hospital room as she contemplated what lay ahead for herself and her family. How baffling, how maddening her plunge from vibrancy to dependency must have been.

The physical and mental punishment of those months tested the ingenuity, resources and faith of Sara and Tom as nothing before. "I remember her going down," Barbara told me. "She'd be outside, and at first she was just walking more slowly. Then, after a while, your Daddy was having to help her." I find the image hard to bear. Sara's description of trying to care for me alone one day while Tom was on a furniture-buying trip to Chicago reveals a shocking decline.

July 15, 1948
Lynch, Kentucky

Dearest Eleanor,

Tom comes home tomorrow afternoon, and though we haven't had any except the most minor of tragedies, nevertheless, I hope most earnestly that I'll have no more "in-bed-six-days" with the two liveliest Edds I know, with him gone. I'd gladly have pawned them on any willing member of either family for that time. But we have survived all right, though it was impossible to follow Dr. Gordon's rest instructions to the letter or spirit either part of the time.

Last night Mrs. Thomas left a few minutes early, and Mrs. Goss was over an hour and half late. Everything was fine until Margaret, in playpen in my room, messed up her panties. I waited and waited, knowing how uncomfortable a little fanny, already broken out, was getting. After one and a half hours neither she nor I could stand it any longer, so I got her oil and cotton and bathrag and towel and sat down in a chair by the playpen and pulled her up in my lap. You wouldn't believe just 3 weeks in bed could make a person so weak, but the slight effort of pulling her up made me feel faint and start perspiring. However, I felt sure I'd be able to finish up, when I realized I had forgot to get a clean diaper. That would involve more than I thought I could make, so I told Rachel to run over and tell Pauline to come over. I don't know exactly what Rachel said but think she called a cheery invitation from our yard for Pauline to come for a visit, but didn't mention "Mama said." Anyway, she didn't come, and in a few minutes, I felt better and let Margaret slip down sans panties and went to let Rachel in the back door. Mrs. Goss heard me call her and came over then, so all was all right.

. . . Margaret's wary one or two steps have changed to firm and many ones, and after her meals, I can hear her come pattering back to the bedroom. She's in my sight most of the time, except her nap times, *and is so sweet. Rachel has slept with me this week to her delight. Even during the night when she rouses slightly she reaches over and gives me love pats and you never heard such endearing good nights. . . . I mostly don't do anything—read, write and mend a little. I feel good most of the time, but fever hasn't decreased. Nor are aches gone, nor ankles entirely down. I eat good, but have lost a pound. Wish you and Charles were in "dropping in" distance.*

    Love,

      Sara

That letter must have frightened Eleanor. Soon afterward, she and Charles, newly married, made plans to visit Lynch for the first time.

July 24, 1948

Lynch, Kentucky

Dear Eleanor,

    We were glad to get your letter today; and you know we're thrilled at the thought that you all are actually coming. I wish I could welcome you with a clean house and a good meal (you missed your opportunity for that last summer) but neither will be the case. . . .

    I read "Peony" by Pearl Buck this week. I've read more than anything, but not even that a great deal. I usually sleep during the day besides all night. The aches in joints are about gone and last night I was thrilled for my fever to be down to 100 degrees and even more so tonight as it was down to 99 degrees. That's the best two days in a long time. . . .

    Neither Rachel nor Margaret have been feeling very good the last 2 or 3 days. Rachel crawled in bed with me this morning and slept 4 hours. (I slept most of that time too—how can I help but get well.) . . .

    Love,

      Sara

The improvement did not last. Sara wrote her next letter from the Lynch Hospital, a dispiriting setback. Two days after my first birthday, she rejoiced in her sister's anticipated arrival. Sara also allowed herself a rare admission of the emotional toll of her illness.

August 20, 1948
Lynch Hospital
Lynch, Kentucky

Dearest Eleanor,

How are you and Charles? We're so "elated" that you all are coming next Saturday night! Couldn't it be for longer? Three nights away from a farm is a pretty long time though, especially when a honeymoon has already come. . . . We're going to let Rachel return with you and Charles, if it's still O.K. with everybody. She's staying this week at Grandmother Edds, quite happily, so I believe she won't mind a month or so down home without Tom or me. . . .

Little Margaret is 22 pounds at 1 year—fatter than Rachel by 6 ounces at that age. She cuddles down to me when Tom brings her at night. Occasionally she comes out with a short sentence like "Dar it is" (there it is) to a question of Tom's. She's adorable and I think she likes me.

Although I've been pretty sick and pretty "blue" too, I'm definitely better of both now. Just wish I could be home when you all come, but I won't be, as Dr. Sonne says a full 4 weeks of penicillin (already 123 shots and more than a hundred more to go). But the last X-rays—two days ago—showed great improvement. . . . I've a tremendous appetite now, and keep Tom busy bringing me things besides meals here with juice and crackers in mid-morning and mid-afternoon. I've seven lovely bouquets this morning. Visitors have been allowed since Tuesday, and I enjoy them. I've started reading

again this week. Tom has been wonderful, as always. Can hardly
wait to see you all.
    Love,
      Sara

So what is this mother-killer, this rheumatic fever? How could
it snuff out so youthful and energetic a life?

Dave Propert, professor of internal medicine and a former
director of the cardiology division at Eastern Virginia Medical
School in Norfolk, Virginia, explained. Rheumatic fever is an acute
inflammation of the heart muscle, brought on by an infection,
but not an actual infection itself. It begins with streptococcal
pharyngitis, a bacterial infection commonly called "strep throat."
Antibodies that develop in response to the strep sometimes attack
the heart, joints and other connective tissues. The resulting
inflammation—rheumatic fever—can be lethal, either in the
short term or later due to heart damage. Rheumatic fever most
often affects children between the ages of five and fifteen, and
recurrences are common later in life. Resulting rheumatic heart
disease can last a lifetime. Scottish poet Robert Burns, who
passed away at thirty-seven, died of the ailment. Some scholars
believe that Wolfgang Amadeus Mozart, dead at thirty-five, did
as well. About fifteen thousand Americans, including Sara, died
of rheumatic fever or rheumatic heart disease in 1950, according
to the American Heart Association. By 2003 that number had
dwindled to about 3,500 due to improved treatment of strep
infections and damaged hearts.

Sara's medical records no longer exist. So, playing medical
detective, Dr. Propert created a timeline of her illness, a standard
clinical way of reviewing pathologies. He recorded the April fatigue,
followed by the June diagnosis, trailed by weeks of bed rest at home,

and then a hospital stay of about four weeks. Her exhaustion, fever, aches and high sedimentation rate (an indicator of inflammation in the body, determined by how quickly red blood cells separate from plasma) point to a correct diagnosis of rheumatic fever.

And what of the theory that childbirth contributed to Sara's death? I winced at asking but wanted to know. Propert proved reluctant to buy into the speculation. I welcomed his dismissal, but felt nagging doubt. Was he being straightforward or was he reluctant to fuel guilt over a fifty-year-old death? What does the evidence say? My birth, about nine months before rheumatic fever struck, could have affected Sara's condition, but probably only if the pregnancy further weakened a previously damaged heart. Did she suffer rheumatic fever as a child? Mild cases at an early age sometimes went undetected. Nothing in her letters indicates any awareness of an earlier attack. A serious round of rheumatic fever often left a heart murmur, and Sara never mentions having a leaky value. Still, a daughter of John O. (Johnny) tells me that her father believed Sara's rheumatic fever first surfaced in childhood. It would be unusual, though not unheard-of, for the first episode to occur as an adult, Propert said.

I found it hard to let go of the fear that he was shielding me from a real, though remote, possibility.

In the 1940s and early 1950s, according to the era's leading medical textbooks, the link between rheumatic fever and strep was suspected, but not confirmed. Bed rest, in some cases so extreme that patients weren't allowed to feed themselves or walk to the bathroom, was the primary treatment. Today, steroids would help manage the inflammation, but in 1950 there were no effective medications. Why Sara received in excess of two hundred penicillin shots that summer remains a mystery. Once the connection with strep throat was affirmed in the 1950s, post-rheumatic patients often took a penicillin tablet daily to ward off future infections. So excessive a dose in the midst of Sara's illness might have been a trial therapy. Or it might have been prescribed because some clinicians still suspected an active infection caused the fever. Doctors also may have feared bacterial endocarditis, an infection that occurs when bacteria in the bloodstream lodge in abnormal heart valves or other damaged heart tissue. Propert's view that Sara received quality medical care for the times is consistent with evidence that the Lynch Hospital and medical staff were among eastern Kentucky's best.

As the summer and fall of 1948 wore on, Sara reported slow but steady progress toward recovery. Almost daily letters to Rachel, visiting in Tennessee, recorded her maternal devotion and her longing to be well.

> *August 30, 1948*
> *Lynch Hospital*
> *Lynch, Kentucky*

Dear Rachel,

You, Aunt Eleanor, and Uncle Charles are still in Morristown, but soon you'll be ride-ride-riding again toward Belvidere. Do you like to look out the car window and see the big lake with little boats on the water? And the roadside cabins with their gay bedspreads and fox furs for sale?

Daddy and Margaret came to see me last night. Margaret had on a little flower-sprigged dress that used to be yours. When Daddy said they had to go, Margaret began to wave her hand and say,"Bye, Bye." They brought me a big bowl of watermelon, yum-m-m and a piece of chicken.

Jim Bill's Grandmother came to see me yesterday afternoon. She brought a lovely bouquet of red and orange zinnias, lavender phlox, yellow and orange marigolds, cream gladioli, and black and yellow daisies. Aunt Eleanor has pretty flowers, and she will tell you their names.

Dr. Sonne came to see Mother this morning. He said I could go home next Sunday, and maybe sit up to eat dinner and supper. Someday I will be well and strong again, and that means you and I can go walking again and gather sycamore balls maybe, and in the wintertime we will make a snowman.

It would be nice if you could help Aunt Eleanor. She doesn't know you can dry silverware and put it away, so you show her.

Daddy, Margaret, and I love you dearly; and we are glad you are having such a good time.

Love,

Mother

[In a note to Eleanor, she added:]

Dr. Sonne says the last blood test shows improvement in everything but the sedimentation chart, which has not changed since my admission to the hospital. It is 45. The correct sedimentation rate is from about 1 to 10. Until that goes down I'll have to continue to stay in bed. However, I can go home Sunday and possibly sit up for 2 meals a day. He was disappointed that the blood activity hadn't lowered, and of course I was; but it usually is last to get normal and I am better in so many ways. . . .

. . .

August 31, 1948
Lynch Hospital
Lynch, Kentucky

Dearest Rachel,

. . . And what have you done today? Did you go to the barn and see the Hampshire pig? Maybe you will be there when the little pigs are born. You'd like to see them.

Last night I heard somebody coming down the hall fast. They went pit-a-pat, pit-a-pat. It sounded like you, but I knew you were in Belvidere. Guess who? It was Margaret, first a-running, all by herself (well, Daddy came along in a minute).

This morning a little boy came in my room with a basket of asters his mother had sent. They are pink and purple and white. Next summer you and I will plant some aster seed, then put the little plants in our yard and watch them grow.

Daddy came by to see me on his way to work this morning and brought me a big, red tomato.

Mother thinks of you every single hour of the day. . . .

Love,

Mother

. . .

September 6, 1948
Lynch Hospital
Lynch, Kentucky

Dearest Rachel,

This is the day I'm going home, and I'm so excited I can hardly wait for Daddy to come get me. Then when you come home, I will be there. . . . It was as windy here yesterday as though it had been March, maybe the tail end of the New Orleans hurricane. . . . Mother and Daddy miss you and love you.

Mother

. . .

September 8, 1948
Lynch, Kentucky

Dearest Rachel,

I'm home again, in my own bed, and happy as a lark. Daddy came for me Monday night. When we got here little Margaret was sitting in your green and yellow chair in the living room. She clapped her hands, and stomped her feet, and sang a song, and grinned broadly and happily. All in all, she gave her mother a real welcome home.

Mrs. Thomas had a good dinner for my homecoming yesterday, and I got to sit down at the table and eat with Daddy. She had stuffed sweet peppers, which I like.

Sally [a neighbor] came to see me yesterday. Have you worn the dress with the ballerina skirt that she made for you? Barbara came too, with a bouquet of dahlias from her mother. The prettiest flower I have now is a pink rosebud that Daddy cut this morning from the rosebush by the back steps.

Are you being a good girl? I hope so.

Much love from Mother

.   .   .

September 18, 1948
Lynch, Kentucky

Dear Eleanor,

. . . At noon yesterday Tom took me to the hospital for the nurse to take a little blood for checking. Dr. Sonne came last night and was very pleased, as my sed [sedimentation] rate had gone down 15 points in 3 weeks. It's 30 now, after being 45 all the time I was in the hospital. I've gained 5 lbs. since being home, which makes me 128 and still zooming. I enjoy the days so much now—seeing little Margaret, taking long morning naps, eating heartily, working on my *recipe file, sorting photographs, finishing my crocheted wool scatter rug of 1940 origin, planning to finish state flower quilt of the same era, mending, writing, reading. So many things!*

. . . Margaret, the precious, is in playpen with the tea set, phone, and little green and yellow striped chair. She loves the chair and has just recently acquired the know-how of gingerly letting her little behind down to the seat instead of climbing in feet first and then having to execute a turn-around. In Rachel's words, I believe she loves me, but she doesn't associate me with anything helpful, and so when in need she sallies to either Tom or Mrs. Thomas.

. . . Now that I can be up for all 3 meals and double my previous time, and am getting along so splendidly, we're planning for Rachel to come home. . . . I know it's all been a great experience for her and it has really been a help for us too. We haven't worried about her, since we knew she was getting along fine; or been lonesome, since we knew she would soon come home. . . .

　Love,

　Sara

A letter to Delina just before Rachel's return to Lynch reveals the logistical complications in an era when telephone use was still limited and buses were a principal form of travel.

October 3, 1948

Lynch, Kentucky

Dear Katherine,

. . . Kay, you know how hard it is to get correct bus information here and how often it changes at home; so we're still in the dark about the schedule. So I'll give you instructions based on what I know, and you must be sure to let me know if you can't follow these instruction and what you will do instead.

If there's still a bus that leaves Fayetteville about noontime and gets to Knoxville at 10:00 o'clock p.m. (or about that time), then it would be best for you and Rachel to come on it Saturday, and Tom will meet you in Knoxville Saturday night and bring you on home. This would be good all around, as it would be easiest for you all, possible for Tom to get to Knoxville by leaving after work Saturday, and Ruby could come over to stay with Margaret and me. That would work on Saturday, but not Sunday, as then there wouldn't be anyone to stay with Margaret and me, and Tom would be up almost all night Sunday before a work day.

If there isn't any such schedule, and you leave in the early morning from home then it would be almost as easy for you to come on to Harlan, and have Tom meet you there. . . . So you could come either Saturday or Sunday. That way Margaret and I could manage fine, and Tom wouldn't have to miss work either. So be sure to check the schedule, and let us know definitely the time and day you're coming and write us Wednesday, so we'll know certain. . . .

Love,

Sara

A week later the Edds family was again intact. Hopes ran high that Sara's rheumatic fever finally was subsiding and that a return to normalcy lay just ahead. Sara reported to Eleanor on Rachel's return and the latest medical news. In a small aside in that letter, I see yet again how instrumental Eleanor was in preserving a family history that could so easily have been lost.

October 17, 1948
Lynch, Kentucky

Dearest Eleanor,

"She's" been here a week and I've feasted and feasted my eyes upon her. . . . I was looking out the window when they arrived (9 p.m.).

I heard Rachel give a shout and say "There's Mama!" Then she came flying in with curls following after, and oh, there was never anyone sweeter. She was so excited and had to see everything. I took her into Margaret's room where she gushed and exclaimed, "Oh, see her new teefies; oh look how long her hair is." Margaret looked at her solemnly a long while, then slowly a little grin started, swelled into a whopping big one and stayed there solid. She follows her around the house, grinning.

The first night Rachel stayed up till almost midnight. She set up the tea set and fed me and herself breakfast. And over and over again she'd finish up a sentence by saying "cause I'm the girl who 'tays (stays) here." . . . She had so many experiences this summer that she couldn't have had at home, and we're grateful for her visits and more than grateful to have her home safe again. . . . I started to throw away my letters in her suitcase and she said, "No, they're still fresh." And later, "Aunt Eleanor told me to keep them."

Next to Rachel's being home, I guess the next biggest news is that Dr. Sonne says I'm almost well. From 8–15 is normal for women on the sedimentation chart here and I was 19 ten days ago. He says to stay up longer, not to push myself, but to gradually start getting on a more normal schedule. He said in two weeks he thought I would be able to get breakfast and that we could have Mrs. Thomas on an 8-hour day instead of an 11-hour one. Now I'm taking everything slowly and will continue to for a long while, but eventually Dr. Sonne says I will be able to go back to normal activity. I feel completely rested and just grand and weigh 9 pounds more than when you were here.

Everybody seems to be having water trouble since it's been so dry. Lots of people in Lynch have been having water for only 2 or 3 hours a day. We have had it most of the time since we're on the lowest level in town. Saturday it was off most all morning. . . .

Lots of love,

Sara

As they entered the sixth year of their marriage, Sara and Tom cautiously returned to a more active schedule. In December Sara pronounced herself "completely well," and gleefully reported that "we'll need help only one day a week, for hard things, after Christmas." Afternoon rest for Sara remained a staple, and her continuing fatigue was a precursor of troubles to come. But for the next year, the family fully believed that she was on the mend. She joyfully resumed preparing meals ("I just love my new Mixmaster. It makes wonderful creamed potatoes"), attending church, visiting friends and performing her cherished role of wife and mother. "My really mainest worry all summer has been how much Tom has had to do," she confided in a letter that makes me cringe at my comparative selfishness decades later. "It's wonderful to be able now to take a few things off him. For one thing I get up when the children cry out at night, and he can get unbroken rest then at least. He had been getting up a half dozen times a night or more." A half-dozen times? I know my father well enough to say with near certainty that he never complained. I remember with shame my own irritation when, after his stroke at age eighty-five, he cried out repeatedly for attention some nights. Though I did not realize it at the time, life had come full circle. I was doing for him only what he had done for me, but I was showing less patience in the act.

Throughout 1949, Sara's letters record domestic details, amuse her family with favorite sayings of Rachel's and—increasingly— mine, and offer glimpses of possibilities, never fulfilled, as she and Tom dreamed of their future life.

One night Tom was gone to Appalachia to buy some china from Dean & Kite representatives there. I went in Rachel's room after she had been in bed awhile and she asked if Tom was home. When I told her

no, she said, "If you want somebody to hold on to, you just come right
on in here and sleep with me." She said it so sweetly that I hurried
and wrote it down verbatim. Another time when I told her I was well,
she said, "Stay that way, Mommy, and don't get sick a time more."

On New Year's Day, with an abandon that would have been
unimaginable a few months earlier, our foursome packed into the
Buick and drove several hours to size up a farm for sale in northeast
Tennessee. "We took a mad, but gay, jaunt into Tennessee—down
to Talbott, 3 miles from Jefferson City," she wrote to Eleanor.

Tom was intrigued with an ad he'd seen in the paper about a farm
for sell there—100 acres and an 8-room brick house with a tenant
house. He'd written a letter or two about it, and though we knew it
to be way out of our reach, we still wanted to see this place that "has
to be seen to be appreciated." We ate our Mrs. Thomas-prepared
lunch at Rogersville, and how good those sausage biscuits and tuna
sandwiches tasted (though we're still wondering where she got the
horseradish that was in them.) The candy bar dessert was good too,
for in Margaret's lingo, it was a "told, 'told day," and we had sharp
appetites. Even if we'd had $40,000 though, we wouldn't have
wanted the farm.

Almost certainly, I think, a farm would have figured in Sara
and Tom's future. Farming remained my father's lifetime passion,
fulfilled temporarily for a few years after Sara's death, but more
happily in the final two decades of his life.

With the focus diverted from Sara's illness, attention to the
larger world returned. The nettlesome labor-management tensions
that ran through Lynch erupted in violence in February 1949.
Tom found himself at center stage for one of the worst days in the

town's history. Throughout the 1930s, Lynch avoided the deadly confrontations that spawned the county's reputation as "Bloody Harlan." Superior living conditions, combined with company control of the streets and the security force, kept the worst clashes at bay. That reprieve expired on Saturday, February 5.

February 8, 1949
Lynch, Kentucky

Dear Kay and all,

I hardly know how to begin on this letter, and it's further compli-cated by Rachel having a book here for me to read between sentences. This has been a very sad and a very hectic weekend for Lynch. I'll have to start at the beginning. When I came here to work the store members were not organized, which means they did not belong to any union. Of course, the coal company employees, other than the foremen and officials, belong to the United Mine Workers. Shortly after I left Lynch for Oak Ridge, some of the store employees organized and became members of the United Construction Workers. However the majority of the store employees, disapproving of the tactics which union leaders have often used and also realizing that the United Supply Company (the store here) has always dealt fairly with them, have not joined.

Tom, being a department manager, is not eligible, as no one who can hire or fire employees is ever allowed to be a member of a union. You may remember at the time Tom and I came back to Lynch, a store strike had just ended. That's the only time I know that there's been a strike at the store. Ever since they first organized it's been a thorn in the flesh to the members that there have been so many non-members in the store. And they have tried everything in the form of persuasion and even threats to get them to join. The last few weeks, they, joined by the coal company union, have put on a drive to have the store members go a 100 per cent union. By worry and threats they gained a few members, but the most resisted.

Saturday afternoon about an hour before store closing time 5 cars of armed men—union agitators from nearby coal fields—came to Lynch. They were 35 men, later estimated by police. They were asked to come by the 2 unions here. They gathered around the store entrance just before closing time. Inside the store, it was known that union agitators were outside, but of course it was not known that they were armed. Nevertheless, in order to keep the different clerks from being molested in any way, they decided to all come out together at closing time—that is, all the non-union members, the managers of the different departments, and the assistant manager of the store and chief clerk. (Mr. Kirby, the store manager had left earlier in the day for Pittsburgh, along with 3 department managers.)

Since most of the men employees work in the restaurant, service station, and 2 branch grocery stores, there were only 3 boys in the store that were non-union members. There were a number of girls, but the 35 men had come primarily to force those 3 boys into joining—2 in the grocery department and one in Tom's department—Darnell Ball. So when the store group all walked out together, those 3 were quickly spotted by the men and roughly ordered to sign the cards they held. When they refused, pandemonium broke out in different places. Tom and Mr. Farmer had come out with Darnell Ball. When the men grabbed Darnell, Mr. Farmer, the assistant store manager, told Darnell to get away. Then one began to fight Mr. Farmer. He—the agitator—pulled out an opened knife behind his back. Tom saw it and grabbed his arm. Immediately another one, wearing brass knuckles, hit Tom hard, squarely in the nose. It broke his nose and a wisdom tooth and his face and mouth became a bloody mess.

Another group of men about 10 ft. away had grabbed a little grocery boy and began to beat him up. There were 2 policemen arrived by this time. One, John Yelenosky, stepped in to intervene. Although he was naturally armed, he never withdrew his gun. But when he started to separate the fighting group, he was shot four times, twice in the head and twice in the chest. He died instantly. The second policeman shot one of the murderers in the leg, and he was shot himself in the thigh. When Mr. Yelenosky dropped dead, the other groups quickly broke up, and all the union men fled—all except the one wounded man. The others will probably never be found and probably couldn't be identified if they were—so the riot was over.

Mr. Farmer drove Tom home first so that I could hear about it first from Tom. Then he took him on to the hospital. The doctors dressed and set his nose. Although his face is swollen and the upper part a dark purple, he hasn't suffered a great deal. He stayed in bed most all day Sunday, but went to work yesterday. I've hardly had a minute since it happened, as there have been people coming in almost constantly. Mr. Yelenosky's funeral was yesterday. He was 40 years old, a member of the police force here for 17 years—father of three children.

Perhaps you've seen something about this in the papers. The Knoxville papers carried it in the headlines Sunday and Monday. It's all tragic, and almost unbelievable for a free country.

I must stop—Rachel and Margaret have neither been very well. Margaret has 3 new teeth. You should hear her sing "Bye, Bye, Blackbud."

> *Lots of love,*
> *Sara*

A half century later, details of that day had faded in Lynch. One version circulated by an old-timer suggested that Yelenosky was killed by "friendly fire," a stray police bullet. Newspaper annals for the *Sentinel-Echo* in London, Kentucky, where the trial was moved, do not bear that out. According to that record, after a four-day trial, United Mine Workers organizer Lawrence Pennington Jr. was convicted of voluntary manslaughter in a special term of the Laurel Circuit Court and sentenced to two years in the state reformatory. According to eyewitnesses, Coroner Henry Skidmore testified, Pennington was brandishing a pistol when Yelenosky grabbed him and was shot in the chest. The defendant was shot twice, in the left leg and the chest, and a second police officer was wounded in the thigh.

Such a shocking episode must have reinforced Tom and Sara's interest in eventually leaving Lynch. When that departure came two years later, labor tension was one of the things Tom did not regret leaving behind.

Fifteen months after her first daughter was born, Sara had been pregnant with her second. By January 1949, I was seventeen months old and a third pregnancy was on her mind. Her own mother had given birth roughly every two years for a decade. Early in 1949, Sara confided to Eleanor her frustration with the recommendation of a family doctor in Tennessee that she forgo future pregnancies. "I simply refuse to accept Dr. Gordon's advice," she wrote. "It's a subject my doctor did indeed mention, but he gave me another version—not a child right away, tis true, but every reason to think I can have another in time. That promise, along with my joyous responsibility with what I already have, makes me remember to take care of myself."

Dave Propert smiled and shook his head at her next suggestion, which to his knowledge had no medical validity. "Many doctors even go further than mine, and recommend pregnancy for rheumatic patients," Sara wrote. " Now don't worry about this. Neither Tom nor I would let me take on more than I would have a good chance to be able to manage, and whatever we do will be with a good doctor's sanction."

In March, during a visit home to Tennessee, Sara and Tom sidetracked to Nashville for an appointment with a renowned cardiologist, Thomas Frist, whose son Bill later became the GOP majority leader of the U.S. Senate. The elder Frist helped found the Hospital Corporation of America in the 1960s and is sometimes called the father of the modern for-profit hospital system. His advice proved no more to Sara's liking than that of the family physician. Through all her travails, she never expressed greater sorrow than in a letter to Eleanor after Frist's examination, though—typically—she began her account of it with a joke.

April 5, 1949
Lynch, Kentucky

Dear E. B. and Charles,

Dr. Frist was wonderful—just the most likeable person you'd ever meet. I couldn't wait to write you that we arrived with checkbook but no means of signature, and had to borrow a fountain pen from him! Not really him, but one of the girls—anyway it makes a better story the 1st way. We felt our time—2 to 6—and money, $50.00, were well spent. Nevertheless, I have had a hard time not feeling pretty miserable part of the time since. He said, with care, I could expect a normal life span; but it's a hard price. He said, among other things, no pregnancies. The other things were 8 hours sleep at night, a full hour rest every afternoon, flu shot each fall, stopping all colds and sore throats with sulfur, vitamin tablet each day, avoiding going upstairs a lot, proper masticating and elimination, a diet which includes daily several specified things.

He wrote all that list out for me, in detail. All the last things I don't mind, too much, only the 1st; and that I told him I wouldn't accept as the final word. So he told me to come back next March. If my heart were improved or no worse, then maybe. But I don't see how I could bear to ever hear definitely and finally, without further hope, that I could have no more children. I love Tom so dearly that I want many, many children of his to make the world a better and sunnier place. But I feel I could be almost satisfied with just one more. . . .

I'm almost ashamed to say what we've got on the front porch, as yet uncrated. It, too, though is something Dr. Frist told Tom to get for me. It's a General Electric automatic dishwasher. The other thing he told Tom to buy was a clothes dryer. With those things added to what I have, he said, I could do my own work. However, we have dishwasher and Evelyn. I feel like I have too much heaped upon me.

Spring is overtaking Lynch at last. Green hedges, white cherry trees, redbud, tulips. I'm happy to see it come.

Lots of love,

Sara

She wanted a son, and in that wanting lies evidence of the strength of her marriage—just as the purchase of an endless array of appliances reflected Tom's determination to do anything possible to secure Sara's well-being. Clothes dryers and dishwashers became standard fare a generation later, but they were luxuries in postwar Lynch. I have not known anyone else, before or since, who acquired a large electric ironing machine for home use. Yet that lumbering piece of equipment, bought for Sara, trailed us through childhood along with many of the rest of her belongings. A letter to Tom after Sara's death from Mary Bowman, an elderly friend who adopted them during their year in Greenville, repeated Sara's craving for a son. "In one of her letters Sara said 'my life is so rich and happy that I can think of only one thing in the world that could add to our happiness, and that is a little son. Such a man as Tom, so good and generous and fine in every way, should have a son to carry on his name and his character—for he is the kind of man who should father the next generation.'"

I have about a half-dozen photographs of Sara taken in 1949 and while, as Virginia might have said, I believe she looked the worse for wear, her smile had not lessened. If anything, it radiates more fully against a thinner face and unstyled hair. As Sara entered her thirties, I see more of me in her. Those photographs in which her grin dominates are the ones in which I can most glimpse myself at a similar age. My father, in contrast, looks less carefree, more solemn in those 1949 photos. It may be risky to read too much into a handful of snapshots. Then again, how could the anxiety and pressures of Sara's lingering illness not have taken a toll?

Life that year followed an established pattern—twice-annual visits to Tennessee; regular trips across Big Black Mountain ("We stayed 3 days at Tom's house week before last and four days last week. He gathered corn. Margaret and I hulled walnuts in the afternoon"); community commitments to the American Legion, the Masonic Lodge and the Methodist Church and outings to baseball games, weddings and a high school play. "Tuesday night 1/3 of the horizon was red-streaked—all Lynch was out looking. It must have been the Northern lights, which I'd heard about but never seen," she wrote that winter. Monopoly and Flinch were popular family games. Occasional bridge parties at the Lynch country club or dinners at the hotel added spice to daily life. A new pressure cooker brought zip to meals in a pre-microwave era. "It cooks new green beans in 2½ minutes (I put them on after Tom came home to lunch today) and greens in 3 minutes. It takes potatoes, sliced, 3 minutes. I can cook meats, cereals, vegetables, soup or almost anything in it. I'm just carried away."

I turned from a baby to a toddler, carving my own niche in the family constellation. "When we ask Margaret 'Do you love Mother, or Daddy, or anybody?' she says 'I dew,' just like Rachel used to," Sara wrote in January. "And when she's in a bad mood she says 'Nah!' She learned to crow like a rooster tonight. She says lots of words and short sentences." A few days later, after a work-related buying trip to Chicago: "Tom came home unexpectedly Thursday night, a whole day before I expected him, and we were really a tickled household when he stepped in. He brought Rachel a little pink necklace and Margaret one on a chain. But she liked Rachel's best and threw a little fit. She's sweet, but as positive in her likes and dislikes as Rachel." By June, she reported, "Margaret's going through a daddy phase. Everything is 'let daddy do it' from morning to night." And that August, Sara affectionately recorded the events of my second birthday: "Now you are a two-year-old darling, just crazy about your 'Dadee' but pretty fond of 'Murver' and 'Wachie' too. You're precious, our little sweet, and Mother and Daddy just adore you." As parents, Sara and Tom had firm expectations and rules, but if Sara lost patience with childish mayhem, she recovered before putting pen to paper. "Who would start a letter with no ink—Margaret has spilled ours on floor, her, pillow, me and sofa (me being asleep on sofa with pillow under my head.) That girl!" I remember nothing of such moments, but her tolerance and warmth must be embedded in my psyche. So, too, must be the orderliness she expected and the independence she allowed. Both qualities mirrored her spirit; given her physical limitations, they most likely were essential to the family's managing as well.

Throughout 1949 Sara alluded rarely to illness, but occasional references confirm that the rheumatic fever had taken a permanent toll. "I can just imagine how full your days are," she wrote in June to Eleanor, who was ending the teaching year and juggling family and farm commitments. "I rue that mine aren't too, although they're full enough—just not packed (no, I don't rue that they're not full, just that they can't be full). That sentence is complicated now. Guess you heard I went back to bed for four days, but it was just a preventive measure, as I wasn't feeling bad, other than a faster heart. I'm fine again." In September, she mentioned that a hired helper, a black woman, still came four mornings a week. "Evelyn decided she needed work every day (morning) instead of the four only she had here. So she got another job while we were on vacation, but came back to us when I got back; and I've found another place for her Tuesdays and Saturdays. I want to use her one day less, as I know a place she could work the extra day, if Tom will let me. Three mornings would be ample."

By December Sara appeared to have won out on three-day help. Preparations for Christmas were underway.

December 10, 1949
Lynch, Kentucky

Dear Eleanor,

Only two weeks until stocking hanging time. We have two adorable Baby Coo dolls set back, just alike except in size. They are going to be mighty welcome in a house that's been doll-less for weeks except for two bears! . . . How we'd love for you and Charles to be with us on Christmas Day. We're counting on a gift turkey again. I have my presents most all planned, but not all purchased quite. I made a fruit cake last Saturday and am going to splurge with another jam cake and a nut one (cake-eating us!). . . . Tom's working every night and Sundays—the one biggest drawback to December. If it's pretty tomorrow we're going to take a round-about route to Tom's home, in order to gather some holly that was—last year—beautiful with

berries. I'm feeling fine. Evelyn's fairly regular 3 mornings again
after a period of off and one. A few snows. No huge ones yet.

    Love,

      Sara

Sara preserved the holiday in a thirteen-page letter begun
Christmas night. The usual three-cent stamp proved insufficient,
and the letter is stamped "Postage due 3 cents." With her usual
foresight, Eleanor labeled the envelope, "Sara's wonderful Christmas letter, December 1949, Keep for Rachel and Margaret," and
tucked it away.

                        December 25, 1949

                            Lynch, Kentucky

Dear Kay and all,

    A happy Christmas to all, though I'm late in the week and day in
wishing you so. Two little girls have gone tiredly and tearfully to bed,
after a full, exciting, no-nap day. The tears were quick gone, as they
were both asleep in 5 minutes after touching their respective pillows.

    It was a beautiful day here—clear and not so bitterly cold as
yesterday, but with a high wind. It should have been fine for all the
ones coming home today. . . . We have had a busy week, but not
too rushed for enjoyment. All presents were bought by a week ago
Saturday, and most of the main cleaning up was done, so we've had
this week for wrapping presents, going to parties, etc.

    Tom and Rachel fixed the Christmas tree Tuesday night, while
I went to the W.S.C.S. [Women's Society of Christian Service]
Meeting, which we had a week early in order to have a Xmas program.
The preacher's son, a Union College teacher, was home and played
the pipe organ beautifully, both for the Missionary Meeting, and for
a very inspiring cantata last Sunday night.

Back to the Xmas tree, it had the same old lights we've been using since '42, but with three little electric light birds, a yellow, a red, and a blue added. Tom and girls opened Frances' package and put the presents under the tree. Tom's package rattled slightly and Margaret guessed "It could be buttons." . . . They were both very good about not trying to open the packages, but Margaret could hardly keep her hands off the tree. Once when the lights were turned off, she went around the tree, poking her little finger into the branches and touching each light, then proudly announced "Everyone didn't burn me."

I did most of the package wrapping after they'd gone to bed, as their help there was more hindrance. Rachel handed me a seal one night and asked "Are you in desperation for this?" They enjoyed their Sunday School party Thursday afternoon (while the rain poured), and again Friday afternoon, up at the club. There was a Xmas tree there, the biggest I'd ever seen. The colored lights all over it were regular sized bulbs, or almost so. When Santa Claus appeared and all the children gathered around him, Margaret's excited little voice could be heard over everything, exclaiming, "Murver, Murver!" She hugged and kissed Santa and told him she wanted a dollie.

Saturday we stayed home all day. In the morning, I went over the house lightly to get it in final order, in the afternoon I stuffed the turkey with sausage dressing (a 20-lb. dressed one, the biggest and nicest one we've ever had) and cooked it from 5:00 to 12:00. Tom stayed up the last half hour to take it out. It did beautifully. Also I made ice-box rolls. The jam cake was made earlier in the week, and we were given 2 3-lb. fruit cakes, and a roll of nut bread.

I did less decorating for Christmas this year than ever before. Only the tree, and the coffee table fixed up with my very pretty blooming begonia and calla, with pink candles burning on either side. We never did have time to go to Virginia to get any holly, and none was brought around on trucks to sell, as is usually done.

(As you may have deduced, I'm writing this the day after Christmas now. I didn't get far last night, as Tom started reading aloud to me. . . .)

I think this was the best Santa Claus year we've had, or probably will have. Their dolls are the sweetest by far they've ever had, just alike except in size and dress. Rachel saw hers first and was just in ecstasy. Margaret didn't see hers at first, just the one of Rachel's, but little trouper that she is, she said bravely, "See the dollie Santa brought Wachel and me." Then she saw her own, and I'll never forget the look on her face or the tone of her voice as she cried, "a dollie for me!"

They each had to take them to S.S., but were content to leave them in the car for church. After church we had company for about half an hour, then (with Tom helping me some) I made the fruit salad, set the rolls to rising, set the table and put on the potatoes to cook for creaming. Everything else—the turkey, dressing, cranberry sauce, pickles and dessert was ready. Then we had our tree. Rachel and Margaret had been so busy playing with their dolls, doll trunk, and teaset, and 2 little hand sparklers that they had paid little attention to the things under the tree, but once we started opening them, their excitement rose by leaps and bounds. They wound up, dressed in Virginia's socks, with scuffies from Mr. and Mrs. Kirby on their feet, Eleanor's aprons over their overalls, silk panties from Kay on, and little red dress gloves from Verne and Lizelle on their hands. They looked like two adorable clowns. . . .

This letter is so long already that I know I can't cover adequately all the very nice, useful, and pretty gifts received. But we're so pleased. . . . [Four pages of present descriptions followed.] Kay, in case the family is already "dispersed" when you get this, wish you'd save it for them—Not that it's a specially good one, but because I know I won't get to write again of our Christmas in such detail.

Love and a Happy New Year to all,

Sara

January and February 1950 passed in routine fashion. In late March, a flu bug struck, ordinarily enough for the time of year. In a postcard, Sara mentioned Tom's missing the trial of the man accused of murdering police officer John Yelenosky. That was the main consequence of their sickness, she thought.

Sara was wrong. Dr. Frist had warned her against catching colds or flu for good reason. The added stress was more than her enlarged heart could stand.

> *March 31, 1950*
> *Lynch, Kentucky*
>
> *Dear Eleanor,*
>
> *Kay has written of your distressing cough and Charles' infected hand. I do hope both are clearing up. I hardly see how you've made it to school. We've had a "run" too. First Rachel got a bladder infection last Thursday week which kept her with a high fever and pretty distressed with kidney action for a week or more. Then Sat. night Tom came home with the flu. (Thereby missing all 4 days this week at the Pennington trial at London, at which he was a called witness.) By Monday I had the flu too. I'd like to say little Margaret carried on, but what happened was Tom got up and took care of us. I'm still in bed, but the others seem better. Jewell is coming today.*
>
> *Love,*
> *Sara*

I want to scream, to rewind the tape, to interrupt the relentless forward motion of the doomed. Consult five more doctors, Sara. Take 1,000 penicillin shots. Get into bed and do not move.

That seemingly innocuous post card spelled the beginning of the end.

9.

Lynch, Kentucky, and
Delina, Tennessee

April 1950–November 7, 1950

Sara spent Easter 1950, the eighth anniversary of her "special day" with Tom, in a hospital bed.

For the first week and a half of her final stay at the Lynch Hospital, Rachel and I visited only once. Her doctor mandated absolute quiet for a patient whose heart was sufficiently enlarged to cause alarm. In a postcard to Eleanor I detect a rare undercurrent of distress and a hint of manic, forced gaiety. Her exuberance at a prospective visit—"Oh, goody, goody . . . we'll have a wonderful time"—seems unnaturally gleeful under the circumstances. Eleanor could be deeply emotional, and I think Sara sought to protect her cherished sister. Once again, she described herself as "on the mend," but she could hardly have avoided a sinking awareness of the seriousness of her condition. In Tennessee, Sara's family seemed instinctively to understand. Unsolicited and unannounced, Katherine arrived in Lynch.

April 13, 1950
Lynch Hospital
Lynch, Kentucky

Dear Eleanor and Charles,

I'm so happy and thankful to be really "on the mend" again. Tom read me your sweet letter last Friday—I believe—and we both appreciated your Sat. call. I was just overjoyed to see Kay, as were Rachel and Margaret. I had wanted you, or V. or Kay more than ever in my life when I was first brought to the hospital, and when she stepped in Thursday, I could hardly believe it.

I've just seen the little girls once in the 10 days I've been here— Easter Sunday. They looked so sweet with new sister dresses, new socks and ribbons, but they seemed so different in just that length of time. Margaret clings to Tom like a fat little leech.

Everyone has been so good to me. I have a restful room, done in light green, and a big blooming Easter lily and a hydrangea, and a vase of orchid and white gladioli, a pretty new blue gown and 2 bed jackets and lots of cards and visits.

Oh, goody, goody, that you all are coming for a real visit. We'll have a wonderful time. Our own visit home will have to be postponed a month or so, I guess. Are you still coughing? I do hope not.

Love,
Sara

A few days later Sara was still in the hospital and anxious to be home. Kay had taken over Rachel's and my care, a task she would continue for more than two months. One aunt after another visited Lynch that summer as Sara's three sisters and Tom's two unmarried ones took turns managing our household. How many families in today's fast-paced world could rally such support? And how vital it must have been to our family's well-being. Sara could do little more than helplessly watch.

April 16, 1950
Lynch Hospital
Lynch, Kentucky

Dear Eleanor,

. . . The 2 little girls came back today for their 2nd visit. When Margaret left she kissed me goodbye and said "Come home sometime." I'm anxious to go and thought the Dr. might let me this weekend. He might have, but started medicine again on Friday and my tummy reneged on it again last night. No damage done, as he left off the medicine and I've been fine today.

My hair is a worry as it's long, straight, and dirty after 3 weeks of no attention. Kay got out the iron to use and Rachel warned her, "Be careful with it, Aunt Kay; Mother's planning for me to use that when I go to college." I've had good company today—Verne, Clara, Hollingsworths, and my own dear family and others. . . . Try not to overdo.

> *Love,*
> *Sara*

Dave Propert recognized in Sara's 1950 letters the signs of heart failure, a condition in which the heart's pumping action becomes less and less productive over time. Sara had recovered from the rheumatic fever, but her heart muscle itself appears to have been badly damaged in the course of the illness. When she contracted flu (or possibly another undiagnosed strep infection), the illness put additional stress on her compromised heart. Working overtime, with less and less efficiency, the muscle steadily weakened. Propert speculated that the medicine that made Sara ill was digitalis, a modern version of an ancient remedy derived from crushed foxglove leaves. Prescribed to slow a rapid heartbeat, the medicine often produced nausea and vomiting. Curiously, doses in the 1940s were measured by "pigeon units," determined by how much digitalis a pigeon could digest before throwing up. (A postcard discovered late in my research confirmed Propert's speculation about the prescription.) Today, heart failure can be managed and the muscle's deterioration slowed with a variety of medicines from ACE inhibitors to beta blockers. In extreme cases, a patient can even undergo a heart transplant. Diuretics that keep excess fluid from building up in the lungs or the legs and arms are much improved, as well. In 1950, by contrast, Sara's treatment consisted of reduced activity, the problematic digitalis and a diuretic that likely was mercury-based. She and her doctors were playing with an extremely limited hand.

By mid-May, she was home but again limited to bed rest. "Tom took me to the hospital this morning, for an X-ray. My heart hasn't gone down, but otherwise I am feeling better with a good appetite; and I've been sleeping good for a week without sleeping capsules." She thanked Eleanor, who had taken time off from teaching for a short visit. "There was nothing better than your taking a seat by my bed Sat. morning and just staying there. Dr. Sonne says I can write and mend some but stay in bed."

A couple of weeks later her condition was barely improved.

June 7, 1950
Lynch, Kentucky

Dearest Eleanor,

. . . Homefolks are bound to be anxious to know our summer arrangements—if any—and I do want to get at least a short letter

home and one to Virginia written shortly. It goes without saying that I'd hoped to be up—at least sitting part time and going to meals and baths long before this. Since I'm not, I'm trying to take it as philosophically as possible and "not to vex my bosom." There's nothing commendable about that attitude. I just realize that when I do more or less chafe at the bits that I "lose" a day or so.

I still have to take kidney shots to drain off excess fluid. By the end of the week I don't sleep well, and am pretty short of breath. Personally I feel that I'd make more progress and conserve more strength if I were allowed to be sitting up some, but Dr. Sonne and Tom are firmly on 'tother side; and as they have the better of me, I do their way. Now don't you fret; all this is temporary, and in the meantime I enjoy all the attention, flowers, company and mail. . . .

Love,

Sara

The mention of kidney shots, excess fluid and shortness of breath supports the diagnosis of heart failure. Much as Sara longed for more activity, she could not have withstood it.

Life at 503 Lynch Road that summer was a swirl of comings and goings. On the national front, once again, the nation was at war. On June 25 North Korean forces crossed the thirty-eighth parallel into South Korea. Within a week, the first U.S. combat troops set foot on Korean soil to help resist the invasion. Sara's letters do not mention far-off events. Instead, they are consumed with home-front logistics—juggling another work trip by Tom to Chicago, shipping Rachel off to Jonesville for the interlude, arranging for Katherine's return to Tennessee, Eleanor's and Virginia's pending arrivals and various stopgap visits by Tom's sisters Ruby and Jewell. My mother's hospital disappearances must have confused, even frightened, a toddler. The presence of so many other loving adults surely cushioned the absences.

With her energy diminished, Sara began to substitute postcards for letters.

July 2, 1950
Lynch, Kentucky

Dear Eleanor,

Did Kay make her trip without being overly tired? I hope so. We've had a nice Sunday, with weather still not quite as hot as last Sunday. I'm anxious for the doctor to come tomorrow, hoping he'll give me another 5-minute raise [out of bed] or some such boost. Two pretty bouquets today, one of nasturtiums and one of dahlias, from Mrs. Beets and Pauline. . . . Of course we were all glad to see Tom and Rachel home. Did Kay tell you what Margaret said, that "when Daddy and Sister get home, they can't go anywhere but work and Sunday school. Not anymore!"

Love,

Sara

. . .

July 8, 1950
Lynch, Kentucky

Dear Eleanor,

So tickled to get your card, saying you're coming (but kindly grieved that this will be your 3rd trip up here and each time me not even able to cook one meal for you). . . . It seems like a long time to get from there to here, but guess it's the best there is. Tom will check on when the 10:10 Harlan bus gets to Cumberland and meet you

there, as there will be a change. . . . I'm getting along O.K.—sit up
two hours a day now. We've enjoyed all your canned goods so much.
Pickles wonderful.

 Love,

  Sara

Eleanor's visit allowed a firsthand report on Sara's progress.

       July 14, 1950
       Lynch, Kentucky

Dear Charles,

 I am already looking forward to your coming as I am missing
you so very much. . . .

 I don't know that Sara looks much better than when we were here
[in May] but she seems a great deal better. She enjoys sitting up for an
hour three times a day. I didn't have so much trouble taking over the
cooking and things. Ruby was still here and had dinner and supper
the day I came. Tom took her home the night I got here.

 Rachel asked me this morning if I could make sausage. If you think
we could spare a can, I wish you would bring her one along with the lard.
Rachel wants to go home with us but I doubt they let her go since they
don't know how they would get her back. . . . The children are darling.
I got them off to a birthday party today in little pink and blue dresses.

 I told Ruby that I would be here till Friday or Saturday of next
week. I'm surely glad to be able to help them out for this time. . . .

 Very much love,

  Eleanor

Eleanor's visit was barely ended before Sara dashed off welcome
news.

July 22, 1950
Lynch, Kentucky

Dear Eleanor and Charles,

I'm losing no time in writing, as I'm sure you're not at Morristown even yet. Dr. Sonne came, said my heart sounded better, and that I was looking better also (thanks to lots of good meals, I know.) He said I might go to one meal a day (Sorry I did not get to make it while you were here) and go to bathroom for bowel movements. So I feel real jubilant, as do Tom, Rachel, and Margaret.

Naturally, I'll go to supper tonight. He said to continue two digitalis pills a day until he returned the middle of next week, as they had seemed to help. Rachel gave him a full report on how I'd changed beds, also sat in other bedroom without permission! . . . It was a grand week, and I'm excited already about [Eleanor's planned return at] Christmastime.

Love,

Sara

Except for a few hours each day, bed rest remained mandatory for the next six weeks. As August approached, Sara reported that she was still allowed only limited bathroom privileges and one meal per day with the family. "I'm on the same schedule, except for one digitalis instead of two, and two extra pills," she wrote. A week later, she noted, "I think the 2 extra pills were to 'even up' irregular heartbeats." That information, combined with an aside in a September postcard to Eleanor ("I have had no more 'spells' as bad as the Tuesday you were here"), led Dave Propert to conclude that the "extra pills" probably were quinidine, the primary drug used in 1950 to correct an arrhythmia. An irregular heartbeat could be a common consequence of heart failure due to a serious bout of rheumatic fever.

Once again, I find myself revisiting the thorny question—did childbearing contribute to Sara's death? Might all this heartache have been avoided if Sara and Tom had resolved to stay childless or been content with a single child? Patiently, Propert reviewed the evidence. If Sara's first bout of rheumatic fever occurred in 1948, after my birth, then there was almost surely no connection. If it occurred when Sara was a child, and some degree of heart damage was done then, it's possible that pregnancy further weakened the organ. "Pregnancy puts an increased load on the heart," he said. Did that happen? Nothing in the medical record indicates heart problems during Sara's pregnancies. Family and community speculation is the only known link.

Ultimately, he concluded, "the role of pregnancy is unknown. It could have played some [role]—or not." The detached journalist in me concludes, most likely, no. The daughter? That is a tougher sell.

A casual telephone conversation with Barbara Tiabian produces an exhilarating discovery, a nearly miraculous chance for clarity. Dr. Sonne, so often mentioned in Sara's letters, is alive. His wife's sister lives not far from Lynch. Barbara has heard that the Sonnes recently visited. I can hardly believe my luck. Elated, brimming with questions, I begin the search to track them down. A few days later, I take a deep breath and dial the 812 area code number in New Albany, Indiana, where the man who treated my mother more than a half-century earlier now lives. No one responds, so I leave a message explaining my mission. After several weeks of missed telephone calls, a courtly voice answers. "Yes," Irvin Sonne tells me, he is indeed the doctor who monitored Sara through her illness many years ago. Questions pour out of me. What does he remember of her personality, her attitude during her illness? Was he surprised when she died? Why two hundred penicillin shots? Did Sara have a history of rheumatic fever as a child? Did he think, at the time, that Sara's pregnancy with me contributed to her death?

Irvin Sonne is warm, soft-spoken, apologetic. "I remember that she was a lovely lady, and I think I remember going to the home a few times," he says. As for the rest, "I'm sorry to say, I don't remember."

Don't remember? How is that possible? How can he not remember the most important patient of his early career? Surely to have a young mother die so tragically could not have been a usual occurrence. I cannot have come this close to an answer only to have it denied.

"Of course," I murmur. Fifty-odd years and all that. We exchange pleasantries; he reminisces about an era when he was on call every fourth night and made six-to-eight house calls per night. Of course, no one could remember all those details. We hang up. I want to weep. My final answer is no answer.

In mid-September 1950, a youthful Irvin Sonne—then on the verge of his thirtieth birthday—issued Sara's long-awaited reprieve from confinement. At last, she would be able to resume normal life, to dress again, to leave the house, to be more than an invalid mother and wife. She responded with joy.

September 19, 1950
Lynch, Kentucky

Dear Eleanor,

Tra la la la la, la la, la la—My sedimentation rate is down to 11. (Would have used an exclamation point, but was afraid of a misreading.) I'm dismissed as a home patient. Dr. Sonne said I could "push myself" as much as I pleased, so long as I do not tire myself. I'll continue very slowly, but will go to all meals, take baths, use sewing machine, and get out in the sunshine, and go for rides and visits.

"He" said yes to a trip over to Virginia soon, and probably yes to a trip to home in October. (His warning was that my heart was still very enlarged and sounded no better so—). I had my teeth checked too at the hospital and such as they are, they're in good shape. Margaret and Rachel had theirs checked too. To the dentist's inquiry as to how many times she brushed her teeth a day, Rachel answered, "Every night, and whenever we have blackberry pie." I have finished two little fancy, ruffled and lace-bedecked slips for Rachel by hand—one nylon, one batiste. Margaret's content to know "next they will be mine."

Love to all,

Sara

Did Sara know?

Were all those tra la la's a ruse?

I cannot say for sure, but I think she recognized how precarious her future had become. It was her nature to be optimistic. But despite the bravado of reducing bad news to a parenthetical phrase, a "very enlarged" heart that "sounded no better" was a clear forewarning. She urged Tom to remarry, he once told me, if she should die.

Of all her letters, I cherish none more than the next-to-last. In its tone, I detect a sobriety uncommon to Sara, a hint of wistfulness at life's caprice, but also an acceptance of what lay ahead. In it, she mentioned her delight in *Beyond Sing the Woods* and *Wind from the Mountains*, works by Norwegian writer Trygve Gulbranssen that would be the last novels she read. I found the first shelved deep in the stacks at the Richmond Public Library. No one had checked it out for years, and the librarian who assisted me was delighted for a customer. "There are so many good books down there," she said, "so much better than many of the ones" on the main floor.

Turning the yellowed pages, I was astonished by the degree to which the story's conclusion tracked my own nearly finished search. Tracing the evolution of three generations of a Norwegian family living deep in the north woods, *Beyond Sing the Woods* speaks of man's quest to make peace with the impermanence of life. As the book ends, the central character Dag, once youthful, has become an old man with a grown son of his own. I imagined Sara, reading, contemplating the same words my eyes now traced, reflecting perhaps, as I did, on how any single life in the march of generations passes in a instant but forges a permanent, unbreakable link with the rest. Gulbranssen wrote:

> *His thoughts were not quite as they used to be. People's deaths no longer seemed like punishments upon himself. . . . None of those dear to him had lived or died in vain. All of them, in life and death, had contributed something towards what he afterward became; he felt them all within him, going forward with him now in the work he had undertaken.*

I, too, felt Jennie May, Sara, Eleanor, the other aunts, Rachel and my own children moving beside me, each larger than a single self, fortified by the strength of our interconnectedness, as I approached the end of Sara's life.

September 28, 1950
Lynch, Kentucky

Dear Eleanor and Charles,

At long last I'll start this oft-planned letter. Your own three long, interesting, and avidly read ones, as well as all cards, since you were here, we've been so glad to get and have enjoyed them every one. I don't see how you have managed them really, for I know just how busy you stay.

The last week has been so eventful for me—not all the old familiar places and things, but at least some of them. Last Wednesday morning I arose at 7:30; and Margaret, coming into our bedroom on Tom's arm saw an unfamiliar happening. Her eyes practically popping out, she asked breathlessly, "Mama, are su going to take off your gown?" She and Rachel have since been most interested in what Mama was going to wear next day.

It's been good to walk in the yard again and to see all that Tom has done with the flowers. The potted flowers are beautiful. Tom moved them in Tuesday afternoon after frosts on Monday and Tuesday morning. The begonias are just covered with blooms; and the sultana has been too. The big angel-leaf begonia has one bloom the size of a man's double fist, and two more beginning. Geraniums are blooming too. Outside the chrysanthemums are budded, and there are a dozen or more buds on the rose bushes. We still have hardly used our own flowers for bouquets, for I've had the loveliest dahlias, asters, mari-golds, and other fall flowers brought in.

The past week I've had three "broads"—a ride up the Whitesburg road—a highway out from Cumberland to the northeast—Sunday afternoon; a trip to the cleaners Wednesday, and a very short shop-ping jaunt into one store to buy hose; and today (after both Tom and I had our 1st installment of flu shots—six more to come) we all four went down to "The Store" for the last 15 minutes. I at last saw the cherry bedroom suite and a part of the cherry dining-room set, which has just come in, also the mahogany bedroom suite that Tom said you liked. I didn't see many people—we went upstairs on the elevator—but it seemed just wonderful to be going with Tom, Rachel and Margaret again. I'm just going to forget, as far as worrying, I mean, that I'm less strong than once, and enjoy this autumn as the most exciting of my life, and savor every single second of it.

I've written Margaret's sweetest sayings home, so you may have read them, but I'll repeat one or two in case you haven't. Sometimes I've been letting her go to the store with Rachel, though she slowed them down some. Last week they returned from an errand there, and Rachel brought the sack in to show me she'd bought the right items, and Margaret marched in behind her to say proudly, "I wasn't much pokey." A day or two ago when she wanted help with her shoes, she said coaxingly, "I want su to help me, nobody but my old Kentucky Mama."

Did you hear the fight last night? All I wanted to begin with was no knockout, but by the 11th or 12th round I was beginning to wish old Joe L. could make a comeback. Anyway the world champion made a nice little speech at the close of the fight. . . .

Your jam and preserves you made us were so good. One pint is saved back for Tom's birthday jam cake. The other, along with Ruby's applesauce and Virginia's plum preserves, has brought us up to this week, when I ordered some cherry preserves. Also last week we ordered lard for the 1st time since your gift of same. . . . With clothes and a sweater on this afternoon I weighed 126, which means I am beginning to gain at last. . . .

I just loved "Beyond Sing The Woods" and "Wind from the Mountains"—even had Virginia let me borrow them so I could let Sally and Mr. Carter read them. Your bedroom sounds so good and inviting.

Much love to both,

Sara

In postcards over the next month, Sara reported happily that the family was planning an early November visit to Tennessee.

The first few days of the vacation would be spent in Virginia while Tom "goes to see two or three farm prospects." She looked forward to buying a winter hat at a favorite millinery shop in Fayetteville. She and Tom celebrated their seventh wedding anniversary on October 23 with "a silver pin of horses' heads and $10 for me, a cake for Tom. Poor men!!"

Sometime in the first week of November, our foursome arrived at Hilltop View farm in Delina, Sara's beloved home place where in autumns past she gathered hickory nuts and took refuge beneath her favorite apple tree. In a quick turnaround, Tom headed back to Virginia; I have never known exactly why—perhaps to see another farm, perhaps to help out his mother. He planned to return in a few days. That weekend, the clan gathered in—Johnny and Frances with seven-year-old Nancy and their new baby, William; Eleanor, Charles and his mother from Belvidere; and Virginia from her librarian's job at Martin College in nearby Pulaski. Combined with the current occupants of the farmhouse—Katherine; my grandfather; his sister, Ozella, and her husband, Clarence; and Jennie May's surviving sister, Lillie—the crowd swelled to sixteen people. I imagine the rooms rang with laughter, conversation and the inevitable tensions of so large a family gathering.

Monday would have been a quieter day. I hope that, as promised, Sara savored every single second.

Shortly after midnight on the morning of Tuesday, November 7, she got out of bed to take either Rachel or me to the bathroom. Four of us were sleeping in the same room, Rachel with Mother, me with Katherine. Soon afterward, Katherine heard Sara groan.

That quickly, she was gone.

Through the dim haze of decades, I remember flashes of that night—the lights, the commotion, the hands that guided me elsewhere when I tried to climb into bed with my mother. Five-year-old Rachel provided the information that allowed the long-distance operator to track down a physician-cousin of my father's. "Southgate" Ely set off into the Virginia countryside to deliver the news to Tom. Rachel recalled listening to my grandfather's solemn voice speaking into an old-fashioned telephone box, the conelike receiver pressed to his ear. "Sara just passed away," he said over and over. Did that mean "died," Rachel wondered, or was "passing away" a better, less permanent state?

What caused the sudden death? Sara's damaged heart may simply have collapsed in a spasm of electrical disorganization known as ventricular fibrillation. Or she may have suffered a pulmonary embolism, in which a blood clot, perhaps in a leg, broke loose and traveled to her lungs, blocking an artery. Risk factors for a clot include prolonged bed rest and inactivity, sometimes brought on by a long car ride such as that from Lynch to Delina. "Both are reasonable possibilities," said Dave Propert.

What does it matter anyway? She died.

In the day and a half after Sara's death, scores of relatives and neighbors visited Hilltop View, where she lay in a casket in the living room before a funeral service at the Methodist Church. A small, grieving caravan traveled on to Lynch for a second service on November 9, followed by burial at the Edds family plot ten miles west of Jonesville. "I thought the service yesterday very lovely. The beauty of those many yellow flowers, the prettier day and the comforting words made me feel better than the service here on such a desolate day," Virginia wrote to Tom on November 10, a few hours after arriving back in Delina with her father and Katherine.

It's hard for me to know whom I feel sorriest for but Katherine feels just desolate. She sometimes takes crying spells and is hard to console. . . . I think Daddy is very brave. He tells everybody he

*sees about the abundance of flowers and how nice they were and
about how much everybody did. He has always bragged about Sara's
achievements and now all he has is the funeral. He was just amazed
at the friends she had in Lynch. Of course they are the combination
of yours and hers.*

. . . I think he would feel much worse if he had not gone.

What can I remember of that time? Precious little. A funeral
song, "The Lily of the Valley." An image, perhaps, of the Delina
church. A sense that Sara was present, but soon would not be.
Rachel recalled playing with other children on the large, flat
rocks, down from the house, where the milk cans were set each
day to be picked up by a local dairy. She was supposed to be sad,
she knew. But was she? Rachel was uncertain.

In her book about early parent death, *The Loss That Is Forever*,
psychiatrist Maxine Harris says children often recall some discrete
event near the time of a death as the point when they recognize
that life has changed. For Rachel, that may have been later in the
day of November 7, after Sara's passing, when our father and his
sister Ruby arrived from Virginia. Rachel remembers him getting
out of the car and then—as others hurried to greet him—sagging
against it, sobbing, "Oh, Sara. Oh, Sara."

That is a memory I am glad not to share.

For me, the moment came sometime earlier that day, before
dawn. Rachel and I finally were being put back to bed, in another
room. My great-aunt Ozella, whom we called Auntie, tucked the
covers around us, and then she said something I did not understand, but instantly disliked: "Poor little girls."

That scene is perhaps my clearest early childhood memory.
Even as a three-year-old, I knew she was not describing an envi-
able state.

10.

1950–2009

The letters did not end quite there.

A handful from my father, saved by Eleanor and labeled "Tom carries on," reveal the courage and acceptance with which he shaped an unsought future. Surprisingly, the letters from Sara herself had not ended either. There was one more, written to Eleanor on Sunday evening, November 5. What compelled Sara to write just then, when the sisters had spent the day together? A premonition? Loneliness? What? Rachel vaguely recalls the scene—us gathered in the sitting room at Delina, she and I playing on the floor, Granddaddy in his customary rocker, and Sara with pen and paper. The next morning, someone placed the letter in the mailbox; fewer than eighteen hours later, she was dead.

Eleanor received the news in a 2 a.m. telephone call. Approaching her own death fifty-three years later, she remembered the day that followed as the worst of her life. How astonished she was then, returning home from the funeral in Delina, to find waiting in the mailbox a letter in Sara's own hand. It was as if her cherished younger sister had extended an arm from the grave. Eleanor found herself unable to open the envelope for several days. When she did, the message helped anchor her life. Once, Eleanor read me those treasured words, but they were not in the packets that she passed along, After her death, I wanted nothing more than to find that final letter. On subsequent visits to her home, I checked file cabinets, bedside tables and Eleanor's writing desk. Nothing. I could not imagine my aunt destroying so cherished a keepsake. But I feared that in her large, rambling farmhouse, with its voluminous cubbyholes and drawers, Sara's almost ethereal, last written words would never be found.

As to other questions from that period—How did our lives evolve without Sara? How did the story line go when the woman at its core disappeared?—postcards from my father sketch an outline of the first few months after her death. I am struck by his lack of self-absorption. He wrote not about himself, but about Rachel and me.

November 14, 1950
Lynch, Kentucky

Dear Eleanor and Charles,

Just a note this morning. We, with Aunt Jewell came back to Lynch Sunday afternoon. Pearl is still coming for a while anyway. We aim to go back to Mother's and stay for awhile anyway. Then we will be back home full-time until further plans develop.

I am so glad you came back for the night with us and we hope you got back home safely.

The girls are pretty good except a cold for Rachel. I got medicine for her last night. Dr. Sonne feels about the same as me. The vacation did not hasten Sara's going but gave her additional happiness and us

comfort in knowing that she was home for that short time. I'll write
more later.

Love,

 Tom & girls

. . .

November 20, 1950

Lynch, Kentucky

Dear Eleanor and Charles,

 The girls are in bed and fast asleep as it is almost eleven o'clock.

 Mother and Jewell are both with us this week. We were over there
from Thursday night until last night. We'll keep both of them as long
as they will stay. Pearl will come two days a week now. She has been
so good I wish we could just keep her on fulltime.

 As I see things now, we will go live with Aunts Cora and Bess after
the first of the year. Rachel and Margaret both think they will like
it. We will be getting away from the things we dislike here, but there
will be other disadvantages there. We will just try to make the best of
everything.

 Rachel hasn't been sick anymore except for cold which is better
now. Margaret is all right. They are both excited about the calf mother
gave them while we were there. She intended it to be for Christmas
but couldn't wait. They fed and watered it last thing before we left
Sunday.

 Write us as often as you can.

Love,

 Tom, Rachel, and Margaret

. . .

November 27, 1950
Lynch, Kentucky

Dear Eleanor and Charles,

   . . . Both girls are in bed early tonight. No naps today. They didn't get to Sunday School yesterday because of colds and bad weather. That was their first Sunday to miss since back in the summer sometime.

   They are brave little girls and need more patience than I sometimes give them. I am trying harder every day to give them more loving care and it gets results almost immediately. They are such daddy girls, but I love it.

   Love,

   Tom & Girls

A January furniture-buying trip to Chicago allowed a visit with Mary Crockett, Sara's Oak Ridge friend. I hope that moment of shared grief away from the physical and emotional demands of two little girls was cathartic, a chance to let go and grieve with someone else who loved Sara and felt his loss.

January 17, 1951
Chicago, Illinois

Dear Eleanor and Charles,

   Tonight this trip's midway has been reached. . . . The weather has been good except for some wind. Last night I saw Mary Crockett and had a long talk with her mostly about Sara. Even now it's hard to realize that she won't be home when I get there Friday night. The girls are with Mother while I am here.

   Love,

   Tom

In early 1951, as predicted, the three of us moved across Big Black Mountain to a white frame farmhouse ten miles west of Jonesville, built by my great-grandfather in the late 1800s and maintained by his daughter Bess. Tom set about farming, and we settled into a second-floor room large enough for three beds, a dresser, two chests, bookshelves, a wood-burning stove and a huge cardboard box for toys. Downstairs, life revolved around an ample, musty-smelling kitchen with an imposing iron cookstove; shelves of vegetables canned in aqua-tinted jars; and—in a house without plumbing—a row of water buckets and boots near the back door. Only rarely, when company came, were Rachel and I allowed in the front parlor with its slippery smooth, matching blue and rose velvet love seats and gilt-framed paintings of stern-faced ancestors and pastoral scenes. Outside, chickens wandered free, and a tiny creek ran at the bottom of a rocky hillside just beyond the edge of the front yard. Grandmother Edds; Uncle James; Aunts Ruby, Helen and Jewell; and Cousins Elizabeth Ann and Jimmy lived on the adjoining farm, and we visited them often. I recall the softness of my grandmother's lap as she held me, rocking in a slat-backed wooden chair by the stove.

My memories of that era stir a medley of emotions—contentment, sadness, joy.

Years later, arriving at the farm, I would sometimes have to push myself past a surge of inexplicable sorrow. Yet, most of my recollections of our life there are benign, even happy. I cut paper dolls from Sears, Roebuck catalogs and for hours vanished into imaginary worlds. While my father milked in the evenings, I climbed dusty steps to the barn loft and scaled the mountain of hay bales to its highest peak. Once, unwittingly, I tumbled down a shoot and landed, a scraped heap, in the stall of a startled cow.

On hot July days, we navigated thickets of briars to pluck ripe blackberries and splatter our tongues with their blood-red juice. Tiny, birdlike Aunt Bess read me chilling, serial newspaper stories about kidnapped children, and I shivered in fright behind the coal house when strangers appeared in the drive. Minus a mother, I latched onto my father and suffered mightily his displeasure when I misbehaved.

And Tom, how was he coping with the collapse of his dreams? I was too young to know. My Aunt Helen, James's wife, told me, when I was an adult, that she thought Tom was sometimes too harsh with Rachel and me as children. I recall two switchings, although that was not unusual for the time and place. What prompted such punishment, whether genuine misbehavior or his built-up frustration, I can't say. He spent long hours in the fields, but we saw him at mealtimes and evenings. He read to us most nights. I never remember feeling anything but loved.

Bucolic joys paled beside the bliss that came to me one night in a dream. In sleep my mother was beside me, as real as flesh. When I woke, I called for her, eager to announce her presence. The sting of reality, when it dawned, smarts still.

We regularly visited her grave on a family plot shaded by woods, across the highway, and I wondered what it was like for her there, buried deep in the ground. I imagined her in her old form, sleeping, or perhaps rising late at night to mingle with spirits from the distant past. Rachel once seized the notion that she could write mother a letter and the contact would be real, as if Sara were merely away, visiting. The idea, so satisfying in its conception, hit a roadblock. How would Rachel mail the letter? And to what address? She resolved to simply leave it on Sara's grave. Such are the ways of children reconciling themselves to death.

Rachel started school, depriving me of my daytime playmate.

In the afternoons, she created a classroom in which I was the only pupil. I learned to read, and two years later, at age six, I entered Flatwoods School in the second grade. My joy in school knew no bounds until a bully named Brenda began confiscating my lunch and demanding packs of Blue-Horse paper. I told no one, boarding the school bus each morning with an escalating sense of doom. The reign of terror continued for months until an astute teacher saw what was happening and put it to an end. Even now, I can feel the sweet astonishment of relief—my first lesson in unburdening troubles. Would a mother have recognized my distress, intervened more quickly? And would I have been better served by such intervention or, as happened, by muddling through alone?

In 1953, in what must have been an enormous scare for my father, Rachel developed the fever and aches that signaled rheumatic fever. I recall winding, mountainous drives to Abingdon for hospital visits, followed by long weeks of bed rest for her at home. Once, in her youth, Rachel accused Tom of caring more about her disease than about her. She could not have realized how closely loving her and controlling the rheumatic fever were entwined.

The following spring we moved to Madison, Tennessee, a Nashville suburb where Tom had been offered a job in a furniture store managed by a Lynch friend. Farming remained his life's passion, but he viewed it as too risky financially for raising two girls. Not until he was sixty-five and nearing the last two decades of his life did he fulfill that dream, returning to the Jonesville farm to raise cattle and plant crops until a stroke felled him at eighty-five. Grandmother Edds and Aunt Jewell accompanied us to Madison for several months.

After that, we were on our own.

. . .

"There's a line down the middle of this bed, and if you put a finger or a toe over it, you're dead."

An arm flings itself defiantly across my pillow and I am on her, pushing, kicking, hoping against hope that my big sister will wind up where she belongs—on the floor. She is stronger than I, older by two years, so my best chance lies in having struck first.

"*Girls*," my father calls from the kitchen.

We retreat to opposite corners of the bed. I mutter vile threats to this person who, to me, epitomizes pure love and pure hate. By morning, the spat is forgotten; we are entwined, arms and legs, breathing in unison in the double bed that we share.

On a summer night, dishes clink and the pre-game sounds of Nashville Vols baseball drift from the radio. Tom clears up after supper. "The Star Spangled Banner" begins. Already in bed, Rachel and I jump to attention at the foot of the mattress, rigid as Popsicle sticks, hands glued to our foreheads in a salute. When "the home of the brave" fades away, we fall straight backward, one at a time. The trick is to do this without bending your bottom. Anyone who sits rather than falls in a straight line is a sissy. We pass the test, neither cracking our skulls nor alerting our father to our antics.

Rachel and I are latchkey children. We do not know that, because—as yet—there is no such thing. Most children in the 1950s and early '60s come home to mothers. We come home to unscheduled afternoons and each other. The independence sets us apart; in most other ways, our lives are strikingly ordinary. We read, daydream, watch too much television, teach ourselves to type, fight, catalog our books into a lending library and form a neighborhood club that plans trips to distant lands. Instead of joining soccer leagues, which also do not yet exist, Judy Mayo, Bobby Huffine and the other neighbor children ride bikes and push scooters down Pierce Road or collect in someone's yard to hit softballs and run bases. Instead of taking ballet classes, I learn the five foot positions from drawings in a picture book. This works well until the lessons progress to en pointe. No matter how long they practice, toes crammed into scuffed oxfords refuse to cooperate.

Sometimes, when a cousin turns up in a pretty, hand-sewn dress or I glimpse a table full of steaming dishes at a friend's house, I wish for a mother. At other times, the hint of tragedy, of sympathy that surrounds our small family envelops me in an aura of specialness that I secretly savor. Most times, I do not think about Sara one way or another. Life is simply how it is.

While our father is at work selling furniture, paint and appliances, Rachel and I invent diversions that few mothers would have allowed. We devise a way to walk from the front door across the living room, through the dining room, and into the kitchen stepping only on sofas, tabletops, cabinets and chairs, not once touching the floor. We climb to the attic, pull the folding stairs closed behind us and rearrange boxes to create the cabin in *Little House on the Prairie*, our favorite book. Rachel plays Mary; I am Laura. Judy Mayo, our red-haired neighbor and closest friend, acts out the role of a visiting cousin, at least on days when none of us is feuding. When we are ready to quit, we push the folding stairs part-way open, step onto the top of a bureau and jump to the floor. I create a private world, as well, deep in a wooded glade across the road. I imagine fairies and gnomes who protect me as I clear pathways through the underbrush and line magical courtyards with wildflowers and stones. No one, not even my father, knows the spot exists. Sometimes, I am happiest there, alone.

For a year, when she is ten and I am eight, Rachel is sent to
a children's convalescent home because of her damaged heart.
I see her only on Sundays through a glass window. Neither of
us remembers imagining that she might die, but we do recall
the void created by the separation. Once again, I adjust to loss.
Twelve months later, Rachel returns home, more temperamental
than I recalled. I warily watch her moods but am thrilled to no
longer spend afternoons at a sitter's house and to reclaim my most
constant, lifelong friend.

Our father comes home every day from his job at McClures
store for lunch as well as supper. Sometimes, during summer
school breaks, he is already in the driveway before we force down
the fried eggs that he cooked hours earlier for our breakfast. It
never crosses our minds to flush the greasy food down the toilet.
Rachel is more likely to challenge Tom's rules or opinions, but
we are both good girls. When your father is also your mother,
disobedience carries heavy risk. No one is waiting in the wings to
intercede if you push *the* parent over the limit. And if *the* parent
should somehow reject you or leave, you would be alone. While I
accept that we have no choice but to live without the dark-haired
woman who smiles brightly out of picture frames and recedes
further and further from memory, I cannot imagine existing
without Tom. I adore him. When he leads the Sunday School at
Matthews Memorial Methodist Church, where he is the superintendent, I am quite certain that his tall, thin frame and humble
manner would make him a good stand-in for Jesus. He is no
public speaker, but Tom is earnest and sincere. I am proud to be
his daughter.

One day when I am about eleven, he calls me in, sits me on a
stool and reads to me from a Red Cross manual, something about
eggs and sperm. "Did you understand that?" he asks. "Yes," I lie,

having no idea what he had just read, but wanting to get back outside to play. That is the extent of my formal sex education. At school we learn about menstrual periods. From friends, books and experience, I piece together the rest.

Some children in Madison think we are poor. I learn this from my second-best friend, Cheryl Wagerman, who lives around the corner and over the hill from our house. Cheryl has dark olive skin and beautiful clothes. I have pale freckles and thick brown stockings held up with garters above my knees. I had nearly forgotten this ghastly detail until Pauline Nunn, our former Lynch neighbor, reminded me. My love for Sara grows exponentially when Pauline confides, "Your mother would never have dressed you that way." The stockings, it seems, were an outgrowth of 1940s farm culture, recommended by Tom's mother and sisters, no doubt in a well-meaning effort to protect Rachel and me from sore throats and runny noses. A host of pictures well into high school affirm that fathers make poor mother substitutes when it comes to hairstyles and fashions. Eight-year-old Rachel helped me curl my hair the night before my second-grade school picture at Flatwoods. The photo features a sweet, snaggle-toothed expression and a tuft of hair extending straight out, like a shock wave, from my head. I remember the day that Tom allowed me to shed the brown stockings for good as one of the most liberating of my life.

My father drives the same 1942 Buick until I am in high school. This is as much a matter of taste as means. My father prefers one quality item to a stream of lesser possessions. His life did not freeze with my mother's death—he maintained friendships, took agricultural and real estate classes and became a mainstay in his church and neighborhood—but his material surroundings largely were fixed. Sara and Tom had carefully planned and purchased six rooms of furniture. Those same original pieces filled Tom's home when he died a half-century later. An astonishing number of the books, tablecloths and dishes that we grew up with turn up in Sara's letters as wedding presents or purchases early in their married life.

When Rachel and I joke about making a movie of Sara's life, she quips: "We have the clothes." She's not kidding; we do. Rediscovering those mothballed dresses after Tom's stroke and shortly before his death, Rachel and I tried on a couple. Jarred by the flash of stricken sadness on his face, we quickly put them away.

What Rachel and I lack in poodle skirts and crinoline petticoats, we make up for in brains. This is our salvation; we are smart. In the eighth grade, I have a pivotal experience. In a schoolwide speech contest, I enter in declamation, reciting a memorized speech written by someone else. I am the only contestant in that category in my home room. I will automatically advance to the next round. All I have to do is deliver the speech. When I stand to speak, my voice shakes so badly that I cannot get beyond the first paragraph. I have to sit down. Moments later, I try again with the same result. Not until the third attempt can I will myself through the entire talk. Miserably, I slink back to my seat. Mrs. Zuccarella sees my humiliation as a teaching moment. "A few years from now," she informs the class, "Margaret will not even remember this day." I know instinctively that I will never forget it.

No mother waits at home to offer sympathy. I alone can resolve this predicament. Some internal resource tells me to make a plan. For the next week, I recite the speech endlessly—before a mirror, in bed at night, during every free moment. My motivation is self-preservation, nothing more. My reward turns out better. I win the speech contest for the entire school, launching a high school focus on debate and forensics. Over time, the interest yields modest acclaim, expanded horizons and a lifelong lesson. I do not break with adversity. Mother or no mother, I myself can chart a way through hard times. I can make a plan.

The strategy falters when Jimmy Beasley (not his real name) fails to call back. We have doubled-dated a few times during my junior year, but he attends another school and does not yet have a driver's license. During the summer, the fledgling romance fizzles. Then in the fall, he calls. He picks me up after work and we drive around Nashville for hours, talking. I look forward to our next date, but he does not call again. Jimmy Beasley has fallen off the face of the earth, and I have no idea why. In 1963, for a girl to dial the telephone and ask does not seem an option. One night I feel as if a 2,000-pound weight is crushing me from every direction. My first panic attack, triggered—a psychologist might observe—by inexplicable abandonment, lasts two days. Many years, and a few more episodes, pass before I learn that the miserable feeling has a name and, most likely, a cause tracing back to a far more pivotal loss.

My friend Judy's mother, Lucille Mayo, provides a friendly female presence. From her, I learn the basics of basketball prior to a botched tryout for the high school team, how to scramble an egg and the way 1960s mothers create a steady, background hum in their children's lives. Opal Stout, the wife of one of my father's best friends, volunteers to see me off to the prom on a night when Tom is working. The thought that I might need a woman's touch never crosses my mind. Still, it proves nice to have someone snap photographs and fuss over my dress. My aunts dispense adoration, advice and a lifelong love of Rook, Scrabble and politics when we see them on holidays and summer vacations. It is a running family joke that Eleanor always cries when we leave. For years,

I ignorantly think the tears fall simply because she is sorry to see me go.

In 1961 the movie *West Side Story* debuts. I am enchanted by the love story and the music and cannot wait for Tom to see it as well. Afterward, I ask what impressed him most about the movie. "Stick to your own kind," he says, repeating the lyrics of one of the songs. I am appalled by his lack of imagination. For the first time, I recognize that he is not perfect after all.

By the time I graduate from high school, Sara seems as distant as a long-dead aunt or third cousin, familiar only through photographs or stories that Eleanor and Tom love to repeat but that, for me, have lost their intrigue. My life lies grounded in the here and now, in college plans and budding romances. Except perhaps on the Sunday nearest to Mother's Day, when Tom buys us white rose corsages—signaling death—instead of the vibrant red or pink my friends wear, I seldom think of her and never in concrete terms. She could be a character in a nearly forgotten novel. A warm spot remains, but Sara seems as irrelevant as she is absent in my day-to-day life. How can one miss what one has never really known?

Over the next few years, life takes wing. When Tom visits me at Tennessee Wesleyan College, I am happy to see him and happier when he leaves. My world has moved beyond childhood and the people and places it contained. I read Plato and Karl Marx, plan sorority skit nights, feel the jolt of the assassination of Martin Luther King Jr., listen as my boyfriend and our male classmates contemplate draft numbers and ROTC. As graduation approaches, I ponder graduate school in journalism or political science and accept a diamond engagement ring instead. Olive green and gold are the colors for our autumn wedding. My china is Royal Worcester "Serenade." My new addresses are a string of naval flight training facilities. In Norfolk, Virginia, I land a newspaper job, writing a weekly column for navy wives that evolves into a full-time job. A three-month interlude in Europe, following an aircraft carrier from port to port, opens a new world. On a train in Italy, I hear of the shootings at Kent State. "Your country is exploding," a stranger tells me. I feel disconnected, afraid, anxious to be home. My disdain for our government's Vietnam War policy grows; my husband's support for it cements. There are other signs of trouble—long silences, flashes of anger, a detachment with which I have no experience and that I do not understand. On the night when the break comes, paralyzed with grief, I find myself sucked backward into some deep, primordial well of the soul. From out of the blue, I am three years old and attending Sara's funeral. To my astonishment, my most unattainable longing, my fiercest sobs are for her.

That epiphany launched a personal journey. It culminated many years later in my focused attempt, aided by the letters, to comprehend the impact of Sara's death.

A mother's loss, I have come to understand, is a defining experience at any age, and the impact is especially acute when much of one's life has yet to be defined. Initially, in the short term, it may be easier to adjust to death at a very young age, rather than a slightly older one. Friends whose mothers died when they were teenagers or young adults tell me that they felt numbness, anger or intense grief for a long while, followed by a certain disintegration when they reached the age at which their mother died or when their children arrived at their own age at the time of the death. It was as if the blueprint for adulthood or motherhood suddenly evaporated and they were on their own. In contrast, I cannot remember the immediate aftermath of Sara's death, though I do recall the ache a year or so later of waking to find that her imagined presence was only a dream. Nor do I remember experiencing any particular confusion when I reached thirty-four and my daughter, Kate, coincidentally was three. Growing up, I knew Sara as an icon, not as an actual guide to real-life decision making. My models of femininity were my aunts, my friends' mothers, the women I saw on television or read about in books. Those substitutes might at times provide inadequate or incomplete guidance, but I never felt as if my one, true role model had disappeared.

Even so, the loss of a mother at around age three has a particularly profound impact. While an infant knows the sensation of a mother, and the strength of that attachment and its loss may reverberate throughout life, by three the connection probably has evolved into some level of permanent memory. The relationship has existed long enough to have produced a deep bond, but at the same time, the child has not yet developed the language or the thought processes to verbalize grief and reconcile sadness. For many years, the shock and grief may lie dormant, only to erupt at an unexpected moment of pain, such as a divorce. The catastrophe lodged in my brain at thirty-nine months almost certainly helped trigger the panic I felt later in life at times of significant loss or uncertainty in raising my children. It took me many years to connect the dots and to begin the process of formally grieving Sara. "To have a mother die is an impossible sadness at three," George Hartlaub, a Denver psychiatrist who has focused on early parent loss after losing his father at fifteen, told me. "There's a neurological deficit when you have this kind of loss, but you don't know it."

Ultimately, the degree to which a mother's death damages a daughter's psyche depends on many variables—the nature of the death, the actions and reactions of the surviving parent, the strength of the extended support system and the attributes of the daughter herself.

Many survivors develop an aura of self-sufficiency, an ability to cope that can steady them through both hard times and good. I carry a sense, honed as a child, that I can manage to do what has to be done; I can soldier through. Conversely, such competence can mask inadequacies involving intimacy and trust. Too often, I know, I find it easier to depend on myself than to risk relationships that might be harder work. Loneliness and aloneness are familiar traits in someone who has experienced death at an early age. "You have a deep understanding of loneliness," an eleventh-grade English teacher wrote on one of my short stories. No kidding, I wanted to shout back. You would, too, if you had no mother, your father worked long hours and it was up to you alone to construct a social life. Feeling isolated as a sixteen-year-old hardly made me unique. But the scar of abrupt and genuine loss is more treacherous than run-of-the-mill adolescent angst.

The loss is not limited to a physical disappearance. Death also ends a relationship and the growth that might have attended it. Surely, Sara's extroverted ways would have brightened our home. My quiet father was a man of deeds, not words. He taught us to be useful and to persevere. Livelier joys such as dancing past midnight or talking on and on until an issue is resolved, those I had to discover on my own. Watching a marriage up close, I would have learned different lessons, perhaps taken different paths. I believe, though I could be wrong, that had Sara lived, my first marriage might not have occurred. At a minimum, it would have been informed by better ways to communicate.

Even so, my failings, my mistakes were not insurmountable. That I suffered but did not disintegrate over that divorce speaks to the self-worth instilled by Tom, my aunts and, no doubt, Sara herself. The devotion so evident in her letters surely bore fruit. In my second husband, now my mate for more than three decades, I found a more compatible soul. With conscious effort and sometimes hard work, we can almost always get to a place where we hear each other and understand.

Children who lose their parents early in life share at least one trait that I have long considered a gift—the embedded knowledge that life is temporary. What is here today may not be tomorrow. Such knowledge, I suppose, might breed recklessness or disregard for people or circumstances that cannot be trusted to endure. For me, the opposite is true. Impermanence softens life's edges and makes the imperfections and frailties of myself and others easier to accept.

"One can never repair the hole in the world when a parent dies. However, one can fill in some of the edges," writes psychologist Maxine Harris.

I know that to be true. The loss of a parent at an early age remains forever a pivotal dividing line in one's story. But it is not the whole story. The person who emerges is not ruined; she is simply different—more vulnerable and perhaps more resilient— than she might otherwise have been.

One difference, had Sara lived, is that I would not be sitting in Eleanor's bedroom this hot day in August 2006 asking myself where my mother's final letter might be. I am determined to find it, if it still exists. But where? I have waded through file drawers and boxes of letters on previous visits, and I have made a cursory but not exhaustive search of Eleanor's rolltop desk. Now, I am determined to complete the job. I begin with the top drawers and nooks, tossing a lifetime of thank-you notes, bank statements, check stubs, china and silver brochures, recipes, stickers, duplicate photographs and old negatives as I go. Nothing. Starting down the left-hand drawers, I see in the first only markers, a hole punch, tape and labels. The second drawer appears more promising. A stack of letters, secured with a rubber band, carries a notation in Eleanor's handwriting: "A lot of family history in these letters. Keep." My heart flutters, but the envelopes yield nothing of Sara. Behind that, a second stack promises a treasure trove. Here is a 1901 letter from Grandmother Jennie May to her future husband, John. "My dear friend," it begins. There is the first letter Eleanor wrote home after she and Charles married. I laugh out loud, but tenderly, at an index card taped with a tuft of dog hair from her beloved mutt Mazie, whose death in 1986 she grieved for many years. I can almost cry myself when the stack ends and Sara's letter is not there. The third drawer begins with another group of letters, but the label is more matter-of-fact: "Keep these for early family history." In a second compartment, farther back, I sift through discards, an old insurance policy, a brochure on "Towle Sterling . . . so easy to own."

I give the drawer a final yank, and there, in the third and final section, it lies, a "Zephyr Flight Paper" box unmistakably marked: "Very Important . . . Sara's and Mother's letters . . . Do Not Destroy Ever." The words are underlined two times, and just in case some dimwit misses them still, she has added clear instructions: "Rachel and Margaret, Look in Here, Sara's Last Letter." I am elated. In her inimitable thoroughness and eye to history, Eleanor has shielded and preserved her treasure to the end. A note inside says all: "Very Special. Keep Always. This goes to Rachel and Margaret when I'm gone; But I want to keep it to my very last day. No one will ever know how much I loved Sara. EBM."

Sunday Night
Nov. 5, 1950
Delina, Tennessee

Dearest Eleanor,

Just a short note, 'fore the chillern get in. Right after you all left, Daddy took them with him to the cemetery. However, they were back soon, and then went with Kay down to the Toshes. That brings us up to now.

No sooner had I started writing than they came in. We ate supper immediately, and while Kay washed dishes, I helped first Margaret, then Rachel, with teeth, and face and hands. So now, a quarter past 6:00 we're all through and assembled in the front bedroom—with everyone feeling fine as to health, but a little lonesome I must admit. Both girls are cutting out of catalogs, which will keep them occupied till bedtime, I imagine.

If Mother had been here this weekend, she would have said, "I know there's never been anyone who has married and left home and has a home of her own, who takes the very same interest in everything at the first home, as Eleanor does." She used to say the same about me, but I never came home and did a half of what you have this weekend. And such basic, desirable things, which nonetheless would have gone a long time undone had you not been here. But the very best part of your visit is the way you just make us all happier. You just bring cheer, and laughter, and good common sense, and comfort, and beauty, along with you. (And Charles is the luckiest man in the world I know—and though I can't quite say you're the luckiest woman—I'm that—you are a very, very fortunate one!) After you all left, I read Aunt Lillie part of the Sermon on the Mount and the verse "Blessed Are the Peacemakers for they shall be called the children of God" could have been said just for you. . . .

Tell Mrs. Murray it was so nice to have her here today. Auntie *and Uncle Clarence have been so complimentary of her (and they dote on you and Charles, no matter how loud they bark).*

Little Wilzum is just the cutest thing. Frances took what I'd brought for him (except the plastic panties). They were very few compared to all the many things she's kept us stocked with.

Kay said the Toshes had a good fire tonight (in case you worried). I was truly sorry that you got fussed at about bread (or anything) but as you told me, "You know Katherine doesn't mean half she says."

I could have cried when Tom left, and I could have when you left—but I'm glad I didn't, for after all you're both pretty close and a-loving me!

As I do you all!!

Sara

P.S. Big girl has taken not going with you all O.K., and Little One would have been so lonesome without her.

After all, you're both pretty close and a-loving me. As I do you all. . . .

For Eleanor, a woman steeped in faith in an eternal life, the message of those words was unmistakable. Sara had defied death to say she was nearby in spirit and not to grieve. Without those words, her death would have been much harder, nearly impossible, for Eleanor to bear. Was there a mystical element to Sara's writing? Perhaps. Perhaps not. I take from the letter and its eerie timing a different idea. Over time, in ways unique to each person, it is possible to find what one needs to survive a death. Nothing spares us grief or struggle, but usually something—a belief, a new direction, a letter—makes it possible to go on.

For my father, the key to accepting Sara's death was a decision, I think. My friend Anne, a therapist for many years, says she often sees recurring patterns in families or the lives of individuals.

The pattern I see in Tom's life is the ability to make deliberate, pragmatic, often selfless decisions and live them out. With conscious calculation, I think he decided that he alone could best raise his daughters in the way that he and Sara had planned. A stepmother would have her own ideas. He elected to honor Sara, and to reconcile himself to her death, by completing the task. He must at times have felt grief, loneliness and frustration in that celibate existence. If so, he did not saddle his daughters with worry or guilt. He kept it to himself. After we left home, Tom dated a few other women, including one whose close friendship endured until his death. But while Rachel and I were growing up, he kept his focus on us. He was buried beside Sara in December 1997, forty-seven years after her death.

In Rachel I see both Tom's pragmatism and an aversion to self-pity. From early childhood, she was a confident, independent soul, the letters attest. That was encouraged by Sara and re-inforced by the need to keep shipping her oldest daughter off to relatives during Sara's illnesses. Before she was eleven, Rachel had weathered not only a mother's death but a year alone in a convalescent home. That isolation did not breed happy memories; neither did adolescence particularly, but she came out on the far side professionally accomplished and emotionally intact. I take as a metaphor for what helped her withstand Sara's loss an attitude that has spurred family jokes, but is seriously important. Once, when she and her husband, Elliot, were spending a year in the old Soviet Union, and they were forced to travel by train on a bitter-cold day when he was running a high fever and worried about reaching their destination, Rachel admonished him: "Don't dwell on it." That could be her motto. She is far more sympathetic than the words, even taken in humor, suggest. Her purpose on the train trip was to help Elliot weather his misery until they reached a safe haven. But she does not dwell in blame or self-absorption; life for her is about moving on.

And me? I who believe in the power of stories to illuminate and sustain have been handed, well along in life, the incredible gift of my own. In the years I spent raising my own children, I came to recognize the incalculable impact of a mother's presence and a mother's loss. I welcomed the growing understanding that Sara's passing fed both my shortcomings and my strengths. Gradually, I began to see how my horror of abrupt and unendurable loss stemmed from her death. With time, I could see also that a resilience born of necessity contradicted my fears. What I never expected was to come face to face with her. How grateful I am that that she lived in an era when a three-minute telephone call was a luxury and e-mail did not exist. That Tom preserved his wartime love letters is not so unusual, perhaps, but that Sara held on to cherished mementos from girlhood friends, a former lover and my father, and that Eleanor had enough of a historian's soul to keep almost everything, is good fortune in the extreme. How many future daughters will be able to reconstruct a mother's life in the same way? Very few.

I cannot read Sara's letters without railing against the forces that took her from me, without wanting to spit, scream, kick and cry until every ounce of energy lies spent. How different lives cloaked in all that vitality and warmth might have been. I grieve what should have been and never was, not just for me and Rachel, not even mostly for us, but for Tom and for her. I look at my own children and think of all that I would have missed—almost everything, really—had I left them when they were barely three. No first days of school, no ah-ha moments as jumbled letters shaped into words, no glorious soccer goals or home runs, no late-night silliness, no bumpy rides through first love, no graduations, no magical stumbling onto an adult soulmate or a boisterous free spirit under your own roof.

As for my own possible role in Sara's death, over time my distress at the conjecture lessened, eased by the letters themselves. Sara would have accepted any risk to have children. No one could read her words and conclude anything else.

Sara wrote during the hopeful time of life, in the years before age or disappointment take their hardest toll, and in an era when our nation was largely optimistic as well. My parents' love story, played out in rural and small-town America in the mid-twentieth century, is more chivalrous, more reserved, and more idealistic than many modern romances. But it was spiked with humor and passion and a timeless zest for life. If they were less prone to dissect every neurosis and shortcoming, it may be because they were more intimately familiar with nature's cycles, with hard work and the proximity of life and death.

Through hundreds of pages, written in moments of exhilaration, of tedium and despair, I have come to know intimately the woman who gave me life, a woman about whom I knew so little. That knowledge has not bred, as I once hoped, some supernatural awareness of her presence. Sara has not appeared in my dreams. I cannot feel her touch, smell her skin, as I can Eleanor's sometimes even now. Still, after all these hours together, I think I know her, know her gaiety, her bravery, her heartache, her lapses, her devotion, her solidity. I find strength in the knowing.

Letters are not a neutral commentary on a life. The writer selects what to share and decides the tone. But the sheer volume of Sara's letters allows me to see the essence beneath the veneer. I can take her self-portrait, burnish it with whatever understanding of human nature I have acquired, and construct a woman whole. Such knowledge, now mine, cannot be taken away.

Trust, Sara tells me through her words and her life. Trust in the will to endure.

On an early November day, fifty-six years after her death, I plant *Narcissus* bulbs in the front yard. I press the trowel deep into damp, black soil, creating a small nest, then place the bulb into it carefully, just so. Under a blanket of earth, these bulbs will weather winter's cold. Sometime next spring, about Easter-time actually, if I set them right, their crusty brown shells will explode in an unrecognizable form, all green shoots and butter-yellow crown. A few of these bulbs may not make it, but by some immutable force of nature, most will. Their silent work, buried from view, will erupt as if by magic in a profusion of life. I can hardly wait to count the blooms.

Ideas for (Re)Discovering
Your Mother

CREATE A TIME LINE. Start with the obvious dates: births, deaths, graduations, marriages. Then fill in details. How old was she when her own mother and father died? When did she get her first job? Where was she, and in what stage of life, when major world events occurred? What were the critical turning points in her life?

MAKE A LIST OF THE PLACES SHE LIVED, AND DO SOME RESEARCH ABOUT THEM. What opportunities or limitations were available to her in those places? How might her social and political views have been sculpted by the setting? Did she rebel or conform? What role did the local economy play?

LEARN WHAT YOU CAN ABOUT HER MOTHER. How might your mother have been influenced by the way she was raised? What was the relationship between your mother and your grandmother like? Warm or distant? How did that pattern evolve as they grew older?

TAP PRIMARY SOURCES. Search for her letters, pictures, favorite books, movies and pieces of music. Then spend time with them. What do they tell you about her?

INTERVIEW. What are the questions created or left unanswered by your research? If your mother is alive, ask her for the answers. If not, make a list of the people who knew her well enough to provide insight. Seek them out before it's too late.

MEDITATE. Reflect on all you've learned. Incorporate it into your understanding of who she is and—by extension—who you are. Whether you are physically together or not, you can still talk to her spirit about your frustrations, your grief and your joys.

Bibliography

Lynch, Kentucky

Caudill, Harry M. *Night Comes to the Cumberlands*. Ashland, KY: Jesse Stuart Foundation, 2001.

Duff, Betty. "Twentieth Century Company Towns: The Model Towns of Millinocket, Maine and Lynch, Kentucky." *Khronikos* (on-line journal). http://www.library.umaine.edu/khronikos/default.htm. January 3, 2006.

Goode, James B. "Lynch: A Coal Legacy" (videotape). University of Kentucky, Southeast Community College Appalachian Archives, n.d.

Gulbranssen, Trygve. *Beyond Sing the Woods*. New York: The Literary Guild, 1936.

"Harlan County Coal Camps: Lynch and Benham, Kentucky." Industrial Documentary Photography 1912-1948. University of Kentucky, Southeast Community College Appalachian Archives, 1987.

Harrison, Lowell H. and James C. Klotter. *A New History of Kentucky.* Lexington: University of Kentucky Press, 1997.

Hevener, John W. *Which Side Are You On: The Harlan County Coal Miners, 1931-39.* Urbana: University of Illinois Press, 2002.

Johnson, T.E. "History of Lynch Division, 1917-1957." Paper prepared by T.E. Johnson, Special Representative-Coal Division, U.S. Steel Corp., Lynch, Kentucky, n.d.

London (KY) Sentinel Echo, "Defense Now Testifying in Murder Case," March 30, 1950.

London (KY) Sentinel Echo, "2-Year Sentence Meted Organizer in Murder Case," April 6, 1950.

Oral History Research Center, Margaret I. King Library, University of Kentucky, Lexington. Oral History Tapes of Lynch: Steve Andraiga (86OH275, Tape 020), Lena Brannon (88OH-81), Joey Groeber (88OH-48), Katherine Overbeck (86OH265, Tape 014), Pete and Ann Tiabian (86OH201, Tape 004), Verona Smith (86OH274, Tape 019), Verona Smith, Margaret Andraiga and Steve Andraiga (86OH257, Tape 005).

Tri-City (KY) News, "Eight Murder Trials in Bloody Harlan," December 22, 1949.

Wagner, Thomas E. and Phillip Obermiller. *African American Miners and Migrants: The Eastern Kentucky Social Club.* Urbana: University of Illinois Press, 2004.

Oak Ridge, Tennessee, and World War II

Bird, Kai, and Martin Sherwin. *American Prometheus: The Tragedy and Triumph of J. Robert Oppenheimer.* New York: Knopf, 2005.

Brokaw, Tom. *The Greatest Generation.* New York: Random House, 1998.

Celebrate Oak Ridge. Oak Ridge, TN: Celebrate 2000 Partners, 2000.

Gailer, Joanne Stern. *Oak Ridge and Me: From Youth to Maturity*. Oak Ridge, TN: Children's Museum of Oak Ridge, 1991.

Goodwin, Doris Kearns. *No Ordinary Time: Franklin and Eleanor Roosevelt, The Home Front in World War II*. New York: Simon & Schuster, 1994.

Johnson, Charles, and Charles Jackson. *City Behind a Fence: Oak Ridge, Tenneseee 1942-1946*. Knoxville: University of Tennessee Press, 1981.

Overholt, James, ed. *These Are Our Voices: The Story of Oak Ridge, 1942-1970*. Oak Ridge, TN: Children's Museum of Oak Ridge, 1987.

Percy, William Alexander. *Lanterns on the Levee*. New York: Knopf, 1941.

Present, Thelma. *Dear Margaret: Letters from Oak Ridge to Margaret Mead*. Knoxville: East Tennessee Historical Society, 1985.

Russert, Tim. *Wisdom of Our Fathers*. New York: Random House, 2006.

Smith, Lillian. *Strange Fruit*. New York: Reynal & Hitchcock, 1944.

Smyser, Richard. *Oak Ridge 1942-1992: A Commemorative Portrait*. Oak Ridge, TN: Oak Ridge Community Foundation, 1992.

Westcott, Ed. *Images of America: Oak Ridge*. Charleston, SC: Arcadia, 2005.

Yellin, Emily. *Our Mothers' War: American Women at Home and at the Front During World War II*. New York: Free Press, 2004.

Legacy and Loss

Agee, James. *A Death in the Family*. New York: McDowell, 1957.

Briggs, Dorothy. *Your Child's Self-Esteem*. Garden City, NY: Doubleday, 1970.

Burch, George. *A Primer of Cardiovascular Disease*. Philadelphia: Saunders, 1949.

Commins, Patricia. *Remembering Mother, Finding Myself*. Deerfield Beach, FL: Health Communications, 1999.

Crystal, Billy. *700 Sundays*. New York: Warner Books, 2005.

Didion, Joan. *The Year of Magical Thinking.* New York: Knopf, 2005.

Edelman, Hope. *Motherless Daughters: The Legacy of Loss.* New York: Dell, 1994.

Friedberg, Charles K. *Diseases of the Heart.* Philadelphia: Lea and Febiger, 1953.

Furman, Erna. *A Child's Parent Dies.* New Haven, CT: Yale University Press, 1974.

Goodwin, Doris Kearns. *Wait Till Next Year.* New York: Touchstone, 1997.

Harris, Maxine. *The Loss That Is Forever.* New York: Plume, 1996.

Hughes, Lynne. *You Are Not Alone: Teens Talk About Life After the Loss of a Parent.* New York: Scholastic, 2005.

Kennedy, Alexandra. *Losing a Parent.* New York: HarperCollins, 1991.

Krasnow, Iris. *I Am My Mother's Daughter.* New York: Basic Books, 2006.

Levine, Samuel. *Clinical Heart Disease.* Philadelphia: Saunders, 1951.

Silverman, Phyllis R. *Never Too Young to Know: Death in Children's Lives.* New York: Oxford University Press, 2000.

Smith, Alison. *Name All the Animals.* New York: Scribner, 2004.

Stratton, Joanna. *Pioneer Women: Voices from the Kansas Frontier.* New York: Simon & Schuster, 1982.

Warloe, Constance, ed. *I've Always Meant to Tell You: Letters to Our Mothers.* New York: Pocket Books, 1997.

Yardley, Jonathan. *Our Kind of People.* New York: Weidenfeld & Nicolson, 1989.